The Cage of Form

Likeness and Difference in Poetry

Horace Hamilton

Rutgers University

Dickenson Publishing Company, Inc.

Encino, California and Belmont, California

Library of Congress Catalog Card Number 73-170680
ISBN: 0-8221-0008-8

Printed in the United States of America
1 2 3 4 5 6 7 8 9 10

COPYRIGHTS AND ACKNOWLEDGMENTS

WILLIAM BLACKWOOD & SONS LTD.—for 5 lines from "The Highwayman," by
Alfred Noyes, from *Collected Poems of Alfred Noyes*. Reprinted by permission of
William Blackwood & Sons Ltd.
CHATTO & WINDUS, LTD.—for 4 lines from "Dulce et Decorum," by Wilfred
Owen, from *The Collected Poems of Wilfred Owen*. Reprinted by permission of Chatto
& Windus and Mr. Harold Owen.—for "Large Bad Picture," by Elizabeth Bishop, from
Complete Poems by Elizabeth Bishop. Reprinted by permission of Chatto & Windus, Ltd.
THE CLARENDON PRESS—for the verse arrangement by William Butler Yeats of
Walter Pater's "Mona Lisa," in *The Oxford Book of Modern Verse*.
J. M. DENT & SONS, LTD.—for 10 lines from "Sonnet 1," by Dylan Thomas from
Collected Poems of Dylan Thomas. Reprinted by permission of J. M. Dent & Sons and
the Trustees for the Copyrights of the late Dylan Thomas.
DOUBLEDAY & COMPANY—for "In Kyo I am . . ." and "The piercing chill I
feel . . .," from *An Introduction to Haiku* by Harold G. Henderson. Copyright © 1958
by Harold G. Henderson. Reprinted by permission of Doubleday & Company, Inc.—for
"Elegy for Jane," copyright 1950 by Theodore Roethke from *The Collected Poems of
Theodore Roethke*. Reprinted by permission of Doubleday & Company, Inc.
NORMA MILLAY ELLIS—for "Euclid alone has looked on Beauty bare . . ." from
Collected Poems, Harper & Row. Copyright 1923, 1951 by Edna St. Vincent Millay and
Norma Millay Ellis. Reprinted by permission of Norma Millay Ellis.
FARRAR, STRAUS & GIROUX, INC.—for "The Death of the Ball Turret Gunner,"
by Randall Jarrell. Reprinted with the permission of Farrar, Straus & Giroux, Inc. from
The Complete Poems by Randall Jarrell, copyright © 1945, 1969 by Mrs. Randall Jarrell.
—for "Large Bad Picture," by Elizabeth Bishop. Reprinted with the permission of
Farrar, Straus & Giroux, Inc., from *Complete Poems* by Elizabeth Bishop, copyright
1940, 1946, 1947, 1948, 1949, 1951, 1952, 1955 by Elizabeth Bishop.
VINCENT FERRINI—for "A dog ran down the night," by Vincent Ferrini, from
The House of Time. Reprinted by permission of Vincent Ferrini.
HARCOURT BRACE JOVANOVICH, INC.—for excerpts from "The Hollow Men,"
"Portrait of a Lady," "Gerontion," "La Figlia che Piange," "The Waste Land," "Burnt
Norton," and "Dante," by T. S. Eliot. Excerpts from the poetry and prose of T. S. Eliot
are reprinted from his volumes *Collected Poems 1909-1962* and *Selected Essays* by permission of Harcourt Brace Jovanovich, Inc.; copyright, 1936, by Harcourt Brace Jovanovich, Inc.; copyright, ©, 1963, 1964, by T. S. Eliot.—for "Naming of Parts," by Henry
Reed, from *A Map of Verona and Other Poems*, copyright, 1947, by Henry Reed. Reprinted by permission of Harcourt Brace Jovanovich, Inc.—for "Buffalo Bill's defunct
. . .," by E. E. Cummings. Copyright, 1923, 1951, by E. E. Cummings.—for "A Man who
had fallen among thieves" and "Next to of course god america I love you," by E. E.
Cummings. Copyright, 1926, by Horace Liveright; copyright, 1954, by E. E. Cummings.
—for "anyone lived in a pretty how town" and "as freedom is a breakfast food," by
E. E. Cummings. Copyright, 1940, by E. E. Cummings; copyright, 1968, by Marion More-
house Cummings.—for the first stanza of "what if a much of a which of a wind," by
E. E. Cummings. All of the above poems by E. E. Cummings are reprinted from *Poems
1923-1954* by E. E. Cummings by permission of Harcourt Brace Jovanovich, Inc.
HARPER & ROW, PUBLISHERS—for "A Voyage to Cythera," translated by George
Dillon from *Flowers of Evil* by Charles Baudelaire, translated by George Dillon and
Edna St. Vincent Millay. Copyright, 1936 by George Dillon and Edna St. Vincent Millay.
—for "The Red Cow is Dead," from *The Second Tree from the Corner*, by E. B. White.
Copyright, 1946 by E. B. White. Originally appeared in *The New Yorker*.—for 13 lines
from "I Paint What I See," from *The Fox of Peapack* by E. B. White. Copyright, 1933 by
E. B. White. All reprinted by permission of Harper & Row, Publishers.
DAVID HIGHAM ASSOCIATES, LTD.—for "Trio for Two Cats and a Trombone,"
from *Collected Poems* by Edith Sitwell, published by Duckworth & Company.
HOLT, RINEHART & WINSTON, INC.—for "Is my team ploughing," by A. E.
Housman, from "A Shropshire Lad"—Authorised Edition—from *The Collected Poems
of A. E. Housman*. Copyright 1939, 1940, © 1959 by Holt, Rinehart & Winston, Inc.

CONTENTS

iv

PREFACE

The Cage of Form: Likeness and Difference in Poetry is intended for those who may wish for a reintroduction to poetry. It surveys the traditional—prosodic, rhetorical, and conceptual—aspects of poetry, at the same time offering reconsiderations of the more or less set classifications and definitions. Some of my procedures may seem less than orthodox, but the end result, I hope, will yield the desired understanding we seek.

The chapters grew out of my experience both as teacher and as poet. They are essays to stimulate new perceptions in a review of the elements generally touched on in beginning textbooks. The anthologies, handbooks, and casebooks are offering us more material than ever before. Those now in college need never be ignorant of the types by which English verse is conveniently remembered—the ballad, the elegy, the sonnet, the ode—or the kinds of meter and rhyme, or the classification of images, from simile to symbol and paradox to irony.

Interested readers often seem to be of two kinds: those expecting an orderly description of the elements found in poetry, but impatient with any sustained comparative analysis of them, or those too willingly carried by their mentors into a cult of fashionable poets. The reader's indoctrination into fads, of exaggerated concern for the current voices, the polarization of "new" and "traditional," seems incompatible with our function as students and teachers in a heritage as fine as ours. An understanding of the workings of a poem and the cunning forms of its transmission to the reader are surely the insights that devoted scholars should try to pass on. I have arranged some of these "insights" in terms of the values of a poem, or again, the "responses" that a poem arouses in a reader: the aural, the rhetorical, the conceptual or substantive, and the contextual.[1]

Since these values usually function concurrently as we read, the necessity for dealing with successive stages or levels of the poem's art raises a perennial question among students: why ruin a poem by anatomizing it? There are many answers to the question, though perhaps the soundest compromise is for the poem to always be tackled at the outset as a whole and appreciated that way—and not in the reverse order. In most cases I have given illustrative poems in full, even when the successive parts must be taken in segments.[2] The poems usually selected are not intended to represent a survey; they are poems whose art provides the most rewarding analysis. If they seem to stress any particular period, the fact may simply reflect the comparative richness or successful experimentation in that period. The familiarity of the three poems taken up in Chapter 2 was intended to facilitate the demonstration I wished to make of the comparative approaches of three fairly closely related poets.

The exercises ("Practical Criticisms") should be flexible enough to answer various needs. Some are frankly routine and may be passed over for advanced students; others are experimental or meant as a do-it-yourself diversion. A worthwhile exercise that I leave to the instructor is the writing of original poems or the translating of a poem from a second language into English. One often learns more of prosody, rhythms, and verbal economy in this way than from theoretical exposition. For an average group, it may be better to start with free forms, or the imitation of a form like the *haiku*, than to try a sonnet.

The Glossary contains most of the poetical terms used in this text. Some expressions used in general criticism have also been thrown in to provide a complete lexicon for the

---

[1]The Appendix offers some of these approaches in outline form.

[2]To avoid excessive repetition, I have sometimes quoted fragments of poems, though usually only when a cross reference could be made to the complete poem elsewhere in the text.

vii

student of poetics. At moments I was tempted—as many have been before me—to throw out some of the pretentious sounding Greek words that have too long graced English poetics. But always—like many before me—I was cornered by the realization that until there is a concensus on a substitute terminology, the ungainly "anaphore," "anastrophe," "synecdoche," and "hypercatalexis"—or the ugly word "prosody" itself—seem likely to remain with us.

And finally, thanks to my classes in poetry for certain discoveries; to Evelyn, my wife, for her perceptive criticism; to Helen D'Espies for intelligent labors on the typescript; to Michael Snell for indefatigable efforts toward perfection.

H. H.

ONE

Matters of Approach

Past and Present

A Chinese poet and general of the 4th century A.D., by the name of Lu-Chi[1] once spoke of the infinitely complex job of the artist. A clever hunter he must be "to trap heaven and earth in the cage of form"; not, he doubtless meant, to create a cage within the mind, but to confine within the bounds of art the seeming amorphousness of life. Always he must struggle "with the meaninglessness and silence of the world." And his record must be only the inkmarks from "the tip of his writing brush."

This high, almost forbidding conception of an artist's need to master his recalcitrant materials has been dominant in most great cultures. The problem has been to make a likeness of the world, without recreating that material world itself. It must be a likeness with a difference. The difference within that likeness has been the arrangement of a sort of ideal condensation of life's necessities.[2] At various intervals, what was handed down from the past seemed out of step with the present. This made the problem of creating likeness with a difference even more complicated, for it raised the correlative need for dealing with time, custom, and universal values. In our inexperienced view, a "Nun's Priest's Tale" or a "Lycidas" or a "Tintern Abbey" does not invariably explode with glory upon first reading. Only theoretically, we

---

[1] c.275–330 A.D. Author of "Wen-Fu," a prose poem on the art of letters.

[2] As a leading theme, this principle is developed fully in Chapter 5.

1

feel, can an ideal form express man's urgencies in a work for yesterday, today, and tomorrow.

To cut into time, to extricate an ideal form from everyday distractions, to perceive value from fashion and context: these are requirements of a clever hunter indeed. Poetry is a form of literature all too often dispensable in an atmosphere of "relevancy." It seems to be at the farthest pole of pressing affairs. Yet it should be quite the opposite. Poetry should be the constant companion of Everyman. It should be his guide, "in his utmost need, to be by [his] side."[3] In many civilizations it held the most honored place of all the arts. In modern times, we fear it is more honored than enjoyed.

Did poetry ever truly flourish as a popular enjoyment? In Tennyson's time, perhaps. Certainly in Byron's, or Wordsworth's. Then, at least, there was a "romantic era," as can be seen by the richness of anthologies of the period. (Or do we attribute to the general state of mind during that period the tincture of the golden minority we study now?) Or we may move back to the century before that, indeed to an age of enlightenment, if not of poetry, sharing the sensibility of recent times. The metrical emotions of the elite of that period were as polished as their rational discourse, but they hardly constituted a majority of poetry lovers. Not until we look further—to the 17th century and back to the 16th—do we find an era when poetry might have been the nourishment of a literate nation awakening from a long sleep, an imagination fired by images of a new world on the heels of a rediscovered old. So we mark it well: a lyrical age for all but dullards— and, of course, the illiterate masses. And if we go back before this renaissance, with its Shakespeare and its Bacon, there are dark stretches lit only at intervals by verse tales, grim jokes and allegories, churchly rituals, and flashes of other-worldly imagination. For the populace, poetry was at a stage of primitive entertainment, save when a Chaucer found his audience of noble patrons.

Until finally we jump far back, to ancient Greece and to the beginnings of our Western civilization. There, inseparable from public utterance, the aristocrat of entertainment,

---

[3]The quote is from the early English play, Everyman.

and the entertainment of aristocrats, we find the epic minstrelsy, the singing shepherds, and the choric odes of the
plays in the fortnight-long festivals. Was it real? Did a poetry
really exist? Around Homer's time, writing was the magnificent new instrument, and it had already excited the inventive
rhapsodists. By classical times (mostly the 5th century B.C.),
writing had become the glory responsible for transmitting the
epic cycles. Textless, metrical recitation had long become the
chief medium of all serious literature. Yet even so, the Greeks
did not write poetry for quite the reasons that move us today
(reading, analyzing, assessing, as we do, our personal lyr-
icisms). Poetry, then, meant the rhythmic, ordered means for
telling stories, communicating ideas, or arousing rather conventional emotions, as in the celebration of military triumphs
and the praising of the dead in honorific epitaphs. Only by
the middle of the 6th century B.C. had lyric poetry acquired
an independent status. It was also to become the elite medium in the exposition of religion, philosophy, history, and
even the art of husbandry. These functions continued well
into the Roman Empire and after—witness that comfortable
blend of domesticity and poetry, and model for generations
of imitators, The Georgics of Vergil.

Now, in a hora novissima of the cultural wheel, the written
word is being freely discarded for the less painstaking arts
of viewing and listening. Some say we are to leave the
Gutenburg galaxy and reenter an age of primitivism when
there will be neither taste for nor use of the media of print.
(This may not be a bad exchange—if what we revert to has
a Homer in it!) We might as well hope for a return to mon-
etary wampum and the barter system—to further adapt to our
illiteracy. Language, the world's intellectual currency, has
been threatened before by reversals and inflational debase-
ment. Less than a century ago, journalism managed to survive
the much heralded debut of the rotogravure. One picture was
worth a thousand words; so who, it was asked, would bother
to read if he could relax with pictures?

When the great cultural apocalypse is upon us, will it not
come from inanition, the drying up of our inspiration, rather
than from the obsolescence of language? The Greek philoso-
pher Heraclitus anticipated language's defense by seeing in

it the evidence of human stability, the most constant thing in a world of ceaseless flux. The structure of speech itself, he said, must reflect the structure of the world, being a paradigm of that common wisdom which is in all men. Today this conservative force is being assessed again. Poetry, by combining sound and sense to achieve more than the merely graphic, challenges the most active minds to worlds more fabulous than moonscapes.

Poetry exists in language, and language—to all who know theirs well—will lead to poetry. Literary revolutionaries have tirelessly experimented with its forms; critics have hoped to confine it; pedants have set up rules to keep it settled and neat. But it has never submitted for long. Because poetry is the art of language, it may preserve the images of one generation for the next; but even as it conserves, it renews itself, transmitting the germ of life from age to age.

The Essence of Poetry

> The Poet seeks what is nowhere in all the world,
> And yet—somewhere—he finds it.[4]

What definition shall we give it? With the sciences, we can expect describable data, quantitative substance, measurable effects. With poetry, we drift as with the diversity of life itself. Convenient limits are prescribed, but deviations persist. As with the other arts, the changing values of poetry seem to challenge the scientific itch of definers and classifiers. Few arts, however, have tempted so many to formalize an epistomology (as witness this book) and at the same time have induced the artists (the poets themselves) to urge us to "read and enjoy." From the autocratic Saintsbury, who tried to relate English versification to Greek and Latin practice, to the Beatnik-inspired minstrels, who prefer extemporaneous expression, the critics and the poets themselves have greatly mauled the corpus of Poesy.

Some textbooks have devoted several pages to a chrono-

---

[4]Plautus, *The Rope.*

4

logical list of definitions, beginning, perhaps, with Aristotle and continuing through Robert Frost and T. S. Eliot. It is an interesting way to illuminate the shifting values each age brought to its view of poetry. Yet, each spokesman for his time seemed to express cheerful dogmatism about what a poem should be. Critics of venerable standing—Horace, for example—exhibited surprising flexibility, though we think of the classics as rigidly devoted to rules. Then there were Pope's bromides, which in turn gave way to Wordsworth's recognition of the emotions, of a man speaking directly to man, which in turn gave way to Matthew Arnold's magisterial simplification that "Poetry is simply the most beautiful, impressive, and widely effective mode of saying things."

Here at a glance was the evidence that while art might endure, its rationalizers would bring to it the shifting temper of the times. Such a range of attitudes is most illuminating; it is testimony that no art, however fundamental its assumptions, will say quite the same thing to one age as to another. The classically oriented Dryden would urge the logical and symmetrical function, while the nature-lover Wordsworth would insist on poetry's primary appeal to feeling. The empiricists were all for bringing science to the problem, doubtless sensing a certain lack of it among their weak-minded brethren. Others grew legalistic, attempting to plug all the loopholes by which the volatile essence might escape. If someone had spun those hundred or more definitions in a blender, what common amalgam might he have served up? Here is an omnibus definition that might have resulted:

> Poetry is that form of written or oral expression that achieves a unity of effect by sometimes complex means, as by the widening of perception, the heightening of feeling, and the deepening of experience, through language subtly arranged to harmonize the recurrence of motif and sound and a variety of other devices, both dynamic and linguistic.[5]

Against this prescription for all contingencies could be juxtaposed Carl Sandburg's seeming *reductio ad absurdum*: "Poetry is the synthesis of hyacinths and biscuits"—a good illustration of a poet's aptitude for compression.

---

[5]The author's own concoction.

Like the three blind men describing an elephant by the part of its anatomy they touched first, poets as well as critics bring their blind spots to any assessment of the nature of the beast. To one poet, for instance, "All poetry is heightened speech subjected to regular patterns of sound and rhythm" (inadequate, of course, to those for whom the limitation to "speech" would be questionable). And yet, whatever the limitations at one point, certain definitions had a way of sticking. Wordsworth's proved serviceable for over a century: "Poetry is the spontaneous overflow of powerful feelings; it takes its origin from emotion recollected in tranquility."

For some definers, the narrowing of the gap between poetry and prose required added precautions of definitions. But they were willing to admit that poetry had no monopoly on the emotions. Lord Byron, who pretended to curb his emotions, asserts that poetry arises from the process of getting rid of excess feeling: "Poetry is the lava of the imagination whose eruption prevents an earthquake." Verse scribbling, as psychic therapy, has plenty of followers today. It has, indeed, been recommended by one of our contemporaries as a preventative for ulcers.[6] This ulcer school unfortunately offers less of a definition of poetry than a prescription for frustrated authors.

How Poetry May Be Recognized

While there is an understandable satisfaction in naming things, it seems preferable at this time to let definitions emerge from a more inductive approach to the poems. One of these approaches might well be to determine the ways in which poetry differs from nonpoetry. If we grade the kinds of written expression as we do the color bands of the spectrum, we might consider these gradations from prose to poetry:

(1) utility prose
(2) prose in creative forms (essay, fiction, drama)
(3) external verse (rhyme and meter as the only distinction)
(4) elevated prose (literature of nonmetrical eloquence)

---

[6]John Ciardi: "An ulcer, Gentlemen, is an unwritten poem" (the title of an address frequently delivered to gatherings of businessmen).

(5)   poetry (the intensification of language by considered poetic means: prosodic recurrence, image, patterned diction)

Number 1 is not our concern here. Number 2 is of relative interest because of the degree to which some fiction or drama makes use of the intensified language and imagery customary to poetry, but without **prosodic**[7] means. Number 3 possesses obvious distinctions from prose. It is placed *before* Number 4 because its external mechanics of rhyme and meter do not in themselves give the intensity or heightened spirit of poetry. For instance, the rhyme and balladic meter of the following jingle hardly raises it to any degree of intensity:

> To bed, to bed, said Sleepy Head;
>   Tarry awhile, said Slow;
> Put on the pan, said Greasy Dan,
>   We'll sup before we go.

Number 4 includes that which is nominally called prose, but which is heightened by feeling or eloquence, containing varying degrees of the intensifying diction of poetry, even though lacking the more obvious qualities of rhyme and meter. In the lines below are arranged (without alteration of the wording) a short passage from Ecclesiastes as an example of non-metrical eloquence:

> To everything there is a season, and a time
>   to every purpose under the heaven:
> A time to be born, and a time to die; a time to plant
>   And a time to pluck up that which is planted. . . .

In this spectrum, then, we have reversed the order by which the externals of rhyme and meter are viewed as automatic attributes of poetry. Number 4 on our scale may prove a controversial distinction, but it embraces some important aspects of the dynamics that poetry and prose always share.

---

[7] Terms that appear in boldface are defined in the Glossary.

While Number 3 appeals without effort to our childhood habituation (from Mother Goose rhymes to the inanities of many a song hit), its x *a* x *a* rhyme, as well as its iambic ka-plunk-ka-plunk-ka-plunk, belies the mediocrity of its subject (a crude variation of the Ecclesiastic theme above). Even into maturity we perpetuate this confusion of essence and appearance by repeating the simple-minded doublet, "I'm a poet/ And I don't know it." In a larger degree we have the popular tendency to settle for the facsimile rather than the real.[8]

Less apparent as poetry to some, Number 4 possesses a verbal eloquence and underlying rhythm that can be far more moving than verse in its minimal form. It was never more in ascendancy than in the fine prose and sermons of 17th century England. We get an early taste of it in this conclusion to Raleigh's *History of the World*, appearing late in the 16th century:

> O eloquent, just and mighty death, whom none could advise, thou hast persuaded; what none hath presumed, thou hast done; and whom all the world hath flattered, thou hast cast out of the world and despised: thou hast drawn together all the extravagant greatness, all the pride, cruelty and ambition of man, and covered all over with two narrow words: *Hic jacet.*

The unfolding here of a single periodic sentence (common in the subsequent style of John Donne, Sir Thomas Browne, John Milton, and others) raises a rhythmic expectancy similar to the recurrence and expectancy of formal poetry. Rendered into lines of a quantitative metric, the passage affords an example of the link between rhetorical eloquence and poetry:

> O eloquent, just and mighty death,
> Whom none could advise, thou hast persuaded;
> What none hath presumed, thou hast done;
> And whom all the world hath flattered,

---

[8]This is not to dismiss light verse, a genre in its own right, including childhood rhymes, frontier ballads, commercial jingles, and doggerel. The appeal was first to children but did not necessarily end with them.

Thou hast cast out of the world and despised:
Thou hast drawn together all the extravagant
  greatness,
All the pride, cruelty and ambition of man,
And covered all over with two narrow words:
Hic jacet.

Without going into the use here of **personification,** we can see in the lines a play on **antithesis** and **sonority** that anticipates the metaphysical style of the next generation.

While it is doubtful that Raleigh, Browne, or those remarkable scholars who collaborated in translating the Bible thought of themselves as rendering poetry in a prose form, poets of a later time have consciously experimented with it. In his introduction to the *Oxford Book of Modern Verse*, William Butler Yeats offers a passage of Walter Pater's prose as a kind of free verse. The following lines from the conclusion of Pater's *Renaissance*, a prose work, and altered only in the line arrangement, exhibit the **parallelisms** of much archaic poetry:

She is older than the rocks among which she sits;
Like the Vampire,
She has been dead many times,
And learned the secrets of the grave;
And she has been a diver in deep seas,
And keeps their fallen day about her;
And trafficked for strange webs with Eastern
  merchants;
And, as Leda,
Was the mother of Helen of Troy,
And, as St. Anne,
Was the Mother of Mary;
And all this has been to her as the sound of lyres
  and flutes
And lives

Only in the delicacy
With which it has moulded the changing
   lineaments,
And tinged the eyelids and the hands.

Others of Yeats's generation carried their fascination with the interchange between genres beyond the coincidental properties I have claimed for Number 4. Oscar Wilde's "prose poems," John Gould Fletcher's "polyphonic prose," and similar experiments probably lost sight of the virtue of prose for its own sake. Others assumed that mere opulence of style transforms prose into poetry. "Fine writing" is a derrogatory term usually applied to an attempt by nonpoets to adorn ordinary prose, disguising its legitimate function.[9]

Number 5, our final division, is poetry and should possess the eloquence and the heightened feeling of Number 4, but with the concentration, imagery, and prosodic recurrences as needed. It combines, in short, the significant elements of 3 and 4, though not necessarily in measurable proportions. To recognize the authenticity of this degree of poetry requires a sixth sense rather than the quantitative means of scientific analysis. The term **pure poetry** has sometimes been applied here, a satisfactory term as long as "pure" is used generically rather than qualitatively. Indeed, this category must embrace verse as formal as that of Milton or Pope and as colloquial in tone as that of Frost or William Carlos Williams. Blake's "The Tiger" or the broken discourse of Eliot's *The Waste Land* belong in it. Sandburg's free verse image—

The fog comes
on little cat feet.
It sits looking

---

[9]There was persistent criticism in the 1930s of Thomas Wolfe's *Look Homeward, Angel* and *Of Time and the River,* because as a novelist, he indulged too much in poetic flights believed to be inappropriate to prose fiction. The fact that many of his lyric passages could stand alone was demonstrated by a collection of these in free verse or blank verse format in John S. Barnes's book, *A Stone, A Leaf, A Door,* published in 1945.

> over harbor and city
> on silent haunches
> and then moves on....

now takes its place in a canon of verse that includes Shakespeare's sonnets, with its measured lines—

> Let me not to the marriage of true minds
> Admit impediments. Love is not love
> Which alters when it alteration finds,
> Or bends with the remover to remove.

Within the shifts and all-encompassing styles of several centuries, both are total poetry. The formal prosody of the sonnet—new and exciting in Shakespeare's time—afforded a variety of devices now traditional enough. With the fresh discovery of simplicity early in the 20th century, Sandburg's casual-sounding lines afforded a comparable, if lesser, novelty. The extended metaphor for fog gains its poetic appeal from the carefully controlled ratio of stresses and nonstresses and the subtlety of sound pattern by which free verse was to compensate for abandoning a set versification.

Yet just as we found the heightened prose of Number 4 susceptible to poetic arrangement, it must be admitted that Sandburg's lines could also be written,

> The fog comes on little cat feet. It sits looking over harbor and city on silent haunches and then moves on.

Can the poetic potential of prose be transformed at will by the seemingly mechanical factor of linear arrangement? In gauging whether a poem merits our final acceptance, we face the unsettling shifts of emphasis and mode. Sandburg's free verse imagism received approval at a time when highly reductive forms such as the Japanese **haiku** were being translated into English. Coincidentally, the formalized prosody typified in the sonnet (or almost any of the other set stanzas traditional in English) were yielding ground to pure **metaphor (imagism,** as it came to be called) and an *A B C* simpliity.

11

"Fog" would be just one example of the alchemy by which departures from tradition are reabsorbed into our canon—a dilution of the "purity" of poetry, yet representative of its constant renewal.

Number 5 is a most catholic division, as is demonstrated historically. This is why there is no single definition to contain poetry. Its themes may be perennial, but its means and form will change. Wordsworth's "Tintern Abbey" has become a monument of English reflective verse. It also exemplifies a tendency of Western poetry to amplify and protract emotion. Its meditation on the poignancy of time and change—

> Five years have passed; five summers, with the
>   length
> Of five long winters!...
>   That time is past
> And all its aching joys are now no more....

continues for 159 very moving lines. A comparable, although very elliptically expressed, emotion has been compressed in Bashô's *haiku*,

> In Kyo I am,
>   and still I long for Kyo—
>   Oh, bird of time![10]

"Tintern Abbey" is most prominent in our canon; would we accept the *haiku*, supposing it an English poem? It is difficult to sort out the factors constantly being drawn upon to comprehend the nature of true poetry. They seem contradictory at one time; at other times, complementary. It is a competent reader who learns to discriminate the varying elements, acquiring that sixth sense by which he soon recognizes a poem, rather than having to subject it to the still-life test of a single definition.

---

[10]Harold G. Henderson, trans., *An Introduction to Haiku.*

Other Conditions of a Poem

Poetry often may exist for us in unexpected places and in a strictly relative sense. Poetry may, for example, have an accidental existence in another genre, as in certain kinds of primitive eloquence or in the bone-dry concision of logical or scientific deductions, the more striking because no poetry was intended. What a poet intends, and what his poem says, do not always coincide. Even sophisticated writers unwittingly reveal their unconscious to the practiced eye of perceptive readers. In the subliminal state they often achieve a special power by the suspension of the conscious craftsman. The condensation of a poet's images often resemble those images that stir in our dreams, emerge from our past, or reach back into some common racial heritage.[11]

Another relative aspect of poetry is the context in which it is expressed, from which comes the expectancy of poetry or prose. The poet adopts a certain intensity or heightened feeling, and this must be communicated to the competent reader. The simple statement, "The ship is over there, the one with the hoisted sails," carries no special overtones, partly because of the order of the words, but also because no overtones were intended. But consider the words of like content that Tennyson puts into Ulysses's mouth. When the old hero of many an adventure gestures to the ship in which he intends to make his final voyage, Ulysses demonstrates Tennyson's intent to make the most of the whole Homeric context:

> There lies the port; the vessel puffs her sail;
> There gloom the dark seas. My mariners,
> Souls that have toiled, and wrought, and thought
> with me....

Sometimes it is but a slight shift of wording that distinguishes poetic context from that of prose. The general statement of a *haiku* of Buson is, "I stepped on my dead

---

[11]This is discussed at greater length in Chapter 7, pp. 183–191.

wife's comb in the bedroom. I get chills at the thought of her." Whatever evades us through literal translation, the special tension of poetry is suggested by Harold Henderson's translation:

> The piercing chill I feel:
> my dead wife's comb, in our bedroom
> under my heel.[12]

Very little has been added—only a timing and phrasing that concentrate the implied emotion, as in the **ellipsis** (that is, the shortcut of grammatical construction) after the first line, suggesting an instant pause of realization.

But context works not only toward a heightening. It may also achieve a kind of psychological understatement. As early as George Crabbe's and Wordsworth's time, but especially since Browning's monologistic experiments, a colloquial context was deliberately sought. This conversational tone, sometimes with, sometimes without direct discourse, permits an effective understatement, usually leading to a play of irony. Such understatement was practiced in the second and third decades of this century as part of the reaction to the sometimes heavy prosody of the preceding Edwardian and Georgian decades. Masters's and Frost's low-keyed, even flat-sounding poems stressed the psychological rather than the prosodic. The meditations of Spoon River's dead were in a free verse that raised doubts among many as to its being called poetry at all. The opening lines of Frost's "The Death of the Hired Man" (transcribed below in plain prose rather than capitalized verses) could plausibly be read as the first sentences of a short story:

> Mary sat musing on the lamp-flame at the table waiting for Warren. When she heard his step, she ran on tip-toe down the darkened passage to meet him in the doorway with the news and put him on his guard. . . .

Here, of course, we recognize context in its broadest sense: the lines above have an organic part in the poem as a whole,

---

[12]*An Introduction to Haiku.*

which in turn achieves poetic intensity more through the condensing of narrative than through the prosody of lyric poetry. Such a reciprocal movement between the genre in the years just mentioned was taking place on a fairly wide scale. The techniques in James Joyce's collection of stories, *Dubliners*, as in the earlier ones of Chekhov, borrowed the selective imagery and verbal tension—and sometimes heightened mood—of lyric poetry, even as Masters's, Frost's, and Sandburg's techniques acquired the colloquial tones of fiction.

The historical relationships are always shifting. In recent years colloquialism may have reached its ultimate stage in the verse written by the Beatniks for oral recitation. And, as though exploiting the understatement and elliptical tendency of Eliot's and Stevens's generation, many who achieved prominence in the 1960s still seem fascinated with repeating the old counterpoints between the trivia of life and the horrors of contemporary society. The attitudes seem more and more inverted, and while the subjects are often new, the poetics are a simplification of the post-World War I revolution.

Finally, poetry may be said to function in a varying relationship to the art of rhetoric on one side and to music on the other. We have already considered the relation to rhetoric.[13] The connection with music is an ambiguous one. While the word *lyric* means "sung," and the origins of poetry and music are almost inseparable, the kinship today is largely observed in the figurative sense. Unlike music, the determinants of poetry—words—combine the conceptual as well as the aural. Poetry has no physical instrument but the voice; no fixed duration of notes; no established tempo. Its tones, pitches, and stresses are always variable, rather than set, as in music. In poetry there are no harmonies of simultaneous sounds, only the association with natural sounds through the metaphysical transformation of words.

But because poetry, whether read silently or read aloud, evokes the sounds that words have, nothing affects the conditions of a poem more than the way it is read. One who has heard an expert, or has learned to read with authority him-

---

[13]See pp. 8–10.

self, knows what a range of depths and nuances are possible with the spoken word. The oral reading of a poem can mean the difference between apathy and excitement. Once a person has heard a poem, it is never really silent to him again. He may recover it in his **inner ear** at will. And because of the dimension added to poetry by oral reading, the importance of cultivating this inner ear should quickly be apparent.

Practical Criticism

1. Look up two or three samples of "prose poetry" (for example, the conclusion of Robert L. Stevenson's essay, "Pulvis et Umbra") and compare them with any free verse or blank verse of your choice. You will find details about such verse in the Glossary.

2. Compare a passage of muted poetry (for example, the opening of "The Death of the Hired Man," p. 14) with a sample or two of prose that you might wish to defend as having equal poetic quality (for example, the opening paragraphs of "Interlude" in Virginia Woolf's novel *To the Lighthouse*).

TWO

Where the Reader Stands

Statement and Implication

Most people are more comfortable reading prose than
reading poetry. This seems to be a conditioning effected
fairly early in our maturity; for it is in our childhood and
youth—if ever—that poetry seems to leave its sharpest im-
print. To most, prose seems designed to describe things or to
narrate events as they are, rather than to manufacture or
exhibit emotion. The syntax and phraseology of prose are
applied to graspable facts, things comprehendible in a work-
aday, relaxed frame of mind. Poetry frustrates all these aspects of straightforward communication. It tends to be vague
and fanciful, with nothing clear-cut and definite. What the
poet expresses seems to proceed by indirection. When poetry
describes, it goes off on tangents, losing sight of the plain
substance of things.

Of course, none of these distinctions is now, or ever was,
absolute. We saw in Chapter 1 the continual overlapping of
prose and poetry. The distinctions are frequently biased or
highly subjective. Yet every generation makes them, and
some generations more than others. When the bias is strong,
the poets, too, are likely to be influenced. Their poetry is
likely to reflect the prevailing climate by being more direct
or less direct, couched more as statement or expressed more
through implication. William Ernest Henley, for instance,
spoke to his late Victorian contemporaries in the succinct
and unequivocal terms they wished to hear. His poems were
of a robust, declarative sort, favoring the kind of unmistakable prosody that left no one in doubt as to his meaning. We
still quote from his "Invictus," which contains the following
stanza:

It matters not how strait the gate,
    How charged with punishments the scroll,
I am the master of my fate,
    I am the captain of my soul.

Sometimes, disenchanted with the tentativeness of modern values, we may envy the apparent confidence with which
Henley's generation accepted these poetic absolutes. Such
bluffness is very much part of our English heritage. There
are still many who would feel the ring in those lines, or in
these lines by Henley published earlier in *A Book of Verse*:

What is to come we know not. But we know
That what has been was good—was good to show,
Better to hide, and best of all to bear.
We are the masters of the days that were;
We have lived, we have loved, we have suffered
    —even so.

I believe it was his long illness in a hospital that had wrung
from him those blunt phrases. What is noteworthy is that
his choice of style was as suitable to his purpose as a more
involuted style, such as that of Yeats and Eliot was to their
generation.

One poet may move by indirection; another, like Henley,
may express his feelings directly. Still another, like Walt
Whitman, may make a virtue of unrestraint, an impetuous-
ness of style that consorts well with the America he wished
to celebrate. One poet creates images by which whole attitudes are compressed; another prefers the rhetorical sequences, parallelisms, or periodic sentences familiar to
audiences in churches and political assemblies. John Donne
is an example of the latter, a poet working within an **organic**
style, whose ideas, like growing plants, branch from one
another and evolve cell by cell, fed from some central root.
In the stanza below, from his "Love's Growth," we note an
ambivalence of words. These words were not chosen to

18

denote or state literally, as most of Henley's were; they are far more figurative, more **connotative:**

> But if this medicine, love, which cures all sorrow
>> With more, not only be no quintessence,
>> But mix'd of all stuffs, vexing soul, or sense,
> And of the sun his active vigour borrow,
> Love's not so pure, and abstract, as they use
> To say, which have no mistresses but their Muse;
> But as all else, being elemented too,
> Love sometimes would contemplate, sometimes do.

What we may call the denotative poem conveys its ideas, its quality of mind, its sentiment, predominantly by statement. The connotatively structured poem, on the other hand, tries to *suggest* a quality of mind, an idea, or a sentiment. The methods of the second are by indirection, with the attention focused as much on the means of the poem as on the message or conclusion. Henley's poem is denotative (despite the fact that he juggles the meaning of "good"); he talks directly about something that is really vague. MacLeish's "Ars Poetica," below, progresses by a series of similes in a seemingly mechanical way. Yet the relationship of the images is organic, each one (while quite different) evolving from another. By the final couplet, this cellular-like growth reaches fruition—or blossoms.

> A poem should be palpable and mute
> As a globed fruit
>
> Dumb
> As old medallions to the thumb
>
> Silent as the sleeve-worn stone
> Of casement ledges where the moss has grown—
>
> A poem should be wordless
> As the flight of birds
>   . . .

19

A poem should be motionless in time
As the moon climbs

Leaving, as the moon releases
Twig by twig the night-entangled trees,

Leaving, as the moon behind the winter leaves,
Memory by memory the mind—

A poem should be motionless in time
As the moon climbs

       . . .

A poem should be equal to:
Not true

For all the history of grief
An empty doorway and a maple leaf

For love
The leaning grasses and two lights above the sea—

A poem should not mean
But be.

MacLeish's subject is as difficult to enunciate as Henley's "good" in life. Yet despite the indirection of these images, a remarkable clarity emerges from "Ars Poetica." However, despite the seeming bluntness of Henley's terms (and, indeed, they are by no means unmoving), the quality he tries to define remains uncertain. "Tell all the truth, but tell it slant," says Emily Dickinson, expressing in her gnomic way the peculiar nature of artistic communication:

Tell all the truth, but tell it slant,
Success in circuit lies,
Too bright for our infirm delight
The truth's superb surprise;

As lightning to the children eased
With explanation kind,
The truth must dazzle gradually
Or every man be blind.

The ways in which the "truth" has been conveyed in poetry are so complex that it would be foolhardy to attempt any full explanation. In the next section, we shall discuss three fairly typical ways in which three poets—each living about a generation apart—presented their peculiar view of the sea as an aspect of the world around them.

Address and Response

How do the three poets—Wordsworth, Arnold, and Masefield—communicate their feelings about the sea, and how do we respond to them? Let us order our approach according to the distinctions of the previous section. How does Wordsworth address himself to his theme—and, concomitantly, to the reader? And how do we, the readers, respond? Will the poem take shape as sound or sense, as statement or connotation, as meditation or song, as formal structure or free form? Or will it combine several of these, fashioning a complex union of diversities?

While few poems are all of one sort, the dominant pitch will usually evoke one response over another—the sensuous at the expense of the reflective, the aural over the analytic, the imagistic as opposed to the reasonable. In Wordsworth's "The World Is Too Much with Us," a traditional prosody is assured by the Italian sonnet form, replete with its generous recurrences of sound in a rich rhyme scheme. Despite the traditional adornments of **personification** and **metonymy** ("The Sea that bares her bosom," "The world is too much with us"), Wordsworth addresses us directly with the conventional editorial "we":

The world is too much with us; late and soon
Getting and spending, we lay waste our powers:

Little we see in Nature that is ours;
We have given our hearts away, a sordid boon!
The Sea that bares her bosom to the moon;
The winds that will be howling at all hours,
And are up-gathered now like sleeping flowers;
For this, for everything, we are out of tune;
It moves us not—Great God! I'd rather be
A Pagan suckled in a creed outworn;
So might I, standing on this pleasant lea,
Have glimpses that would make me less forlorn;
Have sight of Proteus rising from the sea;
Or hear old Triton blow his wreathéd horn.

Only in the **sestet** (the sonnet's last six lines) is there a shift to an almost dramatic "Great God! I'd rather be / A Pagan..." and to the allusion to Proteus and Triton that achieves metaphorical force. Essentially the poem is *about* the stultification of England's imagination. It addresses itself to a theme, rather than rendering the feel or sound of the sea's neglected loveliness *as* sounds or sensations.

A fairly dynamic idea is neatly packaged in Wordsworth's sonnet. And for what most sonnets are designed to accomplish, that is enough. We can chew over the problem, empathize with the poet's disillusionment, argue its social or cultural implications. But we are less likely to gain the auditory stimulus of the sea itself. For this we turn to a poem in which the poet addresses his subject as though they were in physical contact. The words become active agents rather than indirect symbols. Such a poem may carry scant "meaning" of a sort one could epitomize. Rather, it will be, as in Masefield's "Sea-Fever," below, a reproduction in words of the physical impact of the sea on our senses:

I must go down to the seas again, to the lonely
    sea and the sky,
And all I ask is a tall ship and a star to steer her by,

And the wheel's kick and the wind's song and the
white sails shaking,
And a gray mist on the sea's face and a gray dawn
breaking.

I must go down to the seas again, for the call of the
running tide
Is a wild call and clear call that may not be denied;
And all I ask is a windy day with the white clouds
flying,
And the flung spray and the blown spume, and the
sea-gulls crying.

I must go down to the seas again to the vagrant
gypsy life,
To the gull's way and the whales's way where the
wind's like a whetted knife;
And all I ask is a merry yarn from a laughing fel-
low-rover,
And quiet sleep and a sweet dream when the long
trick's over.

This is not abstract observation; it is concentrated experience, rendered as if at first hand. We hear what is described
—though it be only in that "inner ear" through which most
of us have become conditioned to a verbalized account of
the world.

Many things go into the recreation of experience represented in "Sea-Fever." They would be mostly classed as
what is meant by **prosody**—not so much the *a b a b* rhyme
scheme as the skillfully manipulated rhythm and meter, as
well as the use of syllabic sounds and **phonemes.** As an example, most of the lines are a rocking combination of **anapestic**
and **iambic** feet juxtaposed so as to simulate brisk motion. The
first line of each stanza would be **scanned** like this:

I must | go down | to the seas | again, || for the call |
of the run | ning tide

—where ˘ represents a light stress, ´ represents a heavy stress, and | represents the division of a metrical foot. But when we scan[1] poems, we must expect a great deal of variation within a predominant kind of meter.[2] Note that in the final line of each stanza, Masefield has abandoned the anapests and iambs for a strange double stress, as in the last line of stanza two:

Aňd thĕ | flúng spráy | aňd thĕ | blówn spúme, ||
aňd thĕ | séa-gúlls | crýiňg.

Thus in each final line of each stanza, two unstressed syllables are followed by two stressed syllables,[3] creating the special rhythm of waves breaking along a stretch of shore.

But, besides his physical suggestion in rhythm and meter, Masefield has played upon the sounds of the words themselves to suggest natural sounds of water, wind, bird, and spray. The syllables themselves reveal a breakdown of the sounds by which the phonetic effect is conveyed (in the line above—"fl- -ung spr- -ay," "bl- -own sp- -ume," and "sea-gul- -ls cr-y-ing").[4] This phonetic quality of words is used by poets to control the color and intensity of a poem, frequently unnoted in ordinary reading. The subtleties of these effects are increased by recurrences of similar sounds (in addition to the end rhymes) at the beginning of words. The second line, for instance, sets up a tattoo of initial consonent sounds ("star," "steer") and vowel sounds ("all," "ask"), known traditionally as **alliteration. Consonance,** the recurrence of consonantal sounds (as in the third line—"whee*l*'s," "win*d*s," "*s*ong," "*wh*ite," "sai*l*s," "*sh*aking") may be interspersed within words in different parts of a line. Combine these effects with similarities of vowel sounds *within* words (as in line four—"gr*ay*," "f*a*ce," "s*ea*," "br*ea*king"), known as

---

[1] All the words and symbols related to scansion are in the Glossary.

[2] Sometimes called **substitution.**

[3] This creates what would be respectively **pyrrhic feet** and **spondees,** types of feet occurring only occasionally in English verse.

[4] These are usually referred to in linguistics as **phonemes.** See the Glossary.

assonance, and you become aware of a textured fabrication of sensory impressions.[5]

One would not deny that Wordsworth's sonnet shares with "Sea-Fever" many of these orthographic factors. Both poems make use, for instance, of the musical qualities of **duration, pitch,** and tone. Of these, duration, or quantity, is the way in which we vary the length of the syllables in words—especially of monosyllabic words such as "stone" versus "sit" or "fail" versus "stop," where the first is long, the second short. Masefield's poem is far more eloquent of this durational control than is Wordsworth's, not because the latter could not control it (indeed, the opening of "Tintern Abbey" illustrates such control well),[6] but because Masefield drafts it into his deliberate recreation of physical effects. Note that the juxtaposed long words in the last line of each stanza ("gray," "sea's face," "gray dawn," and "*breaking*") prolong sounds associated with the heavy collapse of waves, while the shorter ones ("and a," "on the," "and a," "-ing") are like the recoil and counterflow between waves. Thus, while length of syllable corresponds in this poem pretty much to stress, the prolonging or abbreviating of time brings out natural rhythms that may underlie the metrical count itself. Notice that in Wordsworth's sonnet, this correspondence is less clear, especially in the second line. If both stresses and duration were marked, the scansion would be something like this in the first two lines [where the **macron** (–) indicates length or quantity and the **breve** (˘) doubles for both light stress and short duration]:

The wórld | ĭs tŏo | mŭch wĭth | ūs; ⸗ lāte | aňd sóon
Géttĭng | aňd spēn|dĭng, ⸗ wé | laÿ wáste | oŭr pówērs.

Sometimes this sustaining of sound corresponds to the **pitch** (the second of the qualities listed above). In the sonnet by Wordsworth, change in pitch seems notably absent until about the middle of the ninth line ("Great God! I'd rather be...") where it seems inevitable that the reader's voice

---

[5]A more detailed discussion of aural recurrences follows in Chapter 4.

[6]See Chapter 1, p. 12.

rises on the scale and probably increases in intensity. In "Sea-Fever," words like "wheel," "wind," "white," (stanza 1, line 3) and "wild" and "clear" (stanza 2, line 2) seem to demand a higher register than the juxtaposed words "kick," "song," "call," which, despite their prominent stress, receive a falling inflection. This recurrent up-down pattern complements the wavelike alternations of long and short duration. The last line of the poem suggests the subsiding of forces, elsewhere so strong. The stresses, syllabic duration, and pitch are muted, but the line exhibits well the harmonious functioning of sound values in concert:

> And quiet sleep and a sweet dream when the long
> trick's over.

If Wordsworth's poem addresses itself to the substance or idea, and Masefield's to the projection of sensory experience, another poem, Matthew Arnold's "Dover Beach," brings the two types of poetic statement together, enlivening a commentary on the times by a personal framework. Arnold's view is as disillusioned as Wordsworth's, but he has chosen to set off his indictment with a background of aural and visual impressions. The setting, as in the other two poems, is the sea. Actually, it is more dominant than mere setting, for it unites the different parts of an otherwise discursive meditation. It is also the cue for a personal glimpse of the speaker and the listener. In substance "Dover Beach" may be closer to "The World Is Too Much with Us," but the studied use of phonetic recurrences, the aural suggestions of the physical world outside the speaker's window, place it within Masefield's technique, or what has been called an "orchestrated" poem:[7]

> The sea is calm tonight.
> The tide is full, the moon lies fair
> Upon the straits;—on the French coast the light
> Gleams and is gone; the cliffs of England stand,

[7]See Chapter 4, pp. 77–80.

Glimmering and vast, out in the tranquil bay.
Come to the window, sweet is the night-air!
Only, from the long line of spray
Where the sea meets the moon-blanch'd land,
Listen! you hear the grating roar
Of pebbles which the waves draw back, and fling,
At their return, up the high strand,
Begin, and cease, and then again begin,
With tremulous cadence slow, and bring
The eternal note of sadness in.

Sophocles long ago
Heard it on the Aegean, and it brought
Into his mind the turbid ebb and flow
Of human misery; we
Find also in the sound a thought,
Hearing it by this distant northern sea.

The Sea of Faith
Was once, too, at the full, and round earth's shore
Lay like the folds of a bright girdle furl'd.
But now I only hear
Its melancholy, long, withdrawing roar,
Retreating, to the breath
Of the night-wind, down the vast edges drear
And naked shingles of the world.

Ah, love, let us be true
To one another! for the world which seems
To lie before us like a land of dreams,
So various, so beautiful, so new,
Hath really neither joy, nor love, nor light,
Nor certitude, nor peace, nor help for pain;
And we are here as on a darkling plain
Swept with confused alarms of struggle and flight,
Where ignorant armies clash by night.

The two middle stanzas (together comprising fourteen lines of **interlocking rhymes** that suggest an originally intended sonnet) are regressions to two great eras of western civilization, one humanistic, the other theistic. They represent two polarities of man's achievement. But to bring them into greater relief, and in greater contrast with his own time, Arnold has taken the role of a speaker who subjectively expresses the deficiency of his own time in the dramatic setting of a seascape and its sea rhythms. This special perspective (as though Arnold had put a personal frame around his sonnet) saves the poem from the declarative flatness that would have resulted from the two central stanzas alone.

Structurally, Wordsworth's poem began with a generalized present, contrasted by allusion to two Greek sea deities symbolic of a picturesque antiquity. Arnold's begins with a particularized moment in the unsatisfactory present, making it a setting within which he invokes two past epochs of world greatness. Then he swings back to the heartless and disheartening chaos of the present. Wordsworth deprecated the crass disregard in his day for the world's natural loveliness; Arnold broods over the alienation of his generation from times either of humanistic richness or spiritual grandeur. The themes are not vastly different, but Arnold's tone gains from a direct transcription of sound and setting comparable to Masefield's. In so addressing himself, Arnold enables us to identify with an otherwise abstract set of attitudes.

From the very outset of "Dover Beach," the sea permeates the speaker's vision. The description, though, is keyed lower than Masefield's. Arnold mingles undulant and muted tones with the speaker's night-bound melancholy. What was for Masefield a total immersion in the sensations of the sea becomes, for Arnold, more of a collaboration between the personal response and the shaping of an idea. Man's turbulence finds its paradigm in nature. It is seen in the opening and closing monologue where the recurrent phonemes (known in linguistics as sibilants, plosives, consonances, and assonances) are almost as dense as in Masefield's poem:

... which the waves suck back, and fling,
At their return, up the high strand,
Begin, and cease, and then again begin. ...

Such is his art, that readers feel the special appeal of this troubled Victorian who combines drama, sound, and sense. Such is Masefield's art that they immerse themselves in his summons to sheer physical experience. By making the reader respond one way or the other, each poet has succeeded in projecting a part of his world beyond himself.

Our original question was how does a given poem first affect the reader. This comparison of three poems involving the sea—Wordsworth's, Masefield's, and Arnold's—represents what may seem an oversimplified answer: as direct statement, pure sound, or the harmony of the two. Most poetry ranges across the field. When lyricism and dramatic enrichment are pressed into the service of pure idea, any resulting degree of success is a matter of balance, and to assess it requires training. Also, any given poem, selected to illustrate specific values, contains many other factors of comparable interest beyond this preliminary discussion (imagery, historical context, and so forth). These will have our attention in succeeding chapters.[8]

Two Aspects of Response

What we experience when first hearing a poem may seem fairly uncomplicated, until rereadings illumine the complexities. The controlling factors may appear as discrete and

---

[8] If Masefield's poem exists independently of context, and Wordsworth's can be enjoyed with or without contextural analysis, Arnold's is the example of a poem that gains stature by our grasp of its conditions. We are bound to gain greater insight by an explanation of his choice of speaker and listener as reflecting something of his own domestic circumstances, or by realization that the contemporary death struggle between science and religion is probably reflected in the pessimistic vision with which the poem concludes, or that the structure of the poem itself reflects Arnold's early interest in Greek plays and his experiments with verse drama.

separate, but they usually prove to be interlocking and inter-
dependent. At what point, for instance, do we become most
aware of the intellectual part of a poem? Or at what point,
in a different kind of poem, do we first discern the concurrent function of means and meaning—that is, when we see
that a poem's aurally stimulating factors are involved in
whatever substantive qualities the poem has?[9]

Undoubtedly each reader's approach to these variables
differs with his conditioning. For many of us, the power of
controlled sound is primary and basic to our initial experience of a poem. Here, probably, poetry comes closest to
satisfying that free masonry we experience in music. Know-
ing little of the German tongue, would a reading of Goethe's
lyric from *Mignon* have any power to please us? Actual
meaning aside, would the prosodic effects, the recurrences,
and the rhythm partially satisfy our conditioning to heard
sounds?

> Kennst du das Land, wo die Citronen blühn,
> Im dunkeln Laub die Gold-Orangen glühn,
> Ein sanfter Wind Vom blauen Himmel weht,
> Die Myrte still und hoch der Lorbeer steht—
> Kennst du es wohl?
> > Dahin! Dahin
> Möcht' ich mit dir, o mein Geliebter, ziehn!
>
> Kennst du das Haus? auf Saulen ruht sein Dach,
> Es glänzt der Saal, as schimmert das Gemach,
> Und Marmorbilder stehn und sehn mich an:
> Was hat man dir, du armes Kind, getan?—
> Kennst du es wohl?
> > Dahin! Dahin
> Möcht' ich mit dir, o mein Beschutzer, ziehn!

What strikes the ear beyond certain stresses and Germanic
gutterals and plosives awkward to the English tongue?

---

[9]These will be examined as individual problems in succeeding chapters.

Mostly, it would seem to be the hard overall rhythm, especially in the doubling back of the refrain ("Dahin! Dahin . . ."), and an **expectancy** we come to feel for the recognizable rhymes, assonances, and consonances that weave through the two stanzas.

These elements, we note, are principally a form of **recurrence,** whether of accentuation, verbal similarity, or whole phrases or lines. It seems possible, then, to derive some pleasure from other languages (certainly those of Romance or Teutonic root) insofar as common prosodic factors are involved. In support of this we have T. S. Eliot's testimony (early in his essay on Dante's *Inferno*) that the sound of poetry had been able to move him long before he could grasp the sense:

> In my own experience of the appreciation of poetry I have always found that the less I knew about the poet and his work, before I began to read it, the better. A quotation, a critical remark, an enthusiastic essay, may well be the accident that sets one to reading a particular author; but an elaborate preparation of historical and biographical knowledge has always been to me a barrier. . . . I was passionately fond of certain French poetry long before I could have translated two verses of it correctly. With Dante the discrepancy between enjoyment and understanding was still wider. . . . It is a test (a positive test, I do not assert that it is always valid negatively) that genuine poetry can communicate before it is understood.

We can say, then, that some readers are intelligently affected by merely the sounds of a poem, whether or not the intellectual or substantive content is ultimately revealed. But the ultimate revelation should always be sought; for even in the seeking, we gain in poetic experience. The question, however, of the order of poetic experience is very much part of both the poet's and the reader's concern—the complementary aspects, again, of means and meaning (see especially Chapters 6 and 7). As was pointed out earlier in this chapter, the realization of the inseparability of such entities has become more and more characteristic of verse in the 20th century.

In our older anthologies we were likely to find the contents divided into "poems of nature," "poems of love," "poems on death," and so forth. This was an understandable classification as long as we wished to, or were required to, approach our poetry at the level of nominal interest. The substantive content became accessible at a glance. As an approach to poetics, however, it overlooked the more complex technical *means* of poet and object. These, as we have seen, involved poet and reader in a dynamic relationship. The poet cunningly prepared the trail, and his reader followed its course, hopefully "experiencing" the result as art (and emerging a keener and, possibly, better man—the poet having already improved *himself* through the creative therapy of his work).

Not too many years ago it was an unusual schoolboy who had not committed to memory sizable quantities of Gray's "Elegy." For his teachers the poem epitomized the acceptable descriptiveness and prayer-like meditation they believed to be any poem's first purpose. A reader knew exactly where he stood as dusk settled on a scene reminiscent of the ever-popular "Angelus" of the painter Millet:

> The curfew tolls the knell of parting day,
>   The lowing herd winds slowly o'er the lea,
> The plowman homeward plods his weary way,
>   And leaves the world to darkness and to me.
>
>   .   .   .   .
>
> Can storied urn or animated bust
>   Back to its mansion call the fleeting breath?
> Can Honor's voice provoke the silent dust,
>   Or Flatt'ry soothe the dull cold ear of Death?
>
>   .   .   .   .
>
> Some village Hampden that with dauntless breast
>   The little tyrant of his fields withstood,
> Some mute inglorious Milton here may rest,
>   Some Cromwell guiltless of his country's blood.

The message was sober, serious, and couched in a prosody and diction so unmistakable as to have held their appeal for two centuries. But, mainly, it was the universal lesson of mortality that made so many recall the poem as a superb statement of its kind. At no point could this central theme be mistaken—ambiguous though the increasingly personal caste of the poem might become.

We may contrast this with a poem of somewhat related theme: life, love, and death of a nobody, isolated from the world of more important people. But in this poem, by E. E. Cummings, the theme has become inseparable from the way of saying it:

> anyone lived in a pretty how town
> (with up so floating many bells down)
> spring summer autumn winter
> he sang his didn't he danced his did.
>
> Women and men (both little and small)
> cared for anyone not at all
> they sowed their isn't they reaped their same
> sun moon stars rain
>
> children guessed (but only a few
> and down they forgot as up they grew
> autumn winter spring summer)
> that noone loved him more by more
>
> when by now and tree by leaf
> she laughed his joy she cried his grief
> bird by snow and stir by still
> anyone's any was all to her

—and so a multidimensional narrative is interlocked with concomitant factors of time, nature, season, and so forth. The recurrences suggest a swirling motion—of bells, days and nights, seasons, weather, human activities, rituals, growth, and anniversaries. The story, like Gray's, is one of mortality, in which the little man ("anyone") reaches marriage and death. But the descriptive elements are inseparable from the fate of the village man. A reader would find it difficult to separate all the essences, intertwined as they are with the sense of environment and the diurnal round:

> someones married their everyones
> laughed their cryings and did their dance

(sleep wake hope and then) they
said their nevers they slept their dream

stars rain sun moon
(and only the snow can begin to explain
how children are apt to forget to remember
with up so floating many bells down)

. . . .

one day anyone died i guess
(and noone stooped to kiss his face)
busy folk buried them side by side
little by little and was by was

all by all and deep by deep
and more by more they dream their sleep
noone and anyone earth by april
wish by spirit and if by yes.

The poem ends with a new beginning (indicated by a period
at the end of the last stanza above, but not after the final
stanza, below) and a cluster of puns on bells, sex, fertility—
all involved as an intertwining **texture** throughout the poem:

Women and men (both dong and ding)
summer autumn winter spring
reaped their sowing and went their came
sun moon stars rain

The meaning merges in the means. The varieties of means
are, of course, very nearly inexhaustible. In Cummings' poem,
not only the ingenious images (a form of **ambiguity** in themselves) or the **incantatory** quality of the **repetends** ("sun moon
stars rain"), but also the intentional shifts in the parts of
speech, the combining of **symbol** and **synesthesia** of "up so
floating many bells down," and the symbol, **pun** and **onomatopoeia** of "women and men (both dong and ding)" all add up
to a rich and powerful combination of mental picture and
sensation. The words are more than denotative. Our associa-

tions with each carefully chosen one commits us to an ever changing, almost cinematic conceptualization.

These qualities, contrasting with or augmenting the familiar devices of many traditional poems, provide most of the themes of the next chapters. The first of these is concerned with the elements of aural recurrence.

Practical Criticism

Aural and Conceptual Emphasis

1. Poems of all sorts contain the distinctions we have discussed, though we need not expect to find them falling into a clear-cut, threefold classification. It would be interesting to take for comparison additional poems of Masefield, Wordsworth, and Arnold to see in what proportion the emphasis is placed, respectively, on the aural, the conceptual, or a structured combination of these. The comparisons made so far in this chapter will serve as an interim pattern for analysis of the three poems, "Cargoes," "I Wandered Lonely as a Cloud," and "To Marguerite—Continued."

   Masefield's "Cargoes," for instance, while resembling "Sea-Fever" in its marked cadence, phonemic color, and marine setting, suggests a theme even closer to Wordsworth's "The World Is Too Much with Us." Its distinction from Wordsworth's, however, is that it expresses contrasts that implicitly criticize modern seafaring, while manipulating the aural effects and contrasting the rhythms to exemplify the idea.

CARGOES

Quinquireme of Nineveh from distant Ophir,
Rowing home to haven in sunny Palestine,
With a cargo of ivory,
And apes and peacocks,
Sandalwood, cedarwood, and sweet white wine.

Stately Spanish galleon coming from the Isthmus,
Dipping through the Tropics by the palm-green shores,
With a cargo of diamonds,
Emeralds, amethysts,
Topazes, and cinnamon, and gold moidores.

35

Dirty British coaster with a salt-caked smoke-stack,
Butting through the Channel in the mad March days,
With a cargo of Tyne coal,
Road-rails, pig-lead,
Firewood, iron-ware, and cheap tin trays.

Like Wordsworth, Masefield compares the commerce of the present with a graceful and elegant past; but his contrasting data require no comment. The poet leaves it to the reader to choose a channel full of smoky shipping (symbol of the day) or an exotic sea of galleons and quinquiremes (like Wordsworth's Triton and Proteus, symbols of a vanished day). The three stanzas are a "tryptich" (that is, three connected pictures) whose relationship tells the tale. The tone and descriptive image of each panel, the assonance and consonance against **cacaphony**, the rich cargo of one against the grubby inventory of the other, leave the listener to judge, just as he would if the pictures were all he had. The **didactic** tendency of the Romanticists gives way here to the more reticent art of exemplification.

2. The following poems by Wordsworth and Arnold, respectively, represent an often recurring theme of each—imagination and isolation. In what respect do they exhibit qualities of the different approaches already contrasted; or in what respect do they exhibit some emphasis we have not yet defined?

I WANDERED LONELY AS A CLOUD

I wandered lonely as a cloud
That floats on high o'er vales and hills,
When all at once I saw a crowd,
A host, of golden daffodils;
Beside the lake, beneath the trees,
Fluttering and dancing in the breeze.

Continuous as the stars that shine
And twinkle on the milky way,
They stretched in never-ending line
Along the margin of the bay:
Ten thousand saw I at a glance,
Tossing their heads in sprightly dance.

The waves beside them danced; but they
Out-did the sparkling waves in glee:
A poet could not but be gay,
In such jocund company:
I gazed—and gazed—but little thought
What wealth the show to me had brought!

For oft, when on my couch I lie
In vacant or in pensive mood,
They flash upon that inward eye
Which is the bliss of solitude;
And then my heart with pleasure fills,
And dances with the daffodils.

TO MARGUERITE—CONTINUED

Yes: in the sea of life enisl'd,
With echoing straits between us thrown,
Dotting the shoreless watery wild,
We mortal millions live *alone*.
The islands feel the enclasping flow,
And then their endless bounds they know.

But when the moon their hollows lights,
And they are swept by balms of spring,
And in their glens, on starry nights,
The nightingales divinely sing;
And lovely notes, from shore to shore,
Across the sounds and channels pour;

Oh then a longing like despair
Is to their farthest caverns sent;
For surely once, they feel, we were
Parts of a single continent.
Now round us spreads the watery plain—
Oh might our marges meet again!

Who order'd, that their longing's fire
Should be, as soon as kindled, cool'd?
Who renders vain their deep desire?—
A God, a God their severance rul'd;
And bade betwixt their shores to be
The unplumb'd, salt, estranging sea.

Can we say either of these poems can be appreciated as an absolute entity? Is the poet simply creating from the abstract, or out of felt experience? Who was Marguerite—and does it matter? Presumably she was not Arnold's wife (whom he addressed in "Dover Beach"). There was an earlier poem to Marguerite. By checking background data (the earlier poem, correspondence, and cross-references), you will be able to place the poem in context.

Assessment of Initial Impact

1. Read the poems below (aloud, if possible) and try to assess their initial impact on you. (Include poems in 2 and 3 for further examples.) Is the primary effect on your consciousness lyrical (in a sensuous way)? Is it primarily intellectual (presenting you essentially with ideas and concepts)? Or is it a combination of these effects? Are there still other ways (not included here) by which each poem reaches you most forcefully?

SONG: "WHEN ICICLES HANG"

When icicles hang by the wall
   And Dick the shepherd blows his nail
And Tom bears logs into the hall
   And milk comes frozen home in pail,
When blood is nipp'd and ways be foul,
Then nightly sings the staring owl,
     "Tu-whit, to-who!"—
A merry note,
While greasy Joan doth keel the pot.

When all aloud the wind doth blow
   And coughing drowns the parson's saw
And birds sit brooding in the snow
   And Marian's nose looks red and raw,
When roasted crabs hiss in the bowl,
Then nightly sings the staring owl,
     "Tu-whit, tu-who!"—
A merry note,
While greasy Joan doth keel the pot.
            William Shakespeare

THE PULLEY

When God at first made Man,
Having a glass of blessings standing by—
Let us (said He) pour on him all we can;
Let the world's riches, which dispersed lie,
    Contract into a span.

So strength first made a way,
Then beauty flowed, then wisdom, honor, pleasure:
When almost all was out, God made a stay,
Perceiving that, alone of all His treasure,
    Rest in the bottom lay.

For if I should (said He)
Bestow this jewel also on my creature,
He would adore my gifts instead of Me,
And rest in Nature, not the God of Nature:
    So both should losers be.

Yet let him keep the rest,
But keep them with repining restlessness;
Let him be rich and weary, that at least,
If goodness lead him not, yet weariness
    May toss him to my breast.

George Herbert

A MAN'S A MAN FOR A' THAT

Is there, for honest poverty,
    That hings his head, an' a' that?
The coward slave, we pass him by,
    We dare be poor for a' that!
      For a' that, an' a' that,
        Our toils obscure, an' a' that:
      The rank is but the guinea's stamp;
        The man's the gowd for a' that.

What tho' on hamely fare we dine,
    Wear hodden-gray, an' a' that;
Gie fools their silks, and knaves their wine,
    A man's a man for a' that.

For a' that, an' a' that,
Their tinsel show, an' a' that;
The honest man, tho e'er sae poor,
Is king o'men for a' that.

. . . .

A prince can mak a belted knight,
A marquis, duke, an' a' that;
But an honest man's aboon his might,
Guid faith he mauna fa' that!
For a' that, an' a' that,
Their dignities, an' a' that,
The pith o' sense, an' pride o' worth,
Are higher ranks than a' that.

. . . .

Robert Burns

2. How much of Browning's "Memorabilia," below, comes through for you in a single reading? Does the poem stand on its own, or do you find yourself wondering about the circumstances, biographical facts, or other background?

MEMORABILIA

I

Ah, did you once see Shelley plain,
And did he stop and speak to you?
And did you speak to him again?
How strange it seems, and new!

II

But you were living before that,
And you are living after,
And the memory I started at—
My starting moves your laughter!

III

I crossed a moor, with a name of its own
And a use in the world no doubt,
Yet a hand's breadth of it shines alone
'Mid the blank miles round about:

40

IV

For there I picked up on the heather
And there I put inside my breast
A moulted feather, an eagle-feather—
Well, I forget the rest.

Robert Browning

This is the sort of poem that often delights a teacher. It requires the special information that he is supposed to know.
William Clyde DeVane's *A Browning Handbook* reports from
Browning's own testimony that the poet was browsing in a
bookstore when he heard a stranger remark to a clerk how he
had once met the poet Shelley. Browning had particularly ad-
mired Shelley, although he had never met him, and was amazed
at the stranger's matter-of-factness. The dramatic shift in the
third stanza to the finding of the eagle's feather in a barren
place is a little allegory that completes the sense of treasuring
something insufficiently valued in a cheapened environment.

3. Try experimenting with the range of vocal expression you can
bring to the poems above. Notice the extent to which your inflection, word emphasis, pitch, and rhythmic phrasing help the
reading or render it stilted and affected.

4. Most of the poems below are in your anthology. At your own
leisure, try applying the questions of 1 (above) to the examples
below:

a. The popular ballad, "Lord Randal"
b. William Shakespeare, "When to the Sessions of Sweet Silent
Thought"
c. John Milton, "Lycidas"
d. Henry Vaughan, "The Retreat"
e. Walt Whitman, "Cavalry Crossing a Ford"
f. Gerard Hopkins, "The Windhover"
g. Rudyard Kipling, "Recessional"
h. Robert Frost, "Fire and Ice"
i. John Crowe Ransom, "Here Lies a Lady"
j. Dylan Thomas, "The Force That Through the Green Fuse
Drives"

THREE

Recurrence—I: Rhythm, Meter, and Lineal Sound

Recurrence and Expectancy

We have said that for most readers the responses to a poem are registered concurrently, though for a particular type of poem one or another characteristic may be dominant. In general, reading is a consecutive process, unlike viewing a painting or sculpture. Poetry, more than prose, tends to counteract this consecutive aspect by the way in which it coordinates experience for the reader. Its merits as an art are chiefly just that: a concurrent manipulation of word sounds, word relationships, and word connotations, along with a preservation of natural cadence (rhythm) and an ordering of recurrent beats or stresses in words (meter).

Only an inexperienced reader might be unaware of those oscillations in our speech (corresponding in part, no doubt, to the cycle of breathing) that we call **rhythm.** By this, we do not mean **meter,** a regular division of verses by stresses and nonstresses. Rhythm is, rather, a recurrence of inflection and tone underlying the speech patterns in any language. Some poems may move primarily by a metrical **cadence** (Pope's **rhymed couplets**), others primarily by a natural speech cadence (the King James Bible or modern **free verse**—whether rhymed or unrhymed). Most poetry has both rhythm *and* meter, the two functioning somewhat in the manner of **counterpoint** in music. Edna St. Vincent Millay's poem "Euclid Alone—" quite apparently conforms to the established sonnet structure, having a set meter and rhyme. But note also the strong cadence that overlaps the pentameter lines. It corresponds to the unregulated lengths of speech phrasing.

Markings of rhythmic units naturally vary according to individual habits of inflection and duration. Brackets have been placed around the word groupings as I might read them.

[Euclid alone] [has looked on Beauty bare.]
[Let all that prate of Beauty] [hold their peace,]
[And lay them prone upon the earth,] [and cease
To ponder on themselves,] [the while they stare
At nothing,] [intricately drawn nowhere]
[In shapes of shifting lineage.] [Let geese
Gabble and hiss,] [but heroes seek release
From dusty bondage] [into luminous air.]
[Oh, blinding hour—] [oh, holy terrible day—]
[When first the shaft into his vision shone]
[Of light anatomized!] [Euclid alone
Has looked on Beauty bare;] [fortunate they
Who though once only,] [and then far away,]
[Have heard her massive sandal] [set on stone.]

In poems that observe conventional punctuation, there is usually a pretty fair correspondence between commas, periods, and dashes and the divisions intended within the natural cadence. This is never absolute, however, as can be seen from some of the phrasings that run on through commas or that occur where there is no punctuation. Many poets, to avoid imposing too idiosyncratic a reading of their work, omit all punctuation. Such omission, contrary to what we might think, is really a gesture toward letting the natural rhythm of the poem assert itself. In much archaic poetry there is a rhythm (often called grammatical **parallelism**) in what Coleridge called the "apparent tautologies of intense and turbulent feeling." He illustrates from the song of Deborah (Judges 5:27), which he says Wordsworth considered to be of extreme beauty: "At her feet he bowed, he fell, he lay down: at her feet he bowed, he fell: where he bowed, there he fell down dead."[1]

---

[1]*Biographical Literaria*, Chapter 17.

The accoustical richness in this sort of recurrence would be the first attraction of much of Whitman's poetry ("Out of the Cradle Endlessly Rocking" or "Song of Myself"), of Masefield's or Lindsay's, and of Beatnik verse modeled on Whitman, such as Ginsberg's "Howl." We often give the name **blank verse** to much verse simply because it is iambic pentameter and unrhymed, but variations and recurrences like the parallelism discussed above may make blank verse quite special.

The basis of meter is syllabic; the basis of rhythm is the succession of phrase and sentence. An analogy of their difference might be that of the difference between the diastole of the heart and that of the lungs and breathing. Thomas Parnell's "A Hymn of Contentment" opens with these lines:

> Lovely, lasting peace of mind!
> Sweet delight of human kind!
> Heavenly-born, and bred on high,
> To crown the favourites of the sky
> With more of happiness below
> Than victors in a triumph know!

This is meter—disyllabic, sharp, and unmistakable. The recurrences come in regular succession. Rhythm without regular meter, on the other hand, is responsible for what cadence the following lines of **free verse** possess:

> My Lord, if I pray,
> Yield at last
> As old men afraid
> With sickness turn
> To the Almighty's safety kit
> In their sixtieth year
> In terror:
>   Will I be
> Content with what will be,
> And sleep?
>   .   .   .   .

> And now, how shall I
> Take it? how take it
> To the Lord in prayer?[2]

Rhythm, in this example, tends to correspond to a kind of recitative division for the reader. Following it, he finds lines 3–7 speeded up, uttered in one breath. Light rests would probably fall as follows—after "Lord," "pray," "last," "terror," "content" (optional), the second "be," "sleep," the first "it," the second "Lord" (optional), and "prayer."

Meter and rhythm, as observed, are most effectively balanced against each other in a sort of counterpoint. In the lines below from "The Highwayman," by Alfred Noyes, rhythm, as distinct from meter, becomes evident in the breaking up of the fourth line, which de-emphasizes the regularity of alternating iambs and anapests in the preceding lines.

> The wind was a torrent of darkness among the
>   gusty trees,
> The moon was a ghostly galleon tossed upon cloudy
>   seas,
> The road was a ribbon of moonlight over the purple
>   moor,
> And the highwayman came riding—
>   Riding— riding—
> The highwayman came riding, up to the old inn-
>   door.

The meter's alternating types of feet express the galloping cadence, while the repetition of "riding" as trochees and the reining-in cadence of the stanza's last line are a jolting reminder of that wider cycle of recurrences, the rhythm.

Rhythm and meter seem to be creative man's echo of the natural recurrences of motion and sound—from the steady sawing of the cricket or cicada to the great cycles of cosmic

---

[2]Horace Hamilton, "Before Dawn," from *Before Dark*.

45

motion. The animal rhythm of bodily function (sistole-diastole, breathing, hunger and satiety, sleeping and waking, weekly work and rest, the menstrual recurrence) is comparable to the physical or environmental cycle of day and night; the rush and subsidence of water; the rise and break of waves; the ebb and flow of tides; the wax and wane of the moon; the rotation of the seasons; the organic burgeoning, insemination, reproduction, ripeness, and fall; the alternations of solar heat and cold, of rain and drought; and the 2000-year ecliptic of earth with the sun.

An **expectancy** accompanies our attunement to the almost infinite manifestations of rhythm and periodicity. Drop one shoe, and we expect the other. Our conditioning from infancy prepares us for completing the series, closing the circle, balancing the rise with a fall and the stress with release. Play two notes toward a chord, and the ear wants the third. Train it further, and the ear seeks the melodic pattern begun when a major chord is diminished by a half tone. As Browning has Abt Vogler say:

> And I know not if, save in this, such gift be allowed
> to man,
> That out of three sounds he frame, not a fourth
> sound, but a star,

so the quality of expectancy in the musician's ear requires completion. As this is true on the level of music, so it is in poetry. We wait for the recurrent stress, the corresponding rhyme sound, the repeated words of refrain, the returning play of image to echo the expectancy begun with a dominant theme. Recurrence, and the expectancy of recurrence: these are powerful stimulants to the liveliness of our response to any poem.

In the poem below, the beginning of almost every line requires a rhetorical conclusion. This repetition of beginning phrases (commonly called **parallelism**) is used here more lavishly than in any other English poem we are likely to read. The syntactical principle throughout resembles the periodic sentences common in the rhetoric of oratory and prayer, particularly of the late 16th and early 17th centuries. Each sentence embodies an **antithetical** balance between purpose and result, condition and conclusion, wish and fulfillment:

> My prime of youth is but a frost of cares,
> My feast of joy is but a dish of pain,
> My crop of corn is but a field of tares,
> And all my good is but vain hope of gain;
>> The day is past, and yet my leaves are green,
>> And now I live, and now my life is done.

> My tale was heard and yet it was not told,
>> My fruit is fallen and yet my leaves are green,
> My youth is spent and yet I am not old,
>> I saw the world and yet I was not seen;
>> My thread is cut and yet it is not spun,
>> And now I live, and now my life is done.

> I sought my death and found it in my womb,
> I looked for life and saw it was a shade,
> I trod the earth and knew it was my tomb,
>> And now I die, and now I was but made;
>> My glass is full, and now my glass is run,
>> And now I live, and now my life is done.[3]

Meter

Accentual meter in English verse is the result of an ordering of regular syllabic stresses. **Quantitative meter** is the measurement of lines of verse according to the recurrent **quantity** (or time duration) of the syllables. As we have seen, meter differs from **rhythm**; yet the two may be complementary to each other.

Most metrical feet contain a major stress [usually indicated by an **ictus** (╱)—or **thesis**] and one or more lesser stresses

---

[3]Chidiock Tichborne (1569–86), "Elegy."

[usually indicated by the **breve** (ˇ), or sometimes the more classical term, *arsis*, meaning a lighter upbeat]. The ratio between heavy and light stresses gives rise to the names of various feet. The commonest in English poetry is the **iamb** (iambic foot— ˇ ´). Three other relatively common feet are the **trochee** (trochaic foot— ´ˇ), the **dactyl** (dactylic foot— ´ˇˇ), and the **anapest** (anapestic foot— ˇˇ´). Only two syllables are involved with iambs and trochees; the result is called **duple meter.** Dactyls and anapests have three syllables and are called **triple meter.**

Less common feet are sometimes substituted in a line consisting predominantly of one of the four commoner feet, such as the **spondee** (spondaic foot— ´´) and the **pyrrhic foot** (ˇˇ). [The concluding line of each stanza of Masefield's "Sea-Fever" (p. 22) contains spondees and pyrrhic feet presumably to accentuate variations desired in the poem's rhythm at that point—"Aňd thĕ | fluńg spráy | aňd thĕ | blowń spúme | aňd thĕ | séagúlls | crýiňg."] The juxtaposition of several heavy stresses produces **syncopation** and a phonetic equivalent of the tumbling effect of waves breaking in rapid succession.

In addition to the effect of doubled stresses and nonstresses is the quantitative factor, or **duration** for which each syllable is held. In the Masefield line (above) the quantity is apparent in the difference in time that it takes to say "and," "the," "blown," "spume," or the two syllables of the final word, "cry-" and "ing."

Since a given sample of verse is seldom more than seventy percent metrically pure, it can be misleading to carry out one's analysis as though the poem's effectiveness depended on the regularity of the prevailing meter. The reasons for the varied **substitutions** (as they are called) within a dominant meter are not entirely clear. Certainly, irregularity is not an indication of laxness on the part of the craftsman; on the contrary, inflexible regularity would be more likely the mark of a straining amateur. It has often been pointed out that logical (or **rhetorical**) stress may not always coincide with the syllabic stresses that regulate the meter. Thus, in reading the lines below from Wilfred Owen's "Dulce et Decorum Est," one must provide the emphasis in the first two lines that the accents of normal speech require (*double, beggars, sacks, knock*-kneed, *coughing, hags, cursed, sludge*), creating the awkwardness intended there; this is in contrast to the smooth iambic meter of the last two lines:

> Bent double, like old beggars under sacks,
> Knock-kneed, coughing like hags, we cursed through
>   sludge,
> Till on the haunting flares we turned our backs
> And toward our distant rest began to trudge.

The meter has been deliberately controlled here to suggest the contrast of distasteful effort (first two lines) and sudden anticipation of return and rest (last two lines).

Meter is the chief device for controlling the speed and movement of lines. The unstressed syllables in a series of feet take less time to sound than the stressed; so triple meters go faster than duple meters, as particularly the lingering **spondaic** stresses of the line—"And the flung spray and the blown spume and the sea-gulls crying."

A poet varies the tempo to let an underlying rhythm become known. Technically speaking, he **substitutes** a foot unlike the predominant meter, but the term makes the act of composition seem more deliberate and logical than it really is.[4] When two or more unstressed syllables come together, they speed up the pace of the line; when two or more stressed syllables come together, they slow it down. The running together of words (**syncretism**) in Cummings's poem below illustrates the intended effect of speed. Note that such words are mostly unstressed:

---

[4]While the nature of the material (as in Owen's lines above) suggests conscious experimentation with the meter, deliberate substitutions probably occur rather rarely. What actually happens is that a basic rhythm carries the composer along, with logical stress and quantitative variation entering the line to suit the poet's desired inflections. The prevailing meter may be thought of as a general level of the spoken word, established by the mood and emotional rhythms of the poet's conception; it is not "chosen" as such, and thus may be interrupted without conscious thought.

Buffalo Bill's
defunct
    who used to
    ride a watersmooth-silver
                stallion
and break   onetwothreefourfive   pigeonsjustlikethat
                             Jesus
he was a handsome man
              and what i want to know is
how do you like your blueeyed boy
Mister Death

While the poem is too irregular to classify according to conventional meter, neither is it truly free verse, because there
is intentional metrical effect. Cummings manipulates the
speed of movement by pushing together several unstressed
syllables, as in the long sixth line with the two groups of
syncretized words. These contribute to a sort of **onomatopoeic**
effect—an acting out of the speaker's monologue (perhaps
an old sidekick's or an abandoned saloon girl's) as he or she
mimics Buffalo Bill's ringing shots as he thunders past. The
shifts in speed, largely controlled by meter and by line
lengths, offer a variety of possibilities in reading the poem.
A glance will also show how the poem's typographical shape
suggests speed.

    English verse of almost any era affords examples of
metrical experiment to assist the intended mood. The effect
is usually to lighten it, as with the crowded vocables in the
lyrics of W. S. Gilbert's light operas. Note the metrics of his
song "Nightmare," sung in hurried desperation by one of the
tenor voices. It begins,

> When you're lying awake with a dismal headache,
>   and repose is taboo'd by anxiety,
> I conceive you may use any language you choose
>   to indulge in, without impropriety....

There are several amusing verses of this, capitalizing on the hop, skip, and jump vivacity of anapestic meter with the extra unstressed syllables at the end (**hypercatalexis**), emphasized by the rather flamboyant **triple rhymes** in each. In the song from *H.M.S. Pinafore*, beginning with the line "I'm the very model of a modern major general," alliteration and assonance effect the slurring over of lesser (or secondary) accents to exaggerate the heavy ones—"I'm," "mod-," 'mod-," and "gen-." Adaptations of verses to song very often result in a distorted prosody. Gilbert's contrivances, however, indicate a purposeful distortion, a practice much imitated in our time by popular humorous poets such as the late Ogden Nash.

The essayist and poet E. B. White carried on Gilbert's light touch in poems such as "I Paint What I See," written in the 1930s about the mural decorations of Rockefeller Center. After a stanza in which he harps on one rhyme made up of badgering questions and distraught answers, the painter Rivera takes off on a goatish refrain:

> "What do you paint, when you paint a wall?"
>> Said John D.'s grandson Nelson.
> "Do you paint just anything there at all?
> "Will there be any doves, or a tree in fall?
> "Or a hunting scene, like an English hall?"
>> "I paint what I see," said Rivera.

And the refrain:

> "I paint what I paint, I paint what I see,
>> "I paint what I think," said Rivera,
> "And the thing that is dearest in life to me
> "In a bourgeois hall is Integrity;
>> "However...
> "I'll take out a couple of people drinkin'
> "And put in a picture of Abraham Lincoln...."

The poem continues thus, shifting back finally to the query and response routine.

Our English prosody seems to go through cycles, relinquishing one discipline of form for a more modish one. Thus, with the Romantic poets, rhythmic and quantitative variations tended to replace the stricter syllabic count of much 18th century verse in which the stresses corresponded to the number of syllables in a line. As noted earlier, any variations were referred to as **substitution**, or sometimes **compensation.** The most common vehicle for the epigramatic, critical verse of the time was **decasyllabics,** usually in **rhymed couplets** (see **rhyme** and **couplet** in the Glossary). Not until quite near the end of the century did the effort to shift to an accentual rather than syllabic count prevail. Blake and especially Coleridge tried to base each line on the number of stresses, regardless of the quantity of syllables. In this, Coleridge seems to have harked back to the so-called "tumbling verse" (or **Skeltonics**) or John Skelton in the 16th century. "To Mistress Margaret Hussey" illustrates the varying or "tumbling" effect of regular stresses augmented in some lines by extra nonstressed syllables:

> Merry Margaret, as midsummer flower,
> Gentle as falcon or hawk of the tower,
> With solace as gladness,
> Much mirth and no madness,
> All good and no badness;
> So joyously,
> So maidenly,
> So womanly,
> Her demeaning;
> In every thing
> Far far passing
> That I can indite
> Or suffice to write
> Of merry Margaret, as midsummer flower,
> Gentle as falcon or hawk of the tower.
> As patient and as still,
> And as full of good will,

> As the fair Isyphill,
> Coliander,
> Sweet pomander....

An incidental effect of **Skeltonics** was to permit the reader to pace himself, the varying line lengths inviting alternating restraint or speed in the reading.

The form of Coleridge's long poem *Christabel* reflects his theory of an accentual control of the verse line. The syllables, he explained, "may vary from seven to twelve, yet in each line the accents will be found to be only four." In the lines below, he seems to have partially demonstrated this count, although the final line has but three stresses:

> Hush, beating heart of Christabel!
> Jesu, Maria, shield her well!
> She folded her arms beneath her cloak,
> And stole to the other side of the oak.
> What sees she there?

The variations of regular iambic **tetrameter** with **trimeter** in the passage below seem to permit modulations of pace and mood, though for the most part, Coleridge sticks pretty closely to the traditional line:

> It was a lovely sight to see
> The lady Christabel, when she
> Was praying at the old oak tree.
> Amid the jagged shadows
> Of mossy leafless boughs,
> Kneeling in the moonlight,
> To make her gentle vows;
> Her slender palms together prest,
> Heaving sometimes on her breast....

What is probably of most significance is the spirit in which Coleridge varied the meter—not as substitutions of anapests and trochees for otherwise iambic feet, but as a means of sensitizing his verses to the shifts of movement and mood.

Quantitative Variations of Meter

As we have said about the variations of meter of "Sea-Fever" (pp. 23 and 48), a conception of added time or **duration** for certain syllables may modify the metrical beat of certain lines. When the line measure is governed predominantly by awareness of this syllabic time, it is called **quantitative meter.** In most English poetry, stress and length of syllable generally correspond, as can be noted in Coleridge's verses. Other poets, including Coleridge's close friend Wordsworth, experimented by opposing stress and phonal duration to achieve a more subtle and brooding effect, as the opening lines of "Tintern Abbey" show (see pp. 57–58).[5]

Quantitative meter was the natural measure in ancient Greek poetry, and was subsequently adapted by the Romans, who imposed rather arbitrary rules for "long" and "short" vowels as found in Latin prosody. English carried on many of the terms (frequently related to these classical meters), but not the meter itself. The incompatibility of quantitative meter to English speech inflections has always been assumed (probably because of the naturally heavy stresses of the Teutonic languages). Yet if one examines any group of English words, he will find that they vary markedly in quantity, with some words (pool, *hunger*, feel, woe, clothe, slow, or ail) taking longer to sound than others (trip, beck, quick, but, of, dip, or cat).

Relative length of a syllable or word usually depends on three things: (1) the position of a syllable in a word or of a word in the sequence of a sentence ("death" is shorter in "death's door" and longer in "sleep of death"), (2) the nature of the final consonant (*l*'s, *n*'s, and *r*'s drawing out the sonority of the vowel, and *t*'s, *p*'s, *d*'s, and *k*'s cutting them short), and

---

[5]Others who have experimented with quantity—for example, Spenser, Campion, Swinburne, and Bridges—seem to have had considerable exposure to Latin poetry as a standard part of the "public school" discipline. Yet the less educated Keats also made quantitative variations.

(3) the coincidence of the vowel sound with the normal accent of speech (the syllable "re" in re*but*" is short and unstressed, but the "rea" in "*reason*" is long and stressed).

In traditional prosody the length of the vowel decides the quantity of the word in question (cāne versus can, báte versus bat, fēēl versus fell, róbe versus rob, and so forth). Thus, the first line in the passage from *Christabel* (p. 153) requires no longer to sound (with its eight syllables) than the sixth line (with only six syllables). Coleridge intended to equate the number of stresses, but the phonal duration of those syllables had a bearing on the equation.

Other poets combined stress and phonal duration to achieve even more pronounced effects than did Coleridge. One was his friend Wordsworth, whose poem "Tintern Abbey" we shall shortly examine in detail. In the meantime, we might note in passing a more recent poet's method of adjusting the durational **equivalence** among verse lines of varying quantitative value. In the abridgement below of Edith Sitwell's "Trio for Two Cats and a Trombone," relatively more time is devoted to those one or two syllables ("See," "Flee," "Tee-hee," "And free," and so forth) that constitute single lines than those syllables would receive as part of the longer lines. In a recording of her poems set to William Walton's music (under the title "Facade"), Dame Edith's reading illustrates this principle as she maintains a balance between the protracted short line and such longer ones as "The tall Spanish jade" and "With hair black as nightshade":

> Long steel grass
> The white soldiers pass
> The light is braying like an ass.
> See
> The tall Spanish jade
> With hair black as nightshade
> Worn as a cockade!
> Flee
> Her eyes' gasconade
> And her gown's parade

(As stiff as a brigade).
Tee-hee!
The hard and braying light
Is zebra's black and white
It will take away the slight
And free

.   .   .   .   .   .

Her flounces as they sweep the ground
The
Trumpet and the drum
And the martial cornet come
To make the people dumb—
But we
Won't wait for fly-foot night

.   .   .   .   .   .

Beside the castanetted sea,
Where stalks Il Capitaneo
Swaggart braggadocio
Sword and mustachio—
He
Is green as a cassada
And his hair is an armada....

Her expressive reading of this demonstrates what a flexible tool metrics can be.

The relationships of metrical and quantitative meter were interestingly demonstrated in Wordsworth's poem, "Tintern Abbey." While most of the poem scans as iambic pentameter, parts of it reveal the poet's dependence on phonal duration for added expressiveness. A scansion of the opening lines, for example, shows how syllabic duration conveys the poet's mood more definitively than the accentual meter. Readers who try to scan according to simple iambic pentameter will find the result unsettling. For more important perhaps than the variations of meter is the responsiveness of the opening lines to control of time, stress, and pitch. These are inter-linked to achieve a tone ideally suited to the meditative engrossment of the speaker. Here are the lines, scanned to indicate both quantity (–) and accentual stress (/):

> Five years have past; five summers, with the length
> Of five long winters! and again I hear
> These waters, rolling from their mountain springs
> With a soft inland murmur. —Once again
> Do I behold these steep and lofty cliffs,
> That on a wild secluded scene impress
> Thoughts of a more deep seclusion; and connect
> The landscape with the quiet of the sky.

Some expected correspondences between accent and duration are evident. But rendering these lines in accentual feet alone would disregard the natural speech rhythms that the poet has been careful to use. Such regularity as Wordsworth sought is confined to the **decasyllabic** count. By this conven-tion he parts company with Coleridge's intentional variation of syllabic line.

While the scansion above accounts for duration and stress (subject, of course, to individual variation), a positioning of a few of the same lines on a simple musical scale will sug-gest possible variations of pitch, as well as some of the finer variations of quantity, including pauses (or rests):[6]

Five   years   have   past;   five   sum-mers, with the length

---

[6]In musical notation o is a full note; ♩ is a half note; ♩ is a quarter note; ♪ is an eighth note; ♪ is a sixteenth note; ᶌ and ᶅ are eighth and quarter rests. This analogy is for clarification only; it is not an attempt to suggest any union of the separate arts of music and verse.

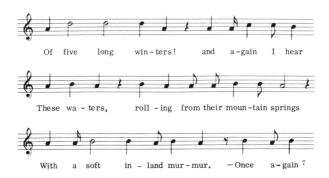

While Wordsworth's inflections cause the notes to range freely on the scale, a stanza from Gray's "Elegy" seems to suggest a more limited range, reflecting a more regularized meter. The arrangement below shows time, stress, and pitch together:

---

[7]This musical notation has been adapted from Franklin B. Snyder, "A Note on English Prosody," *A Book of English Literature*.

Of course, the variance of metrical stress by different readers prevents any meaningful equation of prosody with musical notation. The additional factors of syllabic duration and register of pitch may complicate the problem for the reader. Yet to disregard these coordinate factors—part of the overall **orchestration,** as we might call it—is to ignore the potential by which much poetry achieves its pleasurable effect. A recognition of the acoustical concurrency of duration, stress, and pitch—or as they operate separately—raises some questions about traditionally accepted prosody. It is ultimately for the reader—as so often it is for the poet—to determine the actual modulations by which poetry communicates itself to the physical senses.

Other Mutations of Rhythm and Meter

The interrelation of duration and pitch becomes even more important when we examine the increasing tendency toward a free form poetry. In the last third of the 19th century, aside from the Symbolist trend about to be imitated by English poets, many were trying out the facile **vers libre,** or free verse, with its nonmetrical lines of varying rhythm (and, very often, no rhyme). Its phrasing to the cadences of natural speech may have been in keeping with the increasing taste for a merging of poetry and prose. We have already discussed (pp. 9–11) the acceptance in these years of rhythmic prose (**polyphonic prose**) as a legitimate kind of poetry.

In England, the experimenter to shape meter most fully to his own idiosyncratic rhythms was Gerard Manley Hopkins. In America, Whitman was making a public virtue of rolling over traditional prosody with a free form that combined Biblical devices such as grammatical **parallelism, apostrophe,** and **personification.** Hopkins, possibly because he seldom wrote for publication (and when he did, for only a few select readers) subjected his verse—even forms as conventional as the sonnet—to a highly idiosyncratic emphasis. Few modern poets —with the possible exception of Rimbaud or Dylan Thomas— have modulated poetry as did Hopkins to such a kinetic personal idiom.

One of the strange effects he gave to his verse he called

59

sprung rhythm, an inflection of normal meter by what can be described in part as a spondaic movement (see **spondee**), or conjunction of several stressed syllables. In the passage from "The Leaden Echo" below, however, the sprung rhythm seems to be the syncopation achieved by putting a **head stress** at the beginning of **run-on lines** (the line-end division of such closely linked word groups as "nowhere/Known," "brace,/ Lace, latch or catch," "keep/Back beauty," "wrinkles deep/ Down?"):

> How to kéep—is they ány, is there none such, no-
>   where known, some bow or brooch or braid or
>   bráce, láce, latch or catch or key to keep
> Back beauty, keep it, beauty, beauty, beauty, . . .
>   from vanishing away?
> O, is there no frowning of these wrinkles, rankèd
>   wrinkles deep,
> Dówn? no waving off these most mournful
>   messengers, still messengers, sad and stealing
>   messengers of grey?
> No there's none, there's none, O no there's none,
> Nor can you long be, what you now are, called fair,
> Do what you may do, what, do what you may,
> And wisdom is early to despair:
> Be beginning; since, no, nothing can be done. . . . [8]

The altered effect here on regular meter is emphasized by strong **alliteration** which very soon—even as it deepens the emotional intensity—becomes oppressive or monotonous. The well-worn idea—that beauty and innocence inevitably slip away—gains new poignancy by the cumulative effect of repetition and the concentration of the prosody. He manages to set up a counterpoint of tormented diction with the implacable beat of the spondaic movement (comparable to Chopin's *Rain Drop Prelude*, where a delicate melody is first

---

[8]The accent marks are Hopkin's, presumably to remind the reader of abnormal stresses. While there is scant agreement as to the poet's exact intent by the term "sprung rhythm," we still may speculate about it.

complemented, then dominated, by a monotonous and relent-
lessly intensifying undertone from the bass). The rhythmic
mutations (the "sprung" effect) in Hopkins's poem are like a
physical accompaniment to the morbidity of thought. In addition to the heavy alliteration ("bow or brooch or braid or
brace"), the **assonances** and **internal rhyme** ("Latch or catch
or key to keep") interact with the sprung rhythm, giving an
effect we can only describe as restrained force. All of these
aural devices taken together might be called the **orchestration**
(a general term that has been used to include sound associations and the actual transcription of physical sounds, or **onomatopoeia**; see Chapter 4, pp. 77–80).

Of course Hopkins's mannered prosody carries its own
defects. In its excess of energy it may distract us from the
ideals. One of his later sonnets, "Felix Randal," is crowded
with jolting sonorities, agonized syntax, and disruptive meter
and rhythm:

> Felix Randal, the farrier, O he is dead then? my
>   duty all ended,
> Who have watched his mold of man, big-boned and
>   hardy-handsome
> Pining, pining, till time when reason rambled in it
>   and some
> Fatal four disorders, fleshed there, all contended?
>
> Sickness broke him. Impatient he cursed at first,
>   but mended
> Being anointed and all; though a heavenlier heart
>   began some
> Months earlier, since I had our sweet reprieve and
>   ransom
> Tendered to him. Ah well, God rest him all road
>   ever he offended!
>
> This seeing the sick endears them to us, us too it
>   endears.

My tongue had taught thee comfort, touch had
    quenched thy tears,
Thy tears that touched my heart, child, Felix, poor
    Felix Randal;

How far from then forethought of, all thy more
    boisterous years,
When thou at the random grim forge, powerful
    amidst peers,
Didst fettle for the great grey drayhorse his bright
    and battering sandal!

Despite this sublimity of feeling, the heavily verbalized diction becomes a sort of parody of itself. Possibly, E. B. White was thinking of Hopkins's rhythms when he wrote his piece of light verse, "The Red Cow is Dead." It first appeared under the epigraph of the following news item:

Isle of Wight (AP)—Sir Hanson Rowbotham's favorite Red Polled cow is dead. Grazing in the lush pastures of the Wellow Farm, she was bitten on the udder by an adder.—*The* (New York) *Herald-Tribune*

Toll the bell, fellow,
This is a sad day at Wellow:
Sir Hanson's cow is dead,
His red cow,
Bitten on the udder by an adder.

Spread the bad news! What is more sudden,
What sadder than udder stung by adder?
He's never been madder, Sir Hanson Rowbotham.

The Red Polled cow is dead.
The grass was lush at very last,
And the snake (a low sneak)
Passed, hissed,
Struck.

Now a shadow goes across the meadow,
Wellow lies fallow.
The red cow is dead, and the stories go round.
"Bit in the teat by a dog in a fit."
"A serpent took Sir Hanson's cow—
A terrible loss, a king's ransom."

A blight has hit Wight:
The lush grass, the forked lash, the quick gash
Of adder, torn bleeding udder,
The cow laid low,
The polled cow dead, the bell not yet tolled
(A sad day at Wellow),
Sir Hanson's cow,
Never again to freshen, never again
Bellow with passion—
A ruminant in death's covenant,
Smitten, bitten, gone.
Toll the bell, young fellow!

Echoing something of Hopkins's rhythmic projection, Dylan Thomas uses a spondaic movement in his "A Refusal to Mourn the Death, by Fire, of a Child in London." As with Hopkins's, this meter gives way to studied mutations, each line enriched by a prodigality of assonances, alliteration, and far-ranging metaphors. The unexpected metaphor and phonal recurrences help to carry along the rolling, almost oratorical force of the rhythm. In view of such an aural assault, the marvel is that richly varied ideas still come through (as discussed more fully on pp. 99–100):

Never until the mankind making
Bird beast and flower
Fathering and all humbling darkness
Tells with silence the last light breaking
And the still hour
Is come of the sea tumbling in harness

And I must enter again the round
Zion of the water bead
And the synagogue of the ear of corn
Shall I let pray the shadow of a sound
Or sow my salt seed
In the least valley of sackcloth to mourn

The majesty and burning of the child's death.
I shall not murder
The mankind of her going with a grave truth
Nor blaspheme down the stations of the breath
With any further
Elegy of innocence and youth.

Deep with the first dead lies London's daughter,
Robed in the long friends,
The grains beyond age, the dark veins of her mother
Secret by the unmourning water
Of the riding Thames.
After the first death, there is no other.

Line and Intralineal Recurrence

The recurrence of stress and sound and the expectancy of
the recurrence are an elemental principle of poetry. The expectancy of certain beats (and the mutations that tease that expectancy) has been basic to our discussion so far of rhythm
and meter. The recurrence of words or word units also underlie much of our poetics. Such recurrence may parallel, correspond to, or oppose the rhythmical or metrical cycles
energizing a poem.

Verbal recurrence is the pattern we call **rhyme** and **refrain.**
Here, at least, we see it most in action. Such recurrence is
the dominant form of our oldest ballads and has continued
in our lyric poetry—at least, until quite recently. We see it
in the lighthearted sequences of Mother Goose rhymes, the
rounds ("Frere Jacques" and "Row, Row, Row Your Boat"),
and the grim repetitions woven into time-seasoned popular

ballads ("The Twa Corbies," or "Edward") and 14th century French forms, such as the **triolet** and **villanelle** (notably exemplified in recent poetry by Dylan Thomas in "Do Not Go Gentle into That Good Night"), with repetitions of complete lines and parts of lines. In the early 18th century, prosody was likely to follow classical models, such as the Pindaric **ode,** which allowed scant inventiveness in the uses of recurrence. But verbal recurrences beginning, within, and ending lines (as in parallelism, assonance, consonance, alliteration, and end rhyme) have marked our poetry from Old English to modern times. A revived taste in rich resonances occurred in the late 19th century, especially as manifested in the heavy alliteration of Swinburne and Hopkins.

"Suppose We Kill a King," by the modern poet Robert Horan, is an interesting exercise in the liberal use of a variety of recurrences:

> Suppose we kill a king, and then a king, and then a
> king;
> princes are waiting everywhere.
> Suppose by poison or by water, kill a queen:
> her daughter sits upon the stair.
>
> The beast begun comes back.
> Like shadows or like mirrors where they stand,
> the sun assassinates, the moon refurnishes
> the shadow with a hand.
> Lying alone in midnight, drowned in guilt
> and staggered with emeralds while they sleep:
> the daggers in the bed of silk,
> the devils in disguise,
> the footman with the hand that shakes,
> and when they wake,
> the Dauphin with his eyes.
>
> The king will walk, an antlered ghost, through castle
> halls,

and dukes will turn their heads to see;
the queen will wake to find her face on palace walls
looking down from a tapestry.

A prince, in lighting a taper for a tomb
and putting a sleepy king to bed,
will leave a glistening rapier in his room,
will separate his heart and head
and kneeling at his bleeding crown
and covering his fallen head
will stifle the echo with his gown.

Sidewise in Venetian glass
the mirror shows the murderer, a king.
The bells that rang a funeral
must pause to ring a christening.
The one who killed the king is killed,
assassin, silenced with a stone,
a prison hung around his throat,
a weight upon his tongue.

Like mice beneath a rotting throne, the whispering
    men
sit in the palace sun,
and as the coffin passes through the towns,
lay down their daggers to put on their crowns.

The repetition of "king" in the first line balances "kill a queen," at the end of the third line, and both are counterbalanced by the fourth line, "her daughter sits upon a stair," which completes the cycle of succession. This balancing effect is emphasized by the word beginning the first and third lines ("suppose"), which as verbal **parallelism** alternates with the end rhymes ("-where" and "stair") of the second and fourth lines. The king and queen **antithesis** is further echoed by their respective extensions—princes and daughters ("princes are waiting everywhere" and "her daughter sits upon the stair"). But aside from these counterbalances (which in themselves involve an element of expectancy) is the relentless sound of those parallel repetitions hanging in that first line, beginning again in the third line ("Suppose"), and accumulating as repetitions at the start of all but four lines of the long second stanza ("The beast," "the sun," "the shadow," "the daggers," "the devils," "the footman," and "the Dauphin").

By stanza three, the pattern of parallelism is expanded to a complete subject-verb phrase as an opener for each long line,

> The king will walk...
> and dukes will turn...
> the queen will wake...,

itself a reproduction of the quatrain form of the first and the last stanza. Except for the final couplet of the last stanza, the same rhymes or near rhymes ("king"-"queen" and "men"-"sun") occur, as well as the same alternations of long first and third lines with short second and fourth. Key words repeated in the opening phrases of the third stanza ("and" and "will"—the three lines quoted above) become beginning rhymes for six lines in the next stanza:

> *and* putting...
> *will* leave...
> *will* separate...
> *and* kneeling...
> *and* covering...
> *will* stifle....

This recurrence of line openings (parallelism) has an almost Biblical insistence, and is reminiscent of Whitman's addiction to the device. The *dramatis personae* mostly listed in the opening stanza, point successively to the key actions of "The beast" (line 1, stanza 2), "The king" (line 1, stanza 3), and "A prince" (line 1, stanza 4), with the daughter, the dukes, and the final "whispering men," as accessories after the fact. Most of what has been traced so far has to do with the interlinking effects of recurrence on the pattern of the poem as a whole. Recurrences *within* any two or three lines are to be found throughout the poem. We find **internal rhyme,** alliteration, assonance, and consonance all working together— sometimes doing double duty—as in these two lines from the fifth stanza:

> The one who killed the king is killed,
> assassin, silenced with a stone,

where "killed" matches "killed" (identical internal rhyme), "king" anticipates "killed" (alliteration), and "*one*" and "*who*" or "*kill-*" and "*king*" or "*assassin*" and "*silenced*" and "*stone*" link the dominant vowel and consonantal sounds (assonance and consonance). The total effect of the recurrences—varying from those at the level of phoneme, or those at the word level, to those of whole word groups (at the line and stanza level)—is powerful, and the images and their associations (the overtones of Shakespearean dynastic intrigues) are hauntingly memorable.

The hypnotic effect of this play on recurrences is particularly evident in T. S. Eliot's "The Hollow Men." Here the images are kept sufficently abstract that a reader is perhaps subjected even more to the pure aural recurrences. By the collective "we," the poet probably increases our involvement as readers, even though he sacrifices distinct identity, time, or historical setting, as compared to Horan's poem:

> We are the hollow men
> We are the stuffed men
> Leaning together....
> Shape without form, shade without color,
> Paralyzed force, gesture without motion;
> . . . .
> This is the dead land
> This is cactus land....
>
> . . . . . .

> The eyes are not here
> There are no eyes here;
> In this valley of dying stars
> In this hollow valley....

Parallelism dominates these opening lines, with less addition of the internal recurrences favored by Horan. As in the parallelism so familiar in Songs of Solomon and parts of Ecclesiastes, a tone of despair results. It continues in the fifth section of the poem, emphasized by the powerful rhythm of syntactical recurrences:

> Between the desire
> And the spasm
> Between the potency
> And the existence
> Between the essence
> And the descent
> Falls the shadow
> > For Thine is the Kingdom

Even the marginal gloss from the Lord's Prayer undergoes a fragmental repetition:

> For Thine is
> Life is
> For Thine is the

The section (and the poem) ends on a note of complete futility, the last three lines cheerlessly leading up to the listless admission of the last line:

> This is the way the world ends
> This is the way the world ends
> This is the way the world ends
> Not with a bang but a whimper.

Most of the special stanzaic forms (such as the **sonnet, rhyme royal, Spenserian stanza, villanelle, rondel, rondolet, and triolet**)[9] came into being as formalizations of the principle of recurrence and expectancy that involved meter and rhyme. To balance the more formal stanzaic patterns, an Eliot or a Horan might be thought of as having compensated for his freer verse structure by using more of the intralineal effects (**repetend**, parallelism, assonance, and so forth). Even in writing *free verse*,[10] many poets have had to resort to compensating devices to make up for the forms of prosody they have abandoned.

Of those verse forms mentioned above, the last four (late 14th century French forms, revived in the 19th century) specialized in recurrences of whole lines or parts of lines. A modern example of one of these, the villanelle, is Dylan Thomas's "Do Not Go Gentle into That Good Night." Possibly because he wished to mute somewhat the mechanical quality of so many repetitions (like a cuckoo clock striking the expected hour), and permit more attention to the serious theme, Thomas has blended the parts more subtly than is usual. (The numerals correspond to the alternated lines):

1 Do not go gentle into that good night,
  Old age should burn and rave at close of day;
2 Rage, rage against the dying of the light.

  Though wise men at their end know dark is
    right,
  Because their words have forked no lightning
    they
1 Do not go gentle into that good night.

  Good men, the last wave by, crying how bright
  Their frail deeds might have danced in a green
    bay,
2 Rage, rage against the dying of the light.

---

[9]See Chapter 4, pp. 73–74, as well as the Glossary.
[10]Free verse is discussed on pp. 44–45.

Wild men who caught and sang the sun in flight,
And learn, too late, they grieved it on its way,
1   Do not go gentle into that good night.

Grave men, near death, who see with blinding
     sight
Blind eyes could blaze like meteors and be gay,
2   Rage, rage against the dying of the light.

And you, my father, there on the sad height,
Curse, bless, me now with your fierce tears, I
     pray.
1   Do not go gentle into that good night.
2   Rage, rage against the dying of the light.

At this point it may be seen that recurrences (including those of stress, syllabic duration, inflection, and pitch) have their aesthetic impact not entirely because of the correspondences they embody, but because of the slight differences. These mutations of meter, or an expected type or pattern of sounds, are essential to the pleasure that a listener gains in the cascade of repeated stresses, repetends, verbal similarities, and so forth, that characterize the language of poetry. In this working of mutation we witness that principle of likeness in difference with which we began our first chapter. In our examination of imagery and rhetoric, we will see how the comparison of unequal entities becomes the mainspring of a modern, as well as an ancient, art of imitation.

Practical Criticism

1. Read over E. E. Cummings' "Anyone Lived in a Pretty How Town" (quoted on pp. 33–34) and note the recurrences and overall rhythms in relation to any discernible meter.

   a. List some of the lines or phrases by which metrical mutation enhances (either by slowing or contrasting with) the prevailing meter (for example, "spring summer autumn winter").

71

b. List some of the lines in which syntactical recurrence advances the **antithesis** contained in the poem (for example, "he sang his didn't he danced his did").

c. See how convincingly you can scan the poem.

2. In the following poems, note some of the uses of recurrence and expectancy, as well as any observable ways that rhythm is linked to them:

Anonymous, "Edward"; W. H. Auden, "Law Like Love"; Robert Burns, "A Red Red Rose"; William Blake, "The Lamb"; William Blake, "The Tiger"; E. A. Robinson, "The House on the Hill"; Amy Lowell, "Patterns"; Edith Sitwell, "Still Falls the Rain"; Dylan Thomas, "The Force That Through the Green Fuse Drives."

3. Note the degree to which certain traditional forms (sonnet, villanelle, Spenserian stanza, and so forth) dispense with intraverbal or intralineal repetends or other forms of recurrence. Begin with Shakespeare's Sonnets 12, 18, 30, 73, and 104 and Spenser's Sonnet 75 (from *Amoretti*) and note the recurrence patterns in use other than those of meter and rhyme. Do the same for the popular ballads "Lord Randal" and "Edward."

FOUR

Recurrence—II: Rhyme and
Verbal Phonetics

Rhyme and Phonetic Recurrence

The most familiar element of prosody is the recurrence called **rhyme.** The repetition of sounds in this kind of sequence is by no means limited to the final syllable (**masculine rhyme**) or syllables (**feminine rhyme**) of a line. We noted in Chapter 3 the occurrence of **internal** and **head rhymes** (alliteration) (for example, in Robert Horan's "Suppose We Kill a King," pp. 65–66). Unlike alliteration, consonance, or assonance (which match initial phonemes or phonemes within a word), regular rhymes match the sound of one or more concluding syllables. The most common form of regular rhyme is at the end of a line.

In the course of English literature a score or more of end-rhyme patterns have been invented or borrowed from classical, Italian, and French poetry. The most common of these stanzaic forms are as follows:[1]

Name	Rhyme Sequence
couplet	*a a, b b,* etc.
ballad stanza	*a b a b* or *x a x a* (where *x* marks an absence of rhyme)
bracket rhyme (used in Tennyson's *In Memoriam*)	*a b b a*

---

[1]See the Glossary for a more detailed explanation of each form.

73

Name	Rhyme Sequence
Italian sonnet	*a b b a, a b b a; c d e c d e* variations occur in sestet
Shakespearean sonnet	*a b a b, c d c d, e f e f, g g*
tercet or triplet	*a b a* or *a a a*
sestet or stave of six	*a b a b c c*
rime royal or Chaucerian stanza	*a b a b b c c*
limerick	*a a b b a*
ottava rima	*a b a b a b c c*
Spenserian stanza	*a b a b b c b c c*
villanelle (shorter variations—rondeau, rondel, and rondelet —also limited to two rhymes)	5 tercets followed by a quatrain, all on two rhymes (see example, pp. 70–71)

The meter customarily used in most of these has been iambic pentameter, the most common exceptions being in ballad stanzas, bracket rhymes, and triplet stanzas, which are frequently written in iambic tetrameter or even trimeter.

Rather than duplicating a line's final syllable or syllables (**true rhyme**), many poets prefer to approximate these sounds. This is called, more or less interchangeably, **near rhyme, slant rhyme,** or **approximate rhyme.** The result of these suggested rhymes is a subtler variation on recurrence than the more mechanical effect of steady sound repetition. Emily Dickinson's "As Imperceptibly as Grief" has a prevailing rhyme pattern of *x a x a,* but she avoids the mechanical effect that full rhyme might have in the short trimeter lines by approximating the sounds. In a **rising rhythm** (here, iambic meter), the syllable rhymed is the one receiving the stress (though a slight involvement of the **penultimate** syllable sometimes occurs):

> As imperceptibly as grief
> The summer lapsed a*way*,—
> Too imperceptible, at last,
> To seem like perf*idy*.

A quietness distilled,
As twilight long begun,
Or Nature, spending with herself
Sequestered afternoon.

The dusk grew earlier in,
The morning foreign shone,—
A courteous, yet harrowing grace,
As guest who would be gone.

And thus, without a wing,
Or service of a keel,
Our summer made her light escape
Into the beautiful.

To inexperienced readers, approximate rhymes are often thought to be the result of carelessness or an author's failure to find a "good" rhyme; but, as we have seen, this is not generally the case. Poems dating from earlier times occasionally show "off-rhymes" as a result of changes in pronunciation (as "proved-loved" or "find-wind," from Shakespeare's Sonnet 16 and Donne's "Song"). These are sometimes termed historical rhymes. Frequently, when the spelling itself suggests identical sound (as above), such words are still employed as **eye rhymes.**

Harder to distinguish than slant rhymes and eye rhymes are the barely perceptible recurrences alternating in some of Cummings's poems. In his "What If a Much of a Which of a Wind," the pattern discernible in the first stanza would be *a b c b c d a d*, but some of the elements are actually final assonances or consonances rather than rhymes:

What if a much of a which of a wind
gives the truth to summer's lie;
bloodies with dizzying leaves the sun
and yanks immortal stars awry?
Blow king to beggar and queen to seem

(blow friend to fiend; blow space to time)
—when skies are hanged and oceans drowned,
the single secret will still be man.

Thus "lie" and "awry" will pass for rhymes, but "sun" and "seem," "wind" and drowned," and "Time" and "man" have the shadowy recurrence of consonant sounds (though technically consonance and assonance occur *within* a line of verse). Since both assonance and consonance are interwoven liberally throughout most of the lines above (the "a" recurrences, the "i" recurrences of "if," "which," and "wind," and the consonantal recurrences of "if," and "of," and of "much" and "which"), the poet may have chosen his slant rhymes to reduce too obvious correspondence.

Internal rhyme varies in its degree of correspondence in the same way as end rhyme. First, there are exact correspondences within a line, as in the **leonine rhyme** found in W. S. Gilbert's librettos (for example, "He's so quaint and so *terse*, both in prose and in *verse*," from *The Yeomen of the Guard*), in which the rhyme marks the last syllable of two parts of a **hexameter** line divided by a **caesura.** Second, there are irregularly spaced correspondences, frequently in alternating lines (as in Eliot's "Streets that follow like a *tedious* argument/ Of in*sidious* intent," from "The Love Song of J. Alfred Prufrock"), which tend to camouflage the rhyme into interlocking resonances and echoes. Finally, there are correspondences of phonemes alone (see the examples above from Cummings's first line), which are really the same as assonances and consonances.

Near rhyme, internal rhyme, alliteration, assonance, consonance, and **phonetic color** (or intensives) are all prosodic devices usually supplemental to, yet often alternative to, regular rhyme. With less obvious appeal to the ear (if not the eye) than ordered full rhyme, these devices have been employed more frequently as other adornments have decreased. Such cycles in English prosody are constantly recurring: as one characteristic gains ascendency, another diminishes or falls into disuse. An early example of the process might be the abandonment of alliteration, so prominent in Anglo-Saxon poetry, in favor of other forms of recurrence, notably end rhyme. This has been in use since the Norman Conquest. It would be interesting to learn what linguistic or aesthetic pressures brought it about. Did the cycle complete itself with the resurrection of alliteration by Swinburne in the 19th century (for example, "In a coign of the cliff between low-land and highland...Walled round with rocks as an inland island")?[2] Sometimes the combination of alliteration, internal rhyme, consonance, or assonance can make a line so complex that it is nearly impossible to distinguish the types of recurrence. The familiar tongue-twister "She sells seashells by the seashore" involves the consonantal phonemes *sh-* in an alliteration of "she," "-shells," and "shore," as well as the internal rhymes "she" and "sea" and "sells" and "shells." Such correspondences were concocted essentially for amusement; the result, however, is not technically very different from the combinations Hopkins sometimes achieves, as in the lines from a stanza of "The Wreck of the Deutschland":

> ...How a lush-kept plush-capped sloe...
> Gush?—flush the man, the being with it, sour or
> sweet.

Phonetic Color (or Phonic
Intensification)

Our response to the play of sounds (phonemes and syllables) of words has so far involved their correspondence or *near* correspondence. Another aural aspect of poetic language stems from the peculiar orthography of words.[3] The phonetic extension of a word's spelling (literally its sensory impact, or physical mimicry) has traditionally been called **onomatopoeia**. Analysis, however, shows more than one level of phonetic projection. Taken together (along with the prosodic recurrences already discussed), the complex interac-

---

[2]From "A Forsaken Garden."

[3]See the Appendix for a diagramatic relationship of aural-phonetic values.

tions of sound are sometimes termed **orchestration.** This consists of (1) the sound correspondences (as discussed in the previous section, (2) the **phonetic symbolism** or verbal description of a physically sensed quality, and (3) the actual imitation of sounds or sensory stimuli (the division to which we assign **onomatopoeia**).

We have already discussed sound correspondences. Of the other two divisions above, number three is the attempt at phonetic transcription or imitation of the actual physical sound—as nearly, that is, as orthography permits. Examples would be *buzz, snap, drip, cluck, hiss, crack, burp, tick, ding-dong, jingle, caw-caw, sizzle, moo, thud, meow, purr,* and *boom.* Just as a gesture may intensify the significance of a word, so the physical sounds of some words express in a most elementary sense their meaning. These are closest to what have traditionally been associated with onomatopoeia in poetry.

It is number two, however, that offers the wider range of phonetic exploitation by poets. The two categories are not always distinct. In general, though, words in the second group were originally related to some audible expression of what they now represent only symbolically. The words below appeal to some physical sensation even as they register a dictionary meaning: *bark, bubble, buff, chigger, chunk, cockcrow, dangle, doom, drug, flake, flame, flex, flow, fly, giggle, gloom, gum, hack, hobble hum, hush, jagged, kiss, limp, lollop, lump, miss, moan, murmur, nasal, nick, oil, puff, punk, rant, roar, roll, rollick, scintillate, scrape, scratch, sibilant, slime, slink, slush, slut, tickle, tingle, tomb, twinkle, ugly, uvulate, wail, warble, whine, whisper,* and *womb.* Like so many aspects of poetry, the classification of words in their philological sense is controversial. Indeed, probably one out of three dictionary words (including most of our peculiarly vivid "four-letter" specimens) is suggestive enough phonetically and linguistically to tempt our speculations as to its origin—and prove us wrong about it. Even so, the poet takes advantage of the infinite suggestiveness words offer under careful scrutiny and varying arrangement.

The phonic expressiveness of certain words in the second category above makes them particularly susceptible to the uses of poetry, as in the associative pairing of rhymes with *womb, gloom, tomb, doom,* and so forth. The correspondence in the rhyme itself gains intensity through the phonetic color. Sometimes an inflectional ending (as in the present participles of the poem below) seems to have a phonically intensifying effect separate from either the second or third category above. Thus, "-ing," as used below in James Stephens's "The Main Deep," sets up not so much color as a rhythmic quality, possibly as a result of the usually heavy preceding stress:

> The long, rolling
> Steady-pouring,
> Deep-trenchëd
> Green billow;

> The wide-topped,
> Unbroken
> Green-glacid,
> Slow-sliding,

> Cold-flushing,
> On-on-on-
> Chill-rushing,
> Hush-hushing,
> Hush-hushing. . . .

"Slow-sliding" suggests an unobstructed wave movement more vividly than a more syntactical construction such as "the steady slide of waves" or "waves sliding slowly." This is probably because the phonetic and rhythmic appositive "slow-sliding" (and the parallel adjective-participle compounds "green-glacid," "cold-flushing," "chill-rushing," and so forth) is mimetic as well as descriptive.

This double function of words is fairly common in Tennyson's poetry, as in these two lines from *The Princess:*

> The moan of doves in immemorial elms,
> And murmuring of innumerable bees.

The phonic intensification here by careful choice of descriptive words is somewhat different from the onomatopoeic tendency of Stephens' lines. Had Tennyson wanted a more literal transcription of dove or bee sounds, he could have used "whoo-whoo" and "bzzzz-bzzzz." Rather he suggests the quality of their sounds by words that are the phonetic symbols of that aural quality, rather than a mimetic copy of them. The morphology of words like "moan," "immemorial," "murmur," and "bees" might show actual mimetic origins, but the words have by now attained conceptual rank as well as mimetic.[4]

Even further removed from pure onomatopoeia, but creating an associated effect, are the concluding lines of Arnold's "To Marguerite—Continued" (see p. 37 for the whole poem):

> And bade betwixt their shores to be
> The unplumb'd, salt, estranging sea.

Despite some acoustical quality of assonance and consonance, the first line is verbalized to express itself in the most conventional statement, but is complemented by the phonetic suggestion of the second line. "Unplumb'd, salt, estranging sea," sets up the mingled associations of water, depth, salinity, and distance.[5] Even after the reader has lost the context of this line, it is likely to lodge in his imagination as a permanent image of watery separation.

The orthographic versatility of words is compounded by the variation in the duration (quantity) of syllables. As we noted in Chapter 3, some syllables and single words are shorter in duration of sound than others because of the length

---

[4]See *phonetic symbolism* in the Glossary. A considerable literature has accumulated on this subject. One of the earliest is Otto Jersperson's *Language: Its Nature, Development, and Origin* (London: Allen and Unwin, Ltd., 1922), pp. 396–411. See also, Dwight L. Bolinger, "Rime Assonance and Morpheme Analysis," *Word* (1950) 6:117-36, and Ernest M. Rolson, *The Orchestra of Language* (New York: Thomas Yoseloff, 1959), pp. 17–35.

[5]One is reminded of a parallel kind of symbology between our word "sea" and the richly expressive Greek word for sea, *thalassa*.

of their vowels in relation to the final or enclosing consonants. Thus, the words *bat, cat, had, knack,* and *ran; bet, fed, met,* and *set; bit, it, ship, lit,* and *rig; top, pop, cot, rock,* and *stop;* and *but, hub, buck, rut,* and *sup* contain short vowels surrounded by hard consonants (mostly plosives and dentals, with a few palatals) and are pronounced very quickly. On the other hand, words like *came, crane, fail, strafe, far, march,* and *whale; dream, eve, feel, gene, fear, cream, ordeal, stream, creed,* and *wheel; child, crime, find, isle, mine, repine,* and *shined; cold, dole, enfold, moan, omen, alone, long,* and *stone;* and *dune, fool, fuse, June, mule, use, pure, room, smooth, wound, moon,* and *lose* contain long vowels or diphthongs and terminal consonants or phonemes (mostly labials, nasals, or highly resonated combinations with palatals: *-l, -nd, -ng, -m, -ld, -th, -r,* and the *-z* sound of *s*) that are normally protracted in our speech.

Sometimes a poet compounds the effect of phonetic color with the kind of correspondences we discussed earlier ("green-glacid," "slow-sliding," and "hush-hushing"), so that the color and quantity of the words are further intensified by alliterative or assonantal qualities. Such orchestration obviously appeals to the ear and even evokes a **synesthesia** with sight, smell, touch, or taste. Robert Herrick's little poem "Upon Julia's Clothes" has often been cited for this sort of play on phonetic color:

> Whenas in silks my Julia goes,
> Then, then (me thinks) how sweetly flowes
> That liquifaction of her clothes.
>
> Next, when I cast mine eyes and see
> That brave vibration each way free,
> O how that glittering taketh me!

It is not hard to hear the swish of silks as Julia walks. The three words "silks," "Julia," and "goes" combine "i" assonances with "l" and "s" consonances; but the acoustical quality of "i" is vastly enhanced by the enclosing phonemes —"s-," "-lk," "l-ia," and "-ks"—which guide the vowel sound off the tongue with a smoothness suggesting the shifting folds of fabric. The two words, "silks" and "Julia," also suggest the flow of some creamy liquid. They are mutually associative to the imagination. Even the heavy Latinism "liquifaction" accentuates the earlier phonetic tones (although it is semantically descriptive as well as onomatopoeic, the combination we have already termed **phonetic symbolism**). Acting with the final word "clothes," the word liquifaction" forms a metaphor similar to Tennyson's line noted above—"The moan of doves in immemorial elms." Our aural sense and our semantic knowledge are at work simultaneously.

The aural-phonetic complex by which the skilled word-master gets unique effects is one of the delightful surprises that await any careful analysis of a poem. Far from killing the enjoyment—as is often claimed—analysis trains us not to underestimate the art of a true poet. Only by such care, would we note, for instance, how the metrical mutations in the two lines below (by Frost) may combine with phonetic qualities:

> The old dog | barks back|ward without | getting up.[6]
> I can re|mem ber when | he was a pup

In the first line Frost suggests the rickety movements of the dog by the heavy consonantal stresses of b's, k's, t's, and g's, together with the assonances of a's (in barks backward). The feet emerge almost, but not quite, anapestic. By the second line—as if recalling the dog's youth—the meter changes to a smooth and springy dactylic. Thus, alliteration, assonance, and consonance combine with a kind of sprung rhythm to effect a contrast easily missed at first glance.

Lewis Carroll and Wallace Stevens reveled in sheer phonetic color. Carroll's (Charles Dodgson's) whimsical "Jabberwocky," from *Alice Through the Looking Glass*, with its touch of old balladry, swings into a veritable orchestration

---

[6]The stresses for this line are broken into a secondary (\ ) and a primary (/) stress, since "old," "barks," "-ward," and "get-" seem more than lightly, yet less than heavily, stressed.

of **vocables** (that is, words invented for their *suggestive* sound rather than any established meaning):

> 'Twas brillig, and the slithy toves
>   Did gyre and gimble in the wabe;
> All mimsy were the borogoves,
>   And the mome raths outgrabe.
>
> "Beware the Jabberwock, my son!
>   The jaws that bite, the claws that catch!
> Beware the Jubjub bird, and shun
>   The frumious Bandersnatch!"
>
> He took his vorpal sword in hand;
>   Long time the manxome foe he sought—
> So rested he by the Tumtum tree,
>   And stood awhile in thought.
>
> And, as in uffish thought he stood,
>   The Jabberwock, with eyes of flame,
> Came whiffling through the tulgey wood,
>   And burbled as it came!
>
> One, two! One, two! And through and through
>   The vorpal blade went snicker-snack!
> He left it dead, and with its head
>   He went galumphing back.
>
> "And hast thou slain the Jabberwock?
>   Come to my arms, my beamish boy!
> O frabjous day! Callooh! Callay!"
>   He chortled in his joy.
>
> 'Twas brillig, and the slithy toves
>   Did gyre and gimble in the wabe;
> All mimsy were the borogoves,
>   And the mome raths outgrabe.

Any enjoyment of this mock-ballad is hardly lessened by Carroll's having made up many of the words (as Alice and Humpty Dumpty explain later) by grafting two or more rather colorful words together; thus "slithy," we are told, means "lithe" and "slimy." This pleasant ambivalence is underlaid by a reader's private associations and memory of childhood balladry. To experience the *jeu d'esprit*, one must read it aloud, savoring the playfulness of neologisms like "mimsy" or "brillig," which slightly burlesque real words or half-forgotten Old English ("brillig" suggests O. E. *halig*, "holy," as well as a combination of modern "bright" or "brilliant" with O. E. *blaeddaeg*, "prosperous day") and Beowulf's duels with Grendel or the dragon. The net result is a parody of the English language.

Wallace Stevens's "Bantams in Pinewoods" similarly blends assonances and consonances from verbal amalgams ("if-u-can" and "as-can") to create a pompous and exotic atmosphere. The hypothetical exclamation ("Fat! Fat! Fat!") consists of vocables presumably intended to suggest the incongruous clucks of bantam cocks ambivalent with human pomposity and size:

> Chieftain Iffucan of Azcan in caftan
> Of tan with henna hackles, halt!
>
> Damned universal cock, as if the sun
> Was blackamoor to bear your blazing tail.
>
> Fat! Fat! Fat! I am the personal.
> Your world is you. I am my world.
>
> You ten-foot poet among inchlings. Fat!
> Begone! An inchling bristles in these pines,
>
> Bristles, and points their Appalachian tangs,
> And fears not portly Azcan nor his hoos.

Some poems stress the visual aspect as much as the onomatopoeic. Leigh Hunt experiments at finding words from the human world for the visual oddities seen through an aquarium glass. In the process, his poem "To Fish" becomes a kind of dual-edged parody of both human and creature world:

> You strange, astonished-looking, angle-faced,
> Dreary-mouthed, gaping wretches of the sea,
> Gulping salt-water everlastingly,
> Cold-blooded, though with red your blood be graced,
> And mute, though dwellers in the roaring waste;
> And you, all shapes beside, that fishy be,—
> Some round, some flat, some long, all devilry,
> Legless, unloving, infamously chaste:—
>
> O scaly, slippery, wet, swift, staring wights,
> What is't ye do? what life lead? eh, dull goggles?
> How do you vary your vile days and nights?
> How pass your Sundays? Are ye still but joggles
> In ceaseless wash? Still nought but gapes, and bites,
> And drinks, and stares, diversified with boggles?

Words like "chaste," "wights," "joggles," and "boggles" seem chosen for their sound as well as their absurd connotations. Note that even the frequent punctuation throughout the poem suggests the hesitant, stop-start movement of the goggle-eyed denizens of the tank.

English and American poets have probably not been as attracted to the aesthetics of linguistic sound as certain European poets. Yet, we have had our specialists in this line, from John Skelton—through Milton, Herrick, Burns, Keats, Poe, Tennyson, Swinburne, Hopkins—to Masefield, Lindsay, Edith Sitwell, Wallace Stevens, and Dylan Thomas. Their phonetic and metrical virtuosity has been prompted by different intentions: from Herrick's fascination with words to Burns's exaggeration of linguistic peculiarities of his Scottish tongue, or to the sheer romantic excitement of Keats and Hopkins. Onomatopoeic invention on words was one of Poe's gambits[7] in "The Raven" and "The Bells," although the net result

---

[7]Poe offers a methodology for his poetic creation in "The Philosophy of Composition," in which he pretends to a rather mechanical construction of "The Raven."

from an intellectual standpoint was not greatly significant. Yet, the presence of aural virtuosity in subtle forms has been a distinction of most of the greatest lyricists of our language.

Sound, Sight, and Recurrence

We have noted the poetical method of sound approximation and symbolization as opposed to actual sound duplication. Whenever verbal correspondence is broached, a certain amount of asymmetry or disparity is invited: the requirement of difference in the face of likeness. We shall see the principle still at work in other connections, as in the role of imagery in poetry. In the last section there were many examples of the avoidance of perfect likeness in favor of an imaginative version of it—as in the distinction between onomatopoeia and phonetic symbology. Here, of course, is the underlying inclination of poets to suggest rather than to name and describe, to bring out connotations rather than to be limited to denotations.

Thus, in poetry, language becomes a vehicle for a subtler precision than in many forms of communication that require only limited mechanical resources. The relationship between sound and sense is meant to be gradually revealed, to be discovered by the reader as an imbedded part of the complex of phenomena affecting poetry. This must always be the difference between art and science. No explanation by an acoustics expert, or by a computerized analysis of voice vibrations on electronic devices, has answered the question of what makes three or four words in a row rich and eloquent when the same words in different combination remain undistinguished. The last two lines of Keats's "La Belle Dame sans Merci," which repeat their counterparts in the first stanza, may be cited as an example:

> Though the sedge is withered from the lake
> And no birds sing.

You can change the four words of the last line ("And birds sing not" or "And birds don't sing") or add a word or two to be more explicit ("No more birds will sing" or "The birds are not singing now"), but you will not trigger the same eloquence. Keats's choice of words at this terminal point in the poem brings out the mysterious variables involved in selection. The analogy might be made with music of resolving an uncompleted chord, or of sounding three notes separately as opposed to a chord. The scansion of the four-line stanzas suggests that the short fourth lines (predominantly iambic dimeter) were intended to bring the reader up short, but with compensatory weight of stresses, suggesting disillusion and dejection:

> Though the sedge | is with|ered from | the lake
> And no | birds sing.

The additional quantity or duration of the final three syllables (indicated by the **macrons**) emphasizes the weight and inevitability of those four words.

Practical Criticism

Rhyme Schemes

1. Outline the rhyme schemes of the poems on pp. 19, 26, 30, 32, 35, 36, 37, 38. Use the letter *a* to indicate the first rhyme, *b* the second, and so on. When a final word is unrhymed, use an x. After indicating the rhymes, identify the pattern (for example, ballad stanza, tercet, sestet, sonnet, and so on).

2. Indicate by a suitable notation any slant rhymes in the poems on pp. 19, 61, 63, 84, 103, 115, 132, 148.

3. Identify the stanza form and describe the rhyme scheme of any of the following poems you can find in your anthology: Anonymous, "Lord Randal"; Marlowe, "The Passionate Shepherd to his Love"; Spenser, "The Garden of Adonis"; Donne, "Death Be Not Proud"; Blake, "London"; Wordsworth, "The Solitary Reaper"; Keats, "Ode on a Grecian Urn"; Byron,

"Don Juan"; Arnold, "Thyrsis"; Yeats, "Sailing to Byzantium";
Pound, "Ballad of the Goodly Fere"; Wallace Stevens, "The
Prejudice Against the Past."

Phonetic Color

1. List some words with the following consonental combinations:
   a. beginning *gl, fl, sl, sh,* and *bl.*
   b. medial *nd, ld, ll, sh,* and *rr.*
   c. final *sh, ng, er, le, ine, ing, ion,* and *en.*
   Point out quality, state, or kind of action the types of orthography suggest.

2. As in (1) above, list some words containing these vowels: medial *oo, ee, oa, u, i, e,* and *a.*
   Experiment a bit with them to find how preceding or following consonants (single or double) affect the sound by shortening or lengthening the syllable. Notice the variation in speaking duration.

3. What evidence of metrical mutation by quantitative emphasis (as in our examination of Wordsworth's "Tintern Abbey," pp. 57–58) do you find in Cummings's poem (pp. 33–34), Sitwell's (pp. 55–56), and Stevens's (pp. 121–22)? Also check for quantitative variations on the accentual meter of the following poems in your anthology: Coleridge's "Youth and Age," Keats's "Ode on a Grecian Urn," and Swinburne's "A Ballad of François Villon."

Word Choice

In the following poem, called "Lucifer in Starlight," experiment with the options in wording, to try to discover what the poet probably selected. Your choice will of course be affected by the poem's intended rhyme scheme, and also by the aural qualities of the words within the lines. (Your instructor will tell you where to find the poem as it was written.)

1 On a { bright / starred / cloudy } night { old / Lord / brave / Prince } Lucifer { turned, / uprose, / strode forth, / stretched out, }

2   Tired of his dark { kingdom / region / dominion } swung the fiend

3   Above the rolling ball in cloud part screened,

4   Where sinners hugged their { spectre / warrant / idea / illusion } of repose

5   Poor prey to his hot fit of { anger / lust / hunger / pride } were those.

6   And now upon his western { wing / haunch / foot / continent } he { gazed, / hunched, / leaned, / stepped, }

7   Now his huge { body / bulk / frame / carcass } o'er Afric's sands { amazed, / crept, / hunched, / careened, }

8   { Soon / Then / Now / Later } the { black / burning / ugly / new } planet { covered / melted / produced / shadowed } Arctic snows

9   Soaring through wider zones that pricked his { scars / pride / brows / ears }

10   With memory of old { revolt / arguments / goodness / messages } from { Awe, / God, / Mars, / Death, }

11   He reached a middle height, and at the stars,

12   Which are the { brain / lights / eyes / flowers } of heaven, he { laughed, / looked, / called, / spat, } and sank.

89

13 Around the $\begin{Bmatrix} \text{race} \\ \text{heavenly} \\ \text{ancient} \\ \text{broken} \end{Bmatrix}$ track marched, $\begin{Bmatrix} \text{in formation,} \\ \text{rank on rank,} \\ \text{without a flaw,} \\ \text{hand in hand,} \end{Bmatrix}$

14 The $\begin{Bmatrix} \text{choir} \\ \text{saviors} \\ \text{train} \\ \text{army} \end{Bmatrix}$ of $\begin{Bmatrix} \text{caroling} & \text{heaven.} \\ \text{untouchable} & \text{cars.} \\ \text{unalterable} & \text{angels.} \\ \text{swift moving} & \text{law.} \end{Bmatrix}$

FIVE

Metaphor and Meaning:
Vivification of Language

Image and Reality

In the last section, we spoke of the aesthetic principle of likeness in difference. The further we progress, the more we find this a condition of much that we call art. In one of his essays, Wallace Stevens pays attention to this idea:

> The study of the activity of resemblance is an approach to the understanding of poetry. Poetry is a satisfying of the desire for resemblance.... Its singularity is that in the act of satisfying the desire for resemblance it touches the sense of reality, it enhances the sense of reality, heightens it, intensifies it. If resemblance is described as a partial similarity between two dissimilar things, it complements and reinforces that which the two dissimilar things have in common. It makes it brilliant.[1]

As with the near likeness of the phonetic sound to the natural one it symbolizes, or of poetic recurrences to the natural rhythms of life, so our words connect the infinite differences of the world by matching or contrasting them. By this restless likening or differentiating, we make words into our *lingua franca*, a universal exchange of the imagination. "The wave of the future will be the dead sea of history," expresses in metaphorical terms the more abstract declaration, "the arriving of future events soon moves into the past of history." This reduction of generality to some sort of pic-

---

[1]"Three Academic Pieces," *The Necessary Angel* (New York: Alfred A. Knopf, Inc., 1951).

torial construction—usually into a more particularized analogy—we give the name **imagery**.[2] All speech and writing vivifies itself by some use of images (remember the adage that one picture is worth a thousand words). But poetry lives through its images; and these, of course, may depend not on the visual sense alone, but on any or all the senses or extensions of the senses.

It is not merely the resemblances, as such, that whet our appetite for images. It is more the likeness within the difference that sets up the unceasing play of the imagination with reality. This basic principle, so fundamental to poetry (and perhaps to all art), may well be credited to Aristotle: poetry is an "imitation" (*mimesis*) of the aspects of life. His seeming oversimplification can be usefully qualified by the principle of likeness in difference. Exact reproduction has seldom been intended—and only spasmodically attempted— by genuine artists. Aristotle made this distinction in discussing poetry versus history. The historian, he said, relates the events that have happened, the poet those that might happen. With a slightly different emphasis we might say that the former reproduces the particulars of human action, while the poet catches the universal quality in human action.[3]

Now, we shall consider the linguistic instrument of this universalizing *mimesis*: the way in which a poet associates his words to say, "This tree is like a person; yet though it is actually a tree, because I have seen it this way it will now always be something more than a tree."

---

[2]We shall use the term **imagery** (see **image** in the Glossary), in general, and **metaphor**, in particular, in describing this use of language. Other terms like **figure of speech** or, less frequently, **trope** are sometimes used interchangeably with image and metaphor. For this chapter heading, *metaphor* is used for the implications of its Greek origin: *meta* (change; transfer) + *pherein* (to carry, to bear).

[3]*The Poetics* (The Art of Poetry). He is speaking of poetry in general. By *universal* he probably did not mean that the poet should render actions descriptively abstract or general, but rather that he should select the actual and specific from the complexity of life in such a way that they will represent the universal aspect of life. Here he has in mind verse drama, but the implication applies to all poetry.

Images That Connect: Simile,
Personification, and Metaphor

There is a polarity in the data of poetry. What we want to describe is something that is strange even in its identity—as when early explorers sought familiar terms to describe the exotic. Sir Martin Frobisher, describing sights on one of his arctic voyages in the 16th century, had to transform the strange and unusual into likenesses familiar to his fellow Englishmen at home. Of the huge ice cakes bumping around his ship, he says: "They look like nothing so much as our country or Cheshire cheeses. . ." He was employing the oldest kind of speech figure, the **simile.**[4] The English translators of the Bible brought this kind of descriptive phrase (that is, a grammatical comparison with its preposition—"like" or "as" —introducing an adverbial phrase) closer to the direct equation in which one thing is simply substituted as the equivalent of the other. In Song of Solomon, for example, the object of love is identified repeatedly with natural phenomena:

> Turn away thine eyes from me, for they have overcome me: thy hair is as a flock of goats which go up from the washing, whereof every one beareth twins, and there is not one barren among them. As a piece of a pomegranate are thy temples within thy locks.[5]

The phrases beginning "as"—are each adverbial modifiers of the verbs "is" and "are." If the translators had omitted these prepositions, the resulting figures would have been metaphors: "thy hair is . . . a flock of goats," "thy teeth are . . . a flock of sheep," and so on. As a matter of fact, although metaphor probably seemed too **elliptical**[6] to the translators, they slip into it quite naturally a verse or two further on, as the italics point out:

---

[4]In the earliest Greek literature, the *Homeric simile* could be quite lengthy, serving as an integral element of aesthetic contrast to the narrative proper of the epic. It frequently built up from a series of conditional clauses ("As dry leaves blown before the north wind," and so forth) to a concluding clause ("*so* the Achaeian hosts fled before").

[5]6:5–6.

[6]See **ellipsis** in the Glossary.

> If *she be a wall*, we will build upon her a palace of silver:
> and if *she be a door*, we will inclose her with boards of
> cedar.
> *I am a wall*, and my breasts *like towers* . . .

Note that with the last italicized comparison, the prepostion
has replaced the verb "are," revealing the interchangeability
between simile and metaphor ("my breasts *like* towers," or
"my breasts *are* towers").

The metaphor, then, as a specific kind of image, may be
thought of as a more compact comparison in which the adverbial preposition making the phrase modify the verb (saying *how* the action or state of the verb is qualified) is replaced
by the copulative verb itself. To move a few thousand years
closer to our time, we might recognize the Solomonesque
metaphor in "A tree that may in summer wear / A nest of
robins in her hair," in which the personification of *tree* leads
to a succession of metaphors incident to it. **Personification**
means to give one level of being (usually inanimate) characteristics of one that is animate and, strictly speaking,
human. The metaphorical process makes such a change (or
metamorphosis) tenable to the imagination. In "The Fire
Sermon" of Eliot's *The Waste Land*, almost any half dozen
lines prove to be a veritable fabric of metaphorical conditions, most of which imply a metamorphosis from one identity
to an assumed one:

> The *river's tent is broken*, the *last fingers of leaf*
> *Clutch* and *sink into* the *wet bank*. The wind
> Crosses the brown land, unheard . . .
> *Sweet Thames run softly*, till I end my song.

The italicized passages impute an action not quite generic
to the nouns. To associate "tent" with "river" requires a
basic metaphorical transfer or superimposition: it is the
river's "trees" that make the "tent"—pure metaphor; while
"fingers of leaf" represent personification. And the **apostrophe**
to "*Sweet Thames*," urging her to "run swiftly,"[7] requires

---

[7]Borrowed from Spenser's "Prothalamion" and here imbedded, along
with numerous other borrowings, in *The Waste Land*.

the assumption of personality in a moving mass of water. Curiously enough, in the quotation above from Song of Solomon, the metaphorical transformation of "I am a wall, and my breasts like towers" is actually the opposite of "last fingers of leaf/Clutch. . . ." It is what, for lack of any standard term, we might call "depersonification," and the direction of transformation is from person to thing.

The idea of personification seems to be one of poetry's oldest attributes. Indeed, it seems to be the holdover from primitive animism when men worshipped the forms of nature, investing the evident sources of her primacy, force, and productivity—ocean, rivers, mountains, trees, winds, thunder, rain—with supernatural *animus*. As superstitious associations gradually yielded to a formal theology, man seems to have clung to his pagan animism through his ubiquitous image-making, the emotional component of which he has injected into metaphor and personification.

In modern poetry the metaphor (and, by extension, personification) tends to better express an elliptical quality, as exemplified by Eliot, than the syntactical construction of simile. It is an aspect of the condensation by which drama (a direct transcription of experience) affects our grasp of life more directly than does exposition or description (a secondary and more lineal account of things or happenings). Metaphor is part of the reductive process in literary communication of which the play is the classic example: the components of the image literally act out the momentary play of mistaken identity. At the same time, as with the unexplained dialogue of a play, more is required of the observer. The highly elliptical phrasing of Eliot's verse requires the reader to leap from image to image, grasping the associations without the benefit of connectives or the transitional props of syntax. The five lines that open his "Burnt Norton" (II), for example, are a formidable challenge to ordinary logical thought:

> Garlic and sapphires in the mud
> Clot the bedded axle-tree.
> The trilling wire in the blood

Sings below inveterate scars
And reconciles forgotten wars.

His usage in the context here of "garlic and sapphires"—
that is, to "clot the bedded axle-tree"—calls not only for
some special cogitation but also for the use of a pretty good
dictionary. What does "axle-tree" stand for in this poem?
Certainly not bearings for an ordinary cart. Nor are "sapphires" to be taken literally here any more than "garlic" is.
By looking at the concluding lines of Part I, as well as the
lines that follow, we find the probable context for these
highly elliptical metaphors, which contrast the earthy and
cheap with the rare and priceless. The last lines of Part I are:

Time past and time future
What might have been and what has been
Point to one end, which is always present.

We are in the present, our cart (life's progress, perhaps)
bogged in the mud (our present difficulties), which is made
up of the paradoxical valuable and useless litter of the past.
The metaphors of "the trilling wire in the blood" which
"sings below inveterate scars," link us in our present condition to a vastness of origins and prospects, exalting our continuity with the universe here and elsewhere (as the immediately succeeding lines seem to suggest):

The dance along the artery . . .
The circulation of the lymph
Are figured in the drift of stars
Ascend to summer in the tree

The sum of our hopes is thus strikingly compressed into
these two or three figures, linking us to our past, to our part
in the universal system, and to our identity with nature. And
the line, "And reconciles forgotten wars," is the simple reminder that an inexplicable life force—"the trilling wire in
the blood"—tells us of this link, has power to keep us mov-

ing into an ever-new present, and ultimately, of course, "reconciles" us to "forgotten wars"—our past.

This abruptness of metaphor was not invented by modern poets. Elizabethans and Jacobeans reveled in its power to condense and intensify the abstract. John Donne, for example, achieves a kind of cerebral intensity with his play on seemingly absurd or exaggerated images:

> Go and catch a falling star,
>   Get with child a mandrake root,
> Tell me where all past years are,
>   Or who cleft the devil's foot;
> Teach me to hear mermaids singing,
> Or to keep off envy's stinging,
>   And find
>   What wind
> Serves to advance an honest mind.

By a use of **paradox** and opposition (discussed later in their chapter), he transforms ordinary attitudes and assumptions into a metaphysical (or surreal) perspective. The result is to wring sometimes harsh irony from an accepted view of human behavior. And by forcing words beyond their more conventional usage, he carries on the Elizabethan indulgence in **conceits**—those ingenious and at times wildly fanciful elaborations of a single image. A modern fancier of metaphysical imagery was Dylan Thomas. In his twelve religious *Sonnets,* he narrates the Creation by allusive constructions and **kennings** ("owl-light," "hang-nail," atlaseater") in his metaphors, bending the most farfetched connections to his purpose. The first six lines of Sonnet I begin:

> Altarwise by owl-light in the half-way house
> The gentleman lay graveward with his furies;
> Abaddon in the hang-nail cracked from Adam,
> And, from his fork, a dog among the fairies,
> The atlas-eater with a jaw for news,
> Bit out the mandrake with tomorrow's scream.

The normal recurrences of a sonnet might appear curtailed here, but actually he has added to the more common assonances, consonances, and slant rhymes, a kind of composite effect of anachronisms, whose allusive effect deepens the possible levels of approach. [8] "Abaddon in the hang-nail cracked from Adam" is a combined allusion and metaphor; but its metaphorical success depends upon the reader's breadth of imagination and talent for pursuing farfetched associations.

E. E. Cummings had been in the vanguard with such deviant applications of words, creating bright new mintings out of the worn coin of trite phraseology. In the poem below, note the disassociated or "sur-real" effect he creates by juxtaposing words and modifiers in unusual ways (as in the italicized phrases):

A man who had fallen among thieves
lay by the roadside on his back
dressed in fifteenthrate ideas
wearing a round jeer for a hat

fate per a somewhat more or less
emancipated evening
had in return for consciousness
endowed him with a changeless grin

whereon a dozen staunch and leal
citizens did graze at pause
then fired by hypercivic zeal
sought newer pastures or because

---

[8]Even earlier, Hopkins and Cummings had used the sonnet as a form to break away from. The reader's comparative interest in their variations depends largely on his awareness of the traditional form of the sonnet. Hopkins invented what he called the "curtal sonnet"; Cummings used *tmesis, slant rhyme,* and discontinuous lines to disguise the form.

> *swaddled with a frozen brook*
> *of pinkest vomit* out of eyes
> which noticed nobody he looked
> as if he did not care to rise
>
> one *hand did nothing on the vest*
> *its wideflung friend clenched weakly dirt*
> while the *mute trouserfly confessed*
> a *button solemnly inert.*
>
> Brushing from whom the stiffened puke
> i put *him all into my arms*
> and staggered *banged with terror* through
> a million billion trillion stars

Although the poem begins with the opening words of the most familiar of New Testament parables, the grossly secular context and setting become almost cynically apparent in the deliberate stiltedness of diction and mocking use of clichés. The virtuous gesture of the Samaritan requires more effort in this self-righteous environment, especially because the drunk is not a particularly deserving specimen. The tone of the first five stanzas with their mock-pompous or colloquial metaphors make the sudden shift to the final stanza, with its apotheosis of the friend of the drunk, quite striking and poignant.

Poems such as these reveal the continuing power of metaphor, in these cases with the emphasis of distortion, similar perhaps to the likeness-in-difference of caricature in drawing. Eliot, Cummings, Thomas, Stevens, and others were reviving the piquant quality in language by bending it to new or eccentric purposes. A glance back at Thomas's "A Refusal to Mourn the Death, by Fire, of a Child in London" (quoted on pp. 63–64) will testify to the unusual extractive power his images exert on words. The metaphors are charged with a dazzling richness of prosody and diction, mostly keyed to associations far wider than a child's death. The one lost life is transfigured into a dignity that identifies it with a whole national past. Ordinary exposition could hardly evoke these ideas of an inextinguishable continuity of life: "enter again the round / Zion of the water bead / And the synagogue of the ear of corn," or "Or sow my salt seed / In the least valley of sackcloth," or "Deep with the first dead lies London's daughter, / Robed in the long friends," or "the dark veins of her mother / Secret by the unmourning water / Of the riding Thames."

Images That Connect: Allusion, Synecdoche, and Metonymy

Metaphor is the long-range instrument of poetry. The identification of the immediate thing, or emotion, or state with other things, emotions, or states gives poetry a dimension that it cannot have in formal syntax. When this association ranges into other times and places (historic or mythic), it is usually called **allusion.** In primary form allusion merely names someone or something of associative interest, but outside the immediate context, as in these lines from Milton's "Lycidas":

> Where your old bards, the famous Druids, lie,
> Nor on the shaggy top of Mona high,
> Nor yet where Deva spreads her wizard stream.

Allusions can be more complex than this, functioning metaphorically as a crucial part of the poem.

This more dynamic aspect of allusion as imagery can be seen in Yeats's "Leda and the Swan," in which the reconstruction of Zeus's rape of Leda foreshadows the death and destruction of the Trojan War. The allusions (italicized) are in the **sestet.**

> A sudden blow: the great wings beating still
> Above the staggering girl, her thighs caressed
> By the dark webs, her nape caught in his bill,
> He holds her helpless breast upon his breast.

How can those terrified vague fingers push
The feathered glory from her loosening thighs?
And how can body, laid in that white rush,
But feel the strange heart beating where it lies?

A shudder in the loins engenders there
The broken wall, the *burning roof and tower*
And *Agamemnon dead.*

> Being so caught up . . .

While the references to Troy and Agamemnon are only glancing, that myth, more than Zeus's rape, is really dynamic in the poem. In the first half of the sonnet's sestet they are particularly chosen so as to come at the reader in fragmentary glimpses of hideous fortuity—"the broken wall," "the burning roof and tower," and "Agamemnon dead"— yet at the same time represent to the bewildered Leda the chain of violent consequences to Zeus's self-indulgence:

So mastered by the brute blood of the air,
Did she put on his knowledge with his power
Before the indifferent beak could let her drop?

This metaphoric action of allusion is catalytic—as where the presence of a certain element brings on chemical union. In Homer or Dante, Chaucer or Milton, allusion more often than not has a peripheral function, is nominal, and provides an extension or adornment of what is already complete. All allusion is, in a sense, incidental to a dominant idea or theme, but Milton's or Dante's is not as integral as Yeats's or Eliot's to a total understanding of that theme. With Yeats or Eliot, allusions are more metaphoric, requiring the verbal echo from other voices, other moments, to blend with matter of the present. The five lines ending "The Fire Sermon" of *The Waste Land* come to us as direct discourse, and in tandem, but with even more obliquity than Yeats's allusions to Troy:

To Carthage then I came

Burning burning burning burning
O Lord Thou pluckest me out
O Lord Thou pluckest

burning

The fragments are from St. Augustine's *Confessions* and convey the young man's frustration at his inability to shake off carnal lusts and achieve the spiritual state necessary for conversion. When not annotated, such lines require more than average erudition on a reader's part. The effect, however, once the reader assembles the pieces, is quite different than it would be if Eliot had incorporated the references into the poem syntactically, with something like "—as when the young Augustine fled his burning desire, coming to Carthage."

In *The Inferno*, Dante's personal allusions are a means of shuttling the reader from the causes in life to the results in Hell. Eliot's create a double exposure by which the reader is meant to be in the past and present simultaneously. The net result—particularly in poems like "Gerontion," "Ash Wednesday," and *The Waste Land*—is the psychological equivalent of an old man's confused memory of many superimposed stages of life. Or, in a much simpler way, "Sweeney among the Nightingales" is a reenactment of an ancient event of considerable magnitude in the reductive milieu of a waterfront crime. The allusion in the final stanza to the fabled murder of Agamemnon is meant to lend perspective to the threat to Sweeney's rather gross existence in sordid modern surroundings. Here quite clearly Eliot's allusiveness saves an otherwise paltry poem.

A more specialized form of likeness in difference is the image known as **synecdoche**. Here some part of a more general entity is used to designate or connote the whole, as in "Twenty *head* were selected from the herd" (cattle traditionally having been counted by the head), or where the species designates the genus ("cutthroat" for assassin or "pigskin" for a football, or when the genus is used for the species "creature" for a man). Differing but slightly from synecdoche, **metonymy**[9] is a type of metaphor in which one part becomes emblematic of the thing itself. The part or token aspect of the more general or abstract entity becomes its figurative representation (a kind of symbol of it), as in "How many *moons* since she went away?" or "Ultimately the *Crown* must answer to the People." In Tichborne's "Elegy," repeated below, metonymy abounds in nearly every line:

> My prime of youth is but a frost of cares,
> My feast of joy is but a dish of pain,
> My crop of corn is but a field of tares,
> And all my good is but vain hope of gain;
> The day is past, and yet I saw no sun,
> And now I live, and now my life is done.
>
> My tale was heard and yet it was not told,
> My fruit is fall'n and yet my leaves are green,
> My youth is spent and yet I am not old,
> I saw the world and yet I was not seen;
> My thread is cut and yet it is not spun,
> And now I live, and now my life is done.
>
> I sought my death and found it in my womb,
> I looked for life and saw it was a shade,
> I trod the earth and knew it was my tomb,
> And now I die, and now I was but made;
> My glass is full, and now my glass is run,
> And now I live, and now my life is done.

Most of these lines contain some form of the metonymic principle—"My crop of corn is but a field of tares" or "My

---

[9]The Greek etymology of these terms makes interesting dictionary checking.

fruit is fall'n and yet my leaves are green" serving as natural or vegetative counterparts to the literal facts of the speaker's premature demise (he is awaiting execution in the Tower of London).

The proliferation of this kind of image is vast and very much in evidence from the English Renaissance on (for example, in the language of the King James version of the Bible). In Cummings's poem "Anyone Lived in a Pretty How Town" (quoted on pp. 33–34), the lines "with up so floating many bells down" or "he sang his didn't he danced his did" or "sun moon stars rain" or "Women and men (both dong and ding)" express either a whole by a part, or an entity or condition of things by implicit analogy. Time and the rolling seasons are thus compressed into the four successive words, "sun moon stars rain." Further, singing one's "isn't" or dancing one's "did" uses verbs as nouns to express metonymically a particular quality of continuing activity. Finally, the line, "Women and men (both dong and ding)" combines synecdoche and metonymy with a third kind of image, the **pun**. For Cummings, "dong" and "ding" are slangy variants for male and female genitalia, as well as for the Oriental principle of *yang* and *yin* (male-female, gold-silver, and so forth). They are, at the same time, an echo of the bell sounds of the opening lines and, by implication, metonyms for the bell and its clapper. All together, the elements in that line set up interlinking associations for the entire poem. The overall ambiguity of the poem is neatly epitomized through the likeness in difference of "dong" and "ding."

*Images That Oppose: Pun, Double
Entendre, Hyperbole, Paradox, and
Oxymoron*

The opposition implicit in many of our images—from metaphor and simile through metonymy and pun—becomes part of the dynamics of poetic diction. The opposition is both semantic and aural ("dong and ding"). The **pun** is a humorous use of a word suggesting a meaning of another word of similar sound. Its imagistic effect is to produce possible but incongruous meanings out of another context. The sounds suggest each other but are not quite congruent. Because the pun both connects and opposes, it is ambivalent and should probably be considered an intermediate figure between images of likeness in difference and those that oppose two likenesses (an opposition in likeness). The **valence**[10] of an image can, of course, shift back and forth. The juxtaposition of likenesses or opposites serves the purpose of the image depending on the context: straight comparison, ironical comparison, unnamed comparison, out-and-out contrast, and so on. Even allusion, as we have seen, can evoke ironic contrast —as in the juxtaposition of spiritual vitality and spiritual exhaustion in *The Waste Land*.

Ordinarily, images connect (or oppose) near-likenesses. But also, as we have just noted, many images are ambivalent by their opposing of two possibilities or truths at once, juxtaposing them so that they pull both ways. Our rhetorical term for this is **paradox**. Out of the simultaneous existence of opposing "rightness" or "truth," poetry acquires much of its **tension**, a quality operative in much of the world's greatest literature. The Greek play *Agamemnon*, by Aeschylus, gains remarkable tension by offering the spectator two "rights," that of King Agamemnon, and that of his vengeful queen, Clytemnestra. Psychologically, the tension permits no easy "siding" with one or the other. The conflict actually is not resolved until two more plays have dealt with it. *Oedipus Rex* is another example of the seeming irreconcilables of fate and free will. While the king may extract a grim sort of consolation from his own example, he is still the victim of the adage: "you are damned if you do and damned if you don't." A poem functions in this way by condensing the tensions of coexistent rights within certain of its images.

The psychological effect on us of our language's ambiguity must be left for a different kind of discussion. At this point it is enough to be reminded that images involving puns and

---

[10]The application here is of uniting diverse elements within the terms of a poetic image (see the Glossary).

paradoxes express the opposition discoverable in all things, and, functioning as poetic images, generate a peculiar tension. The lowly pun (the **double entendre** of classic origin), when strategically used, can be greatly suggestive. Its "double meaning" (literally, "to hear twice") evokes our often child-like appreciation of the duality in which so many things may be viewed. It tips off the reader to meaning and counter-meaning simultaneously—as when Cummings relates "Women and men (both dong and ding)" with the dual principle of *yang* and *yin*, the lofty with the slangy.

In other contexts the pun can play the personal against the abstract or intangible, as when John Donne (whose name is pronounced *done*) rings the changes on his own name in "A Hymn to God the Father," using the refrain,

> When thou hast *done*, thou has not *done*,

and ending with the variation on it,

> And having *done* that, Thou hast *done*;
> I fear no more.

Or the pun can balance the secular and trivial against the timeless and universal, as in Dylan Thomas's *Sonnets*. In Sonnet I (the octave quoted on pp. 188–89), God the Father is simultaneously Adam and Jesus and a sort of rogue sus-ceptible to both sex and the Devil. These lines occur in the middle of the sonnet:

> Then, penny-eyed, that gentleman of wounds,
> Old cock from nowheres and the heaven's egg,
> With bones unbuttoned to the half-way winds....

The sexual innuendo of "old cock" does triple duty: it is progenitive of mankind; it is the fowl associated with both dawn of life and betrayal of Christ; and it is the disreputable plaything of the chronic whoremaster unable to do up his fly. It is a word—a pun—that simultaneously unites and op-poses secular and theological, mythical and scriptural, past and present, and finally, the world, the flesh, and the Devil. In its wake come derivative (and derisive) progeny of the parent pun: "heaven's egg," "bones unbuttoned," and "halfway winds."

In an age of the Freudian unconscious, the unintentional verbal slip has been joyfully pounced on by amateur psychoanalysts. With a comparable enthusiasm the poets have sown their work with intended double meanings. **Ambiguity** (present in the very nature of language) has been cultivated for the extra dimension it lends to the literature. In a broad sense, it contributes to the structural tension of a poem as a whole, even though the image in itself is a mere unit of that tension. The Metaphysical poets—especially Donne, Herbert, and Andrew Marvell—developed a fascinating system of images by which otherwise conventional themes—God, death, love, duty, peace, and forgiveness— were complicated by a quasi-physical extension of metonymy, double meaning, paradox, and **hyperbole**. And in their footsteps a number of modern poets have carried on the tradition. A contemporary example of an entire poem based on double meaning or pun is Henry Reed's "Naming of Parts":

Today we have naming of parts. Yesterday,
We had daily cleaning. And to-morrow morning,
We shall have what to do after firing. But to-day,
To-day we have naming of parts. Japonica
Glistens like coral in all of the neighboring
          gardens,
     And to-day we have naming of parts.

This is the lower sling swivel. And this
Is the upper sling swivel, whose use you will see,
When you are given your slings. And this is the
          piling swivel,
Which in your case you have not got. The branches
Hold in the gardens their silent, eloquent gestures,
     Which in our case we have not got.

This is the safety-catch, which is always released
With an easy flick of the thumb. And please do not
      let me
See anyone using his finger. You can do it quite
      easy
If you have any strength in your thumb. The
      blossoms
Are fragile and motionless, never letting anyone
      see
      Any of them using their finger.

And this you can see is the bolt. The purpose
      of this
Is to open the breech, as you see. We can slide it
Rapidly backwards and forwards: we call this
Easing the spring. And rapidly backward and
      forwards
The early bees are assaulting and fumbling the
      flowers:
      They call it easing the Spring.

They call it easing the Spring: it is perfectly easy
If you have any strength in your thumb: like the
      bolt,
And the breech, and the cocking-piece, and the
      point of balance,
Which in our case we have not got; and the
      almond-blossom
Silent in all the gardens and the bees going
      backwards and forwards,
      For to-day we have naming of parts.

The effectiveness of these puns lies not so much in the equation between sexual parts and gun parts as in the irony of a young recruit's foregoing his own potency in the spring world surrounding him. Thus, in the best sense, the *double entendre* serves to sharpen the cutting force of the poem as a whole, over and above the slightly coarse amusement of the puns in themselves. At one level, the punning is a joke; but the poet sets it off with poignant, if not tragic, overtones: the paradox of resemblance between nature's seminal activity and the rifle mechanism of death.

Hyperbole, the Greek origin of which means to "throw too far" or "exceed," is perhaps the most common form of *overstatement* for emphasis (as opposed to *understatement*, which is intended to be subtler, if backhanded, emphasis by de-emphasis). The Englishman with a sabre thrust in his vitals who, when asked "Does it hurt, old chap?" replies, "Only when I laugh," has resorted to emphasis by de-emphasis or reverse hyperbole. Marvell used both ends of the hyperbolic scale for his rueful pleas in the poem "To His Coy Mistress." Beginning with the eleventh line, he mingles this with a good deal of *double entendre*:

> My vegetable love should grow
> Vaster than empires and more slow;
> An hundred years should go to praise
> Thine eyes, and on thy forehead gaze;
> Two hundred to adore each breast:
> But thirty thousand to the rest,
> An age at least to every part,
> And the last age should show your heart.

But thirteen lines further along he reverses the effect, offering the understated conclusion to his exaggerated estimate of the time required for the wooing—

> The grave's a fine and private place,
> But none, I think, do there embrace.

Since the heyday of the English folk ballad, there has been a strong tradition for both extremities of statement. That of understatement is evident in this stanza of "The Twa Corbies,"

"His hound is to the hunting gane,
His hawk to fetch the wild-fowl hame,
His lady's ta'en another mate,
So we may mak our dinner sweet,"

or in the bitter conclusion of "Edward,"

"Mither, mither
The curse of hell frae me sall ye beir,
Sic counseils ye gave to me O."

A good example, combining both understatement and pun, is the mortally hurt Mercutio's answer to Romeo, who has asked if the wound is bad:

No, 'tis not so deep as a well, nor so wide as a church-door; but 'tis enough, 'twill serve: ask for me to-morrow, and you shall find me a grave man. I am pepper'd, I warrant, for this world . . .

One of Donne's best known pieces, "Song," combines hyperbole with paradox to tease the listener's incredulity:

Go and catch a falling star,
    Get with child a mandrake root,
Tell me where all past years are,
    Or who cleft the devil's foot;
Teach me to hear mermaids singing,
Or to keep off envy's stinging,
        And find
        What wind
Serves to advance an honest mind.

If thou be'st born to strange sights,
    Things invisible to see,
Ride ten thousand days and nights
    Till age snow white hairs on thee;
Thou, when thou return'st, wilt tell me

> All strange wonders that befell thee,
>> And swear
>> No where
> Lives a woman true and fair.
>
> If thou find'st one, let me know;
>> Such a pilgramage were sweet.
> Yet do not; I would not go,
>> Though at next door we might meet.
> Though she were true when you met her,
> And last till you write your letter,
>> Yet she
>> Will be
> False, ere I come, to two or three.

The entire poem is constructed on a series of injunctions, all of them more or less preposterous ("Go and catch a falling star / Get with child a mandrake root"), which lead up to two major incompatibles: (1) an honest man's chances of advancing himself, and (2) the likelihood of a beautiful woman remaining faithful in love. Either of these conclusions, if presented as flat and unqualified statements, would sound like irresponsible generalities. But approached through the hyperbolic sequences, they assume, in an atmosphere of contrasts, a kind of violent and rugged honesty rather than mere cynicism. The quality of the hyperbole is such that the speaker seems vulnerable to his own disillusionment rather than a worldy cynic.

Hyperbole is involved, one way or the other, in nearly every form of imagery. Such connective images as metaphor imply an exaggeration or incongruity of the reality of their equation. So staid a metaphor as Gray's "The curfew tolls the knell of parting day" wrenches our sober sense of reality; day simply need not be tolled out like one who has died; day does not die, and it cannot respond to our ceremonies of knelling. Perhaps this means—since we have already called attention to personification as a condition of much metaphor —that the imagistic tendency to personify is itself a form of exaggeration, incongruity, or hyperbole.

We have been noting the affinity of the 17th century English poets for images that oppose each other. Their imaginations played toward an extension of, or antithesis to, natural or human conditions. Naturalism was not especially attractive to them. Rather, their "metaphysical" imagery was an extension of the baroque tradition, amply signalized by Shakespeare and Milton. Certainly, the metaphorical bent of both periods was toward the personative and hyberbolic. The Renaissance poets had assumed that nature was the proper starting place, but that she acquired under artistic imagination the proper kind of adornment through elaborate imagery. Ultimately, in the prescription of an Augustan like Pope, it could be said,

> Those rules of old discovered, not devised,
> Are Nature still, but Nature methodised.[11]

The post-Romantic 19th and early 20th century poets, more empathetic with nature and viewing her as poetic in herself, hardly felt the same enthusiasm for the poetic conceits of Shakespeare's sonnets as did those of the Renaissance and 17th century. Their admiration was more for the didactic and humanistic; the style of the sonnets probably embarrassed the post-Romantic poets. It was a style out of which the metaphysical extravagance was born. Not until the revival of imagism in the second and third decades of this century did such extravagance again seem interesting in itself. Here are just the first pair of lines of half a dozen Shakespearean sonnets. For a full appreciation of their baroque elegance, one may quickly check the entire poem:

> When forty winters shall besiege thy brow
> And dig deep trenches in thy beauty's field
>
> (Sonnet 2)
> Devouring Time, blunt thou the lion's paws,
> And make the earth devour her own sweet brood
>
> Sonnet (19)

---

[11] *An Essay of Criticism.*

Not marble, nor the gilded monuments
Of princes, shall outlive this powerful rhyme

> (Sonnet 55)

Was it the proud full sail of his great verse,
Bound for the prize of all-too-precious you

> (Sonnet 86)

The forward violet thus I chide:
Sweet thief, whence didst thou steal thy sweet
> that smells

> (Sonnet 99)

What potions have I drunk of Siren tears,
Distilled from limbecks foul as Hell within

> (Sonnet 119)

My mistress' eyes are nothing like the sun,
Coral is far more red than her lips' red

> (Sonnet 130)

The last is Shakepeare's mockery of the very convention to which his own poetry paid tribute. Though he accepted its idiom, it is part of his greatness that while assuming the style, he was quite able to transcend it with his own singular voice, and to wink at posterity over its prevailing absurdities.

We have already mentioned paradox in connection with the *double entendre*. We saw that it shared the condition of "opposition in likeness," or opposed likenesses, by declaring the relative forms of truth, the contradictions to the assumed appearance of things. In the dynamics of a poem, paradox may be more than a single image; rather, an ambivalence that runs throughout the poem, generating an overall **tension** to which the metaphors contribute separately.[12]

---

[12]This is related to the tension, or conflict, that generates interest in drama or fiction. It is analogous to the physical force contained in a spring or a bent bow; the tension must be there before two things act upon one another. Homer may be said to have first exploited the dynamics of this principle in his epic poetry; he invented the dualities out of which conflict could be generated.

Paradox exists in condensed or epigramatic form in the **oxymoron**, which capsulizes the ambivalence in a phrase or two. Oxymoron works compressively, expressing in a few poignant words some of our involved and pervasive feelings about life's contradictions. The long legacy of proverbs and maxims in any language is often couched in oxymoronic form ("He who loses his life shall find it," "A fat girl makes a good wife," or "Parting is such sweet sorrow.").

In a slightly expanded form, oxymoron expresses a kind of dramatic reversal, the unexpected twist to an accepted idea, as in the assertion, "The dead are moving among us, and we are the living dead," or "Thy cruel kindness has turned me sweet-sick." In Marvell's "To His Coy Mistress" there is a blend of hyperbole, *double entendre,* and oxymoron, with a powerful irony as end product:

> then worms shall try
> That long-preserved virginity,
> And your quaint honour turn to dust,
> And into ashes all my lust:
> The grave's a fine and quiet place,
> But none, I think, do there embrace.

If hyperbole and pun can be said to satisfy a kind of perverse urge to lie or deceive, oxymoron carries such a perversity to a revolt from conventional acceptance. It gives intellectual neatness to our contradiction of the "tried and true." Emily Dickinson brings a note of defiance and controlled despair in the last lines of her two quatrains below:

> My life closed twice before its close;
> It yet remains to see
> If immortality unveil
> A third event to me,
> So huge, so hopeless to conceive,
> As these that twice befell.
> Parting is all we know of heaven,
> And all we need of hell.

Oxymoron as a form of imagery lent itself to the epigramatic style of the 18th century rhymed couplet, as evidenced from these lines near the opening of Pope's *An Essay on Man*:

> The proper study of Mankind is Man.
> Placed on this isthmus of a middle state,
> A Being darkly wise, and rudely great:
> With too much knowledge for the Sceptic side,
> With too much weakness for the Stoic's pride...
> Born but to die, and reas'ning but to err;
> Alike in ignorance, his reason such,
> Whether he thinks too little, or too much.

In our everyday speech, the oxymoron is formed in such adjective-noun phrases as "wise fool," "hurry up and wait," "elegant disarray," or "lovable rascal." Our wit in seeing things two ways is expressed in colloquialisms such as "You old so-and-so," "He's my little man," or "sense enough to come in out of the rain," which incorporate commonplace hyperbole as much as paradox.

The predilection of poets for irony causes them to lean heavily on elegant contradictions and incongruities. A modern poem that has been virtually constructed on paradoxes is Cummings's "As Freedom Is a Breakfastfood." Following the structure and movement of Donne's "Song," cited earlier in this chapter, Cummings builds up a series of absurd equations, reaching a pivotal line (the fourth line in the first stanza and one line later each succeeding stanza), after which a balancing series of paradoxes carries us to stanza end:

> as freedom is a breakfastfood
> or truth can live with right and wrong
> or molehills are from mountains made
> —long enough and just so long
> will being pay the rent of seem
> and genius please the talentgang
> and water must encourage flame

as hatracks into peachtrees grow
or hopes dance best on bald men's hair
and every finger is a toe
and any courage is a fear
—long enough and just so long
will the impure think all things pure
and hornets wail by children stung

or as the seeing are the blind
and robins never welcome spring
nor flatfolk prove their world is round
nor dingsters die at break of dong
and common's rare and millstones float
—long enough and just so long
tomorrow will not be too late

worms are the words but joy's the voice
down shall go which and up come who
breasts will be breasts thighs will be thighs
deeds cannot dream what dreams can do
—time is a tree (this life one leaf)
but love is the sky and i am for you
just so long and long enough

The first three stanzas are each long conditional sentences (arranged periodically), each clause building up to a set of balancing concluding clauses. The last stanza consists of adversative sentences, summing up, as it were, subtler aspects of the paradoxes. With the pivotal line receding each time, the effect is of slightly ironic symmetry. Some of the paradoxes are a kind of distortion of popular clichés (for example, making mountains out of molehills). Their frivolous tone balances the more satirical line embedded among the concluding clauses (such as, "and genius please the talent-gang"). The pattern of **thesis** and **antithesis** is actually reversed by the final stanza, where the conclusions begin the stanza, and the conditions end it. Taking two representative lines, the syntax could be reversed: "since love is the sky and i am for you" *then* "worms are the words but joy's the voice," and so forth.

Like Donne in "Go and catch a falling star,/ Get with child a mandrake root,/ Tell me where all past years are," Cummings intermingles paradox and hyperbole. Both poets extract considerable irony by arriving at a deeper object of disbelief, after exhausting the fabulous. In the rhetorical sense, all poetical images complement each other: metaphor and personification, allusion and metaphor, metonymy and synecdoche, *double entendre* and pun, hyperbole and paradox. In one way or another they make "a supreme fiction"[13] out of the flat "reality" that the imagination must always begin with—a difference out of likeness.

The Image as Symbol

Images so far have been divided into those that connect and those that oppose. Sometimes an image serves as more than a means of specification: it may attract a reader toward a potential union of a stated or specified thing and its unstated equivalent. Metaphors link things that are different but associated. When something is given or stated, and the associations only hinted at but not linked with it, the part given may be functioning as a symbol: it stands for or suggests the presence of a further relationship. In the lines from Dylan Thomas's "Sonnet" (p. 188), the phrase "that gentleman of wounds" serves as a *double entendre,* or pun, for Adam and the Demiurge, but is also a symbol for Christ, evidence for which we must discern as we read on.

A symbol has *overt* significance when the literal element carries a traditional or universal extension (much as a metaphor may function as allusion). It has gained a stock significance associated with the course of our human history (as when Yeats can merely allude to burning Troy in "Leda and the Swan," to trigger predictable associations of the reader). Taking another example, if the name Waterloo is

---

[13] Wallace Stevens, "Notes Toward a Supreme Fiction," *Transport to Summer.*

117

used metonymously ("He has met his Waterloo") it takes on an abstracted value that now defines the experience of the person to whom it is applied. The overt form of symbol, by virtue of naming something specific, is similar to metonymy; Waterloo becomes the token or emblem that stands for a whole class of terminal disasters. Traditional or archetypal symbols are usually overt ("queen-mother," "the wise old man," "the dark stranger") because they have been in popular use for generations.

Another kind of symbol is not overt; one of its components must be conjectured from the poem's general sense. To say, "My moon is long past due," leaves the usage of "moon" indeterminate. The word "moon" is common enough, but its specific meaning must be guessed by the reader. The manifest or nominal meaning of moon is stretched to serve a personal or subjective association. The association can be understood only by correlations of the image within the poem's context, and final meanings may remain hypothetical. "Moon" is not equated with "month" or "fluctuation," but with any possible number of variables, depending on the poet's intent. To relate this problem to the analysis of dreams: (1) overt or manifest symbols are accepted stand-ins for counterparts of the thing itself; and (2) implied or latent symbols are variable counterparts of the thing itself, their meanings only inferable from context.[14]

The uncertainty of meaning that the latent symbol "moon" takes on may be thought (ideally) to free the reader from the limitations of set usage or literal exposition. Of the two types or stages of symbolic usage, the latent variety best serves the poet who wishes his art to be indirect, suggestive, and connotative, rather than direct, expository, and denotative. It is the overt symbol that has long served poets as a device for allegory or the literary analogue. The difference

---

[14]Some readers will recognize Freud's terminology here, in which *latent* and *manifest* are used for the unrecognizable and recognizable forms through which dreams yield their meaning. When the inhibitor of the sleeping mind restrains the otherwise uncontrollable flight of associative images, it disguises them, transforming them into acceptable forms (that is, into symbols). To interpret the latent meaning of these dreams, the analyst must understand the disguises, substituting the equivalent meanings.

between the overt or manifest usage and the latent or implied usage of symbols becomes more clear by rephrasing
the sentence above, substituting for "moon" the metonym
"Waterloo": "My Waterloo is long past due." The meaning
here can be assessed at face value. The private or latent
symbol has become universal and manifest—in fact, a metonym. With the change—the substitution of the manifest for
the latent symbol—it might be said that the sentence now
calls for a stock reaction.

An intermediate stage between the overt and latent symbol
would probably span much of English Romantic usage. In
Edward Fitzgerald's translation of Omar Khayyam's *Rubaiyat*
we can see how "moon" stands midway between the latent
and the manifest:

> Ah moon of my delight that knows no wane
> The moon of heaven is rising once again....[15]

As early as 1854, Gerard De Nerval, a forerunner of the
French Symbolists, had begun turning his metaphors into
something like metonymy, and his metonymy and allusion
into latent symbols. In his sonnet "El Desdichado" ("The
Dispossessed"), note how the recurrent use of the definite
article alters the status of metaphor parts like "dark," "widowed," "disconsolate"; also, how "tower" in the second line
is used (similar to our example of "moon," above) as an
"open-end" allusion (that is, an allusion with latent symbolism) rather than straight metonymy:

> I am the dark, the widowed, the disconsolate.
> I am the prince of Aquitaine whose tower is down.
> My only star is dead, and star-configurate
> my lute wears Melancholy's mark, a blackened sun.
> Here in the midnight of the grave, give back, of late

---

[15]Some of the above discussion may appear to be hair-splitting. The
intent, however, has been to make the rather stereotyped definitions of
our poetics a little easier to understand. Symbolism represents the
imagination in action and (as a component of the theory of images) has
been the subject of lengthy volumes.

my consolation, Pausilippe, the Italian
sea, with that flower so sweet once to my desolate
heart, and the trellis where the vine and rose are one.
Am I Love? Am I Phoebus, Biron, Lusignan?
Crimson the queen's kiss blazes still upon my face.
The siren's naked cave has been my dreaming place.
Twice have I forced the crossing of the Acheron
and played on Orpheus' lyre in alternate complaint
Melusine's cries against the moaning of the Saint.[16]

Some of the evocations come through in translation, though
the allusiveness sounds more natural, less strained, in Nerval's
French. The allusions, while verifiable, function essentially
as latent symbols, fragmented and haunting. The ambience
is Romantic (on a classical background), much as Eliot's (in
The Waste Land) is anti-Romantic—on a Romantic-anthro-
pological background. The allusions are not merely to identify
the *persona* or "speaker" ("I am the dark.../...the prince
of Aquitaine whose tower is down"); rather, they supply
metonymic counterparts to the speaker's real identity (which
is never clearly revealed). Thus, when he says, "Am I Love?
Am I Phoebus, Biron, Lusignan?" he supplies us with associations that are never too close to any specified person or
state. The possibilities of alternate identities for the speaker

---

[16]Richmond Lattimore's translation. The French text follows:

Je suis le ténébreux,—le veuf,—l'inconsolé,
Le prince d'Aquitaine a la tour abolie:
Ma seule ètoile est morte,–et mon luth constellé
Porte *le soleil* noir de la *Mélancholie.*

Dans la nuit du tombeau, toi m'as consolé
Rends-moi le Pausilippe et la mer d'Italie,
La *fleur* qui plaisait tant à mon coeur désolé
Et la treille ou le pampre à la rose s'allie.

Suis-je Amour ou Phébus? ... Lusignan ou Biron?
Mon front est rouge encor du baiser de la reine;
J'ai rêve dans la grotte ou nage la sirene ...

Et j'ai deux fois vainqueue traversé l'Achéron:
Modulant tour a tour sur la lyre d'Orphée
Les soupirs de la sainte et les cris de la fée.

are intended to increase the poignancy of his alienation from his rightful past ("Crimson the queen's kiss blazes still upon my face"), as well as forfeiture of his inheritance ("the dark, the widowed," and, of course, "the dispossessed"), and, finally, to suggest one for whom death has come more than once ("Twice have I forced the crossing of the Acheron"). Without having to draw on knowledge of Nerval's periods of mental derangement, we can sense the controlled distraction in which loss and desolation are projected in an otherwise formal sonnet.

Symbolic imagery at its best requires an imaginative reconstruction, while a strictly descriptive imagery requires little more than our assent to a matching process. Even when symbolic figures elude our immediate grasp, they may give pleasure. An example of the possible variety of poetic experience awaiting a reader is Wallace Stevens's "Thirteen Ways of Looking at a Blackbird," a poem of thirteen vignettes, each one suggestive of a Japanese **haiku**, and in each of which the delightful presence of a blackbird is both a naturalistic and a symbolic part of the poem. After some familiarity with the author's preoccupation with color symbols—to mention but one category—a reader moves through the teasing little stanzas of the poem absorbed in both the *haiku* aspect of each as a thought in itself and in the discovery, through the recurring blackbird, that the thirteen segments fit together as one:

I

Among twenty snowy mountains,
The only moving thing
Was the eye of the blackbird.

II

I was of three minds,
Like a tree
In which there are three blackbirds.

III

The blackbird whirled in the autumn winds.
It was a small part of the pantomime.

121

IV

A man and a woman
Are one.
A man and a woman and a blackbird
Are one.

V

I do not know which to prefer
The beauty of inflections
Or the beauty of innuendoes,
The blackbird whistling
Or just after.

VI

Icicles filled the long window
With barbaric glass.
The shadow of the blackbird
Crossed it, to and fro.
The mood
Traced in the shadow
An indecipherable cause.

VII

O thin men of Haddam,
Why do you imagine golden birds?
Do you not see how the blackbird
Walks around the feet
Of the women about you?

VIII

I know noble accents
And lucid, inescapable rhythms;
But I know, too,
That the blackbird is involved
In what I know.

IX

When the blackbird flew out of sight,
It marked the edge
Of one of many circles.

X

At the sight of blackbirds
Flying in a green light,
Even the bawds of euphony
Would cry out sharply.

XI

He rode over Connecticut
In a glass coach.
Once, a fear pierced him,
In that he mistook
The shadow of his equipage
For blackbirds.

XII

The river is moving.
The blackbirds must be flying.

XIII

It was evening all afternoon.
It was snowing
And it was going to snow.
The blackbird sat
In the cedar-limbs.

It would seem from the outset that the blackbird is essential in more than an avian or naturalistic context. Except in the plural, blackbird is always designated by the definite article "the," giving it a generic rather than particular value in the poem. It is the only source of movement or animation in the static and lifeless background of snow. It is the element of unity between a man and a woman. It is an essential part of autumn change, whirling in wind-blown leaves. It is the differential between the thing heard or the recollection of it ("The blackbird whistling/ Or just after."). To the successive phases of life (virtually from lifeless pretime, to the quasi-finality of death) the blackbird is involved; and without it, existence would be meaningless. In all its shifting meanings, the blackbird is an imagistic personification of the

abstract, a symbol that is barely translated by the context of
the poem.

In the course of many poems Stevens evolved a fairly
consistent set of associations with color (as also with the
antitheses of latitude, of climatic hot or cold, of moon and
sun, sea and land, music and silence, exotic and domestic
existence, flora and fauna) to the point where the familiarized
reader could empathize in the poet's associations with blue,
green, red, black, and so on. By turning to those of his poems
intrinsically related to color—as in "The Sense of the Sleight-
of-Hand Man" or "The Domination of Black"—we can de-
duce that *black* is a symbol to Stevens for the absence of all
color or life, in short, of finality, of death, perhaps of the
end of time as we know it. Since the *bird* is associated with
mobility, change, aspects of life itself, one comes up with a
symbol compounded of "black" plus "bird"—two entities in
the paradox life *vis-à-vis* death. This has many facets in
the course of the thirteen stages of existence or stanzas of
the poem. In each stanza, the blackbird is the spirit of paradox—of time as the one imperative of life, of change as the
one imperative of beauty—against the empty backdrop of
snowy mountains, life here and life on the wing. What makes
anything exist, and register in consciousness, is the "eye of
the blackbird" (life-death, time-change, nature-order).

But if consciousness belongs to life, it is also the thing
that experiences change and, ultimately, death. Thus, at any
given stage of life—from non-being through infancy, marriage, art, commerce, age, and the expectancy of death—the
blackbird is a relative factor and "is involved/ In what I
know." In the third stanza, it is involved in the change of
season, the coming of autumn, the approach of winter—a
combining of the beauty and the poignancy of life. To life's
special connoisseur in the fifth stanza (Stevens, no doubt),
which should be preferred: the moment of realization ("The
blackbird whistling") or the savor of it in retrospect ("just
after")? In the eighth, the same connoisseur—the poet or
perhaps the critic—is steeped in art, but the one thing he
knows for sure about art is that the blackbird is in it (in other
words, the imperatives of nature and of death determine his
sense of the beauty of life).

By the ninth stanza, "when the blackbird flew out of

sight," the speaker's awareness of life and change (as of the autumn landscape) is arrested. The perspective he has of life at any stage is the center of one of many circles. Though they may overlap, the speaker moves on from one to another. In the eleventh, the speaker is a modern citizen who confuses the shadow of his car with time and change. This seems to be the same man of Haddam, Connecticut (outside Steven's Hartford), who in the seventh stanza is preoccupied with "golden birds." While the caging of money distracts him, he fails to realize the life-beauty and change-death aspect of the women around him. In the twelfth, the river (life-time) is moving like the imminence of death. His present "circle" of perspective must move and change with it. In the thirteenth, the decline of life is darkening toward its latest hour. Snow is beginning to fall (the approach of death), and it will keep on falling (the permanence of death), bringing us full circle from the first stanza and its snowy lifelessness. Even now the blackbird remains ambivalent: he sits "In the cedar-limbs" (evergreen), and we know neither the end nor the beginning, for life will reemerge even as death marks a period to it.

This suggested reading (which need not be taken as final) will demonstrate the psychological complexity of effectively harmonized symbols in a poem. As "Thirteen Ways of Looking at a Blackbird" may illustrate, the value of latent symbols may be their relative rather than definitive or one-for-one equivalency. An irony implicit in this poem is the shifting meaning of the symbol itself. For the blackbird has a varying identity as it enters varying aspects of being. We pursue it through thirteen stages (like twelve hours of clock time—discounting half the beginning stanza and half the end). Yet it is a true bird taking its place in each picture, flying ahead of us, evading all efforts to put salt on its tail. We will never totally grasp it anymore than we can decipher life itself. As we watch it, it has moved; it changes, marking "the edge / Of one of many circles." It will not be reduced to absolute certainties, for life is a condition of time and change; it is a dance in the very shadow of death, and this is part of its haunting loveliness (for "the blackbird is involved / In what I know").

The mystification of poetic symbolism is, at its best, not merely arbitrary. If it is to draw us into its meanings, to involve us, its images must be as effortless, belong as naturally to the scene, as the blackbird in Stevens's poem. It must be a true blackbird and belong naturally to that last perch in "the cedar-limbs." In good art, symbols must be an outgrowth of the state in which the artist is at his best. Working under creative pressure, a poet may find his hand almost guided in fashioning the images from which the latent meanings will emerge in due time. With less creative power another poet may attempt the conscious formulation of symbols as such. Such additives may seem to give his work a greater depth, but it is doubtful that in the end they will serve him well.

Permutations: Private Image, Quasi-Symbol, and Allegory

The obscure, the private, the undecipherable falls like a curtain drawn by the artist across the overt, or manifest. Most poets (as well as painters, sculptors, and interpretive dancers) are tempted to linger in their inner vision. The fascination we have in our own dreams is limitless. In a consideration of the "symbolic" in poetry, we must recognize the converging or merging of what may be clearly a symbol of latent meaning with merely private imagery. In Eliot's phrase, poet and reader come together best when the poem provides an **objective correlative**. Yet the extent to which much verse, especially of a romantic bent, is preoccupied with its inner vision without sufficient objectification impairs our efforts to translate its images, affecting though they often are.

The private symbol is not so much a technical defect as a shortcut. It combines mystery with imagery, as does a note-taker's shorthand in comparison with conventional script. In the free-verse poem below by Vincent Ferrini, the most commonplace details are used to express an uneasy relationship between the speaker and a dog. The images—because they hint at a more significant concept—work symbolically, interacting in a little drama of personification and metonymy:

A dog ran
down the night
with my left hand

I asked
the lamppost
where the dog had gone

The lamppost
hung its head
it had no tongue

I hunted
the dogtrack
down the endless night

And on a hill
I saw the dog
burying the

bone of my
left hand
in the moon.

Because the "left hand" is mentioned twice, semantic connotations of "left" (*sinister*, Latin for "left") occur to one.
Has the master's hand dealt harshly with or wronged the
dog—as implied in the dog's carrying it away with him? And
by burying it, is the dog somehow expiating the master's
guilt? The speaker has lost track, but in a dreamlike futility
he asks the lamppost (naturalistically, an appropriate enough
stopping place). However, the lamppost (sharing the master's
—or perhaps the dog's guilt) hangs its head, lacking (as the
dog lacks) the power of speech. The hunt goes on "down the
endless night"—bringing to mind Francis Thomson's "The
Hound of Heaven," in which a great hound (a symbol of God
or of conscience) reverses the situation by pursuing the
frightened soul of the speaker. But Ferrini's dog, making off
with the hand (an instrument of man's violence to others) is

sighted at last on a distant hill (a little Golgotha?) burying the hand, like a bone, "in the moon." "Moon" is ambiguous, allowing several connotations, such as remoteness in time, an association as the earth's counterpart, or simply moonlight.

Since the Romantic era, poets have used "open-end" images to widen their scope of reference and add a sort of portentous charge to the poem. The professed attention by the Imagists[17] to images as the essence of all poems was simply a belated discovery that the French Symbolists had gained something by withholding explanations. Certainly Eliot had learned much from them in the fashioning of The Waste Land, and Amy Lowell gave her otherwise stereotyped lady in "Patterns" a rather vivid set of reactions by having her meditate in images. With much the same use of repetend as Eliot later used in "The Love Song of J. Alfred Prufrock," she lets the lady describe her own entrapment with mounting hysteria, from—

> In Summer and in Winter I shall walk
> Up and down
> The patterned garden-paths
> In my stiff, brocaded gown,

to the final outburst—

> Christ! What are patterns for?

In reaching the intensity of that final line, we have been subjected to a repetition of metonymous references or quasi-symbols for the universal conditions of constriction—"Up and down," "garden-paths," "stiff...gowns," and "patterns" —which brings on war and the separation of lovers.

---

[17]The group of American and British poets before World War I that included Ezra Pound, "H.D.," (Hilda Doolittle), and Amy Lowell, who urged a simplifying and sharpening of poetry through imagery, chiefly metaphor. Pound, as chief spokesman, offered a prescription in his "An A.B.C. of Poetry," published as part of his critical work *Pavannes and Divisions.*

In a different way, Robert Browning selected details of the abandoned and the ugly as an emphatic understatement of a kind of romantic ideal. In "Childe Roland to the Dark Tower Came" the outlines of a broken and abortive quest are merely suggested, but the details are concrete and vivid enough to animate a shifting scene that would otherwise be unrelieved description. We are willing to empathize with the despairing imagination of such a dogged hero. Old comrades are named, their failure cloaked in merciful oblivion; the old cripple at the gateway is all the more menacing because the images associated with him merely arouse our conjecture; the scars and wrecks along the road are lovingly described by Browning, each as a mute denial of the validity of the knight's quest. In the twilit scene, the tower unexpectedly looms before Roland—squat, inhospitable, unrewarding. What does it stand for? What is the rueful knight looking for? Why is he there?

> Burningly it came on me all at once
>> This was the place! those two hills on the right,
>> Crouched like two bulls locked horn in horn in
>>> fight;
> While to the left, a tall scalped mountain . . .
>> Dunce,
> Dotard, a-dozing at the very nonce,
>> After a life spent training for the sight!

If Browning had an explanation, he left it for others to conjure with. The unexplained images—realistic yet functioning just out of our grasp—lead us on in the futile quest. Nothing much comes of them, but they have had their effect. They raise our speculations about their probable meaning. Psychologically speaking, we have gained an experience from them —largely of our own invention. Browning's purpose was accomplished. And he did it with symbols for which the equivalencies were left completely to conjecture.

Another example, Walter de la Mare's "The Listeners," derives much of its attraction from this quasi-symbolism.

Centered around one limited episode, the poem still seems
pregnant with meaning:

> "Is there anybody there?" said the Traveller,
>   Knocking on the moonlit door;
> And his horse in the silence champed the grasses
>   Of the forest's ferny floor;
> And a bird flew up out of the turret,
>   Above the Traveller's head;
> And he smote upon the door again a second time;
>   "Is there anybody there?" he said.
> But no one descended to the Traveller;
>   No head from the leaf-fringed sill
> Leaned over and looked into his grey eyes,
>   Where he stood perplexed and still.
> But only a host of phantom listeners
>   That dwelt in the lone house then
> Stood listening in the quiet of the moonlight
>   To that voice from the world of men....
> Stood thronging the faint moonbeams on the dark stair,
>   That goes down to the empty hall,
> Hearkening in an air stirred and shaken
>   By the lonely traveller's call.
> And he felt in his heart their strangeness,
>   Their stillness answering his cry,
> While his horse moved, cropping the dark turf,
>   'Neath the starred and leafy sky;
> For he suddenly smote on the door, even
>   Louder, and lifted his head:
> "Tell them I came, and no one answered,
>   That I kept my word," he said.
> Never the least stir made the listeners,
>   Though every word he spake
> Fell echoing through the shadowiness of the still
>   house
>   From the one man left awake:

> Ay, they heard his foot upon the stirrup,
>> And the sound of iron on stone,
> And how the silence surged softly backward,
>> When the plunging hoofs were gone.

A poetic richness is evoked by the scene, its dominant image that of the waiting rider; nor is that dominance dispelled simply because there is no final explanation. As with Browning's poem, the mystification is the more haunting because the explanations seem to lie just beneath the surface. And, like Browning, de la Mare was bombarded with volunteered explanations. Doubtless there would have been disappointment had either poet finally granted his authorized interpretation. Part of the extended meaning by which the poem tantalizes readers can be attributed to simple ambiguity, as in "And a bird flew up out of the turret," or

> Stood listening in the quiet of the moonlight
> To that voice from the world of men,

or the line near the end—"From the one man left awake." While these examples suggest allegorical interpretation, no connected system of them can be counted upon as final or definitive. Even so, the poem rightly survives for its tonal qualities, a piece out of the romantic tradition of dream mood and exoticism comparable to Coleridge's "Kubla Khan."

Our final consideration of the permutations of imagery is given to *allegory*. This is an elaborate and extended variety of metaphor, developed normally as a narrative, with personification as characters. It may contain (as in Spenser's *The Faerie Queene*) a variety of subordinate metaphors growing out of the central equation. It usually represents abstract or philosophical concepts by personifications or symbols, as in Bunyan's prose *The Pilgrim's Progress*: "The Valley of the Shadow of Death" is a dark and dangerous place very concretely surrounded by unpassable mountains, and "The Castle of Doubt" is the physical equivalence of a mental or moral

131

attitude. Spenser, in *The Faerie Queene,* permits people and creatures to play out a story of universal principles at the tangible level. Virture or vices are systematically portrayed by knights and ladies or their monstrous adversaries with little more ambiguity than a character on stage wearing his type-mask. In this sense, allegory could be said to be made up of a *dramatis personae* of evenly matched manifest symbols.

Up through the 18th century, James Thomson's *The Castle of Indolence* and William Blake's almost impenetrable *Visions of the Daughters of Albion* marked something of a last stand for the genre. On the other hand, Blake's more humanistic *Songs of Innocence,* while often allegorical in concept, retain their delight for other reasons. Even Coleridge's *The Rime of the Ancient Mariner* appeals to modern readers for qualties subtler than any overt allegory. Possibly because of its somewhat mechanical form, the device has not been very popular in modern times. When it does appear (as in Baudelaire's "A Voyage to Cythera" or Francis Thompson's "The Hound of Heaven"), the emblems and symbols are frequently reduced to rather naturalistic terms or (in Baudelaire's poem) debased to convey the author's indictment of a life style. Thus the island once sacred to Venus is discovered, in "A Voyage to Cythera," to harbor only a gibbet on which hangs the rotting corpse of an exhausted roué:

My heart, that seemed a bird, was gliding in the sun,
And joyous, free, about the rigging swerved at play;
The ship, too, like a sun-drunk angel flown astray,
Under the clear blue happily skimmed on and on.

What is that sombre island like a low dark wall?
"Cythera" someone says—"a country famed in song,
Trite Eldorado of bachelors no longer young.
Look, it is only an arid country, after all."

—Island of magic love-rites and the sounding lyre,
Shore of delicious secrets! Like a fragrance there,
The shade of Venus glides upon the sea-washed air,
Drugging the very soul with languor and desire.

Fresh-myrtled island, garden still unwithering,
Your long renown, by every human tongue
    confessed,
To the far-scattered nations of the east and west
Diffuses, like the incense of full-blossomed spring

Or a dove's endless cooing.—Cythera was no more
Than a terrain of rock and scrub, a dismal reach
Of emptiness, disturbed by an occasional screech.
I saw one curious object, though, along that shore.

It was no vine-girt temple where, with vague desire,
Robe loosened to the breezes, the young priestess
    went
Among green arbours, mingling with the roses'
    scent
That of her pulsing body and its secret fire;

No, but we did see, following the coast so near
That frightened birds were scolding and beating
    upon our sails,
A solitary gibbet with three branching rails,
Against the sky like a black cypress, sharp and
    clear.

Some fierce birds were destroying in an obsessive
    way
A hanged man, duly ripened—with assured
    technique
Perched on their fare, each planting, like a tool,
    his beak
In every bleeding corner of that rich decay.

The eyes were holes; the heavy coil of entrails fell
Streaming onto the thighs from where the belly
    gaped;

And, taking care no hideous delight escaped,
Those glutted bravoes had unmanned their victim
    well.

Below the feet, a pack of jealous quadrupeds,
Their lifted muzzles trained upon the dwindling
    feast,
Slunk, pivoting upon themselves; one taller beast
Moved like an executioner among his aides.

Son of Cythera, remnant of a world so brave,
How silently, with your black hollow eyes of woe,
You took these insults, paying for I do not know
What shameful cults, what sins forbidding you the
    grave.

Ridiculous hanged creature, who are you but I?
Before your dangling limbs I felt, corrosive, strong,
Rise like a bitter vomit to my teeth, the long
Stream of afflictions suffered in the time gone by.

At sight of you, poor devil, I could feel the fresh
Rage of the past upon me—every beak and tooth
Of those black panthers and large crows that in my
    youth
So dearly loved to lacerate and grind my flesh.

—The sea was calm, the beauty of the sky
    complete,
But from that moment all was desolate to me:
In the black reeking shade of that symbolic tree
My heart was wrapped as in a heavy winding sheet.

Nothing besides, O Venus, in your island—just
That mournful allegory to welcome me, at length.
Almighty God! Give me the courage and the strength
To contemplate my own true image without
    disgust.

The poet, wishing to focus intently on one central image, does not attempt to carry out correspondences beyond that single shocking symbol: the gibbet and its rotting burden of the perversions of natural love. He does not expand the allegory beyond the manifest equivalency, though he implies much that the reader may interpret from the latent equivalences which follow.

Authors have used symbols as clues to the seeming pattern of existence from Homer's time to ours. A few psychologists such as Karl Jung believed such symbols to have been conditioned more by the racial memory than from studied choice by the poet. The Biblical figures of Cain, Abraham, Noah, Moses, Job, Saul and David (not to mention the Garden of Eden and Serpent) and of those famed in Greek myth (Prometheus, Atreus, Philomela, Oedipus, Theseus, Leda, Hecuba, and Odysseus) are prototypes that have served as perennial reincarnations in poetic imagery throughout Western literature. Jung reduced many of these to certain key images that he called **archetypes**—such as the *anima* (the residual feminine paramour) or the *persona* (the mask assumed by those performing the act of life). Many of our words in general use acquire a conceptual or symbolic quality, as with our word *Nature*, which by repeated associations as the source and contriver of life is sometimes capitalized, indicating something beyond the meaning of the simple word.[18]

As part of the so-called "shift in sensibility" of the 19th century, many of the archetypal associations were ironically reversed. Baudelaire's preoccupation in *Les Fleurs du Mal* with whores and the perversions of beauty and love is not pornographic; rather it is a deliberate inversion of this mystical *anima* to emphasize the brotherly share we all have in corruption, be it of innocence, of woman, or of nature's simplicity itself. He prefaces his work with an address "to the reader," insinuating complicity between the author and the reader, much as between one who commits a crime and one who tolerates it, ending with the line, "You! hypocrite reader, —my likeness,—my brother!" So, in the poem about the

[18]See pp. 189–90 for further discussion of Jung's archetypes.

island of Venus, the rotting man hangs from his gibbet as an alter ego of the *persona* himself:

Ridiculous hanged creature, who are you but I?

The collective symbolism of the past, from which poets may unconsciously draw, sets up something like an international code of metaphor. Poetry of this conditioning would seem to have better roots—deeper certainly—than a poetry of symbols that were concocted from limited private or localized data. Indeed, a perennial defect of an over-cultivated poetry in any age might lie in this inadequacy: the alienation from a shared, collective past by which poetry—more than any of the other arts—retains its roots. Poets who have no history very likely achieve little empathy with the past. They become the victims of the immediate in literature, of shifting fashions, hoping to substitute novelty for the magnificent panorama of man's complex experience.

Practical Criticism

Image, Metaphor, and Symbol

1. A variety of images may be found in the poems or parts of poems below. See how many you can identify.

   a. Michael Drayton, "Since There's No Help, Come Let Us Kiss," p. 178.

   b. John Webster, "Call for the Robin-Redbreast"

   > Call for the robin-redbreast and the wren,
   > Since o'er shady groves they hover,
   > And with leaves and flowers do cover
   > The friendless bodies of unburied men.
   > Call unto his funeral dole
   > The ant, the field-mouse, and the mole,
   > To rear him hillocks that shall keep him warm,
   > And (when gay tombs are robbed) sustain no harm;
   > But keep the wolf far thence, that's foe to men,
   > For with his nails he'll dig them up again.

c. William Blake, "The Tiger" (stanzas 1–4)

> Tiger, tiger burning bright
> In the forests of the night,
> What immortal hand or eye
> Could frame thy fearful symmetry?
>
> In what distant deeps or skies
> Burnt the fire of thine eyes?
> On what wings dare he aspire?
> What the hand dare seize the fire?
>
> And what shoulder, and what art,
> Could twist the sinews of they heart?
> And, when thy heart began to beat,
> What dread hand and what dread feet?
>
> What the hammer? what the chain?
> In what furnace was thy brain?
> What the anvil? what dread grasp
> Dare its deadly terrors clasp?

d. Keats, "On First Looking into Chapman's Homer"

> Much have I traveled in the realm of gold,
> And many goodly states and kingdoms seen;
> Round many western islands have I been
> Which bards in fealty to Apollo hold.
> Oft of one wide expanse had I been told
> That deep-brow'd Homer ruled as his demesne;
> Yet did I never breathe its pure serene
> Till I heard Chapman speak out loud and bold:
> Then felt I like some watcher of the skies
> When a new planet swims into his ken;
> Or like stout Cortez when with eagle eyes
> He star'd at the Pacific—and all his men
> Look'd at each other with a wild surmise—
> Silent, upon a peak in Darien.

e. T. S. Eliot, "La Figlia che Piange," p. 182.

f. W. B. Yeats, "The Second Coming," p. 100.

g. Wallace Stevens, "Domination of Black," p. 206, and "Bantams in Pinewoods," p. 84.

   h. Dylan Thomas, "Altarwise by owl-light in the halfway house," p. 188.

   i. Randall Jarrell, "The Death of the Ball Turret Gunner," p. 197.

2. The following poems will be found in most anthologies. Select a few to read (a portion of the longer ones if time is short) and determine to what extent the art of any of them is furthered by their metaphor or, when applicable, by their symbols, and to what extent the extended metaphor or symbol gives more unity to the poem as a whole.

   a. Pope, *The Rape of the Lock*

   b. Blake, "The Poison Tree"

   c. Coleridge, *The Rime of the Ancient Mariner*

   d. Tennyson, "Ulysses" and "Crossing the Bar"

   e. Dickinson, "By the Sea" and "The Snake"

   f. Yeats, "Sailing to Byzantium" and "Byzantium"

   g. Eliot, "Gerontion" and "Sweeney Agonistes"

   h. Stevens, "A Postcard from the Volcano"

   i. Thomas, "The Hand That Signed the Paper Felled a City"

3. Here are some longer poems ranging from allegory to extended metaphor or symbol. As a possible critical study it would be interesting to note the shifts in type or quality of imagery from medieval or Renaissance to modern times, and the degree to which such a device as allegory has been variously favored.

   a. Anonymous, *Sir Gawain and the Green Knight*

   b. Chaucer, *The Romance of the Rose* and "The Pardoner's Tale" (from *The Canterbury Tales*)

   c. Dryden, *Absalom and Achitaphel*

   d. Tennyson, "The Palace of Art"; "Merlin and the Gleam"; and "The Lotus Eaters"

   e. Browning, "Childe Roland to the Dark Tower Came"

   f. Hopkins, "The Wreck of the Deutschland"

   g. Francis Thompson, "The Hound of Heaven"

   h. Hardy, *The Dynasts*

   i. MacLeish, *The Hamlet of A. MacLeish*

   j. Thomas, "Ballad of the Long-legged Bait"

Options in Diction and Image

1. In the following poem, called "Ask Me No More," experiment with the options of image and phrase. One of those bracketed is the poet's choice. In some instances your choice will, of course, be affected by the poem's probable rhyme and meter. (Your instructor will tell you where to look for the poem as the author intended it.)

1   Ask me no more $\begin{Bmatrix} \text{where June bestows} \\ \text{who doth compose} \\ \text{for I cannot say} \end{Bmatrix}$

2   When $\begin{Bmatrix} \text{night} \\ \text{June} \\ \text{love} \end{Bmatrix}$ is past, the fading $\begin{Bmatrix} \text{rose} \\ \text{day} \\ \text{maid} \end{Bmatrix}$

3   For in your $\begin{Bmatrix} \text{treasury's sacred keep} \\ \text{beauty's orient deep} \\ \text{garden through which I peep} \end{Bmatrix}$

4   These $\begin{Bmatrix} \text{flowers,} \\ \text{results,} \\ \text{loves,} \end{Bmatrix}$ as in their causes sleep.

5   Ask me no more $\begin{Bmatrix} \text{how time will betray} \\ \text{how we can stay} \\ \text{whither doth stray} \end{Bmatrix}$

The happy hours for which we pay;
6   The golden atoms of the day;
Every scent that goes its way;

7   For in $\begin{Bmatrix} \text{sick envy} \\ \text{pure love} \\ \text{deep wisdom} \end{Bmatrix}$ heaven did prepare

8   Those powders to $\begin{Bmatrix} \text{bleach} \\ \text{gild} \\ \text{enrich} \end{Bmatrix}$ your hair.

9   $\begin{Bmatrix} \text{Ask me} \\ \text{Tell it} \\ \text{Consider} \end{Bmatrix}$ no more whither doth haste

The sound of song to you so chaste;

10   Summer bees whose honey is waste;

The nightingale when May is past;

11   For in your sweet dividing { breast / throat / limbs

12   She { sleeps, / winters, / warbles, } and keeps warm her note.

. . . .

13   Ask me no more if in { north / life / east / here } or { there / death / west / south

14   The phoenix builds her spicy nest;

15   For unto you { all day / at last / exhausted } she flies,

16   { And in / Then from / And upon } your { bounteous / chaste / fragrant } bosom { rises. / will nest. / lies.

2. In this poem, called "The Soul Selects," you may exercise similar options of image and phraseology. The poet in this instance makes occasional use of slant, rather than perfect, rhymes.

1   The soul selects her own society,

2   { Then asks no more; / Then shuts the door; / Then plays the bore;

3   { In / On / Of } her divine { obscurity / majority / priority

4   Obtrude { no more. / the poor. / as before.

5 Unmoved, she ⎰ turns away, unbidding
⎱ sends the sky thundering
notes the chariots pausing

6 At her low gate;

7 Unmoved, an emperor is kneeling

8 ⎰ Upon her mat.
⎱ Beside her state.
To shape his fate.

9 I've known her from an ample nation

10 Choose one;

11 Then close the valves of her attention

12 ⎰ Like stone.
⎱ All alone.
Her largess done.

3. In the following poem, a leading English Romantic poet expresses in tones both cavalier and wistful, his resignation and relief at the end of a romance. The rhymes and meter are conventional.

1 So we'll go no more a-roving

2   So late into the night

3 Though the heart be still as loving,

4 ⎰ And the moon be still as bright.
⎱ I pray he'll treat you right.
Out of mind is out of sight.

5 For the sword outwears its sheath,

6 ⎰ And roving requires some rest,
⎱ And wenching dulls one's zest,
And the soul wears out the breast,

7 And the heart must pause to breathe,

8   And love itself have rest.

9 Though the night was made for loving,

10   And the day returns too soon,

        ⎧ We'll not be disapproving
11   ⎨ Somehow we'll get a-moving
        ⎩ Yet we'll go no more a-roving

12   By the light of the moon.

SIX

Means Into Meaning:
Concept and Mode

Narrative Modes

When you want to tell a story or express an idea, you look for the best means to that end. Most people start at the beginning and follow through in chronological order: a beginning-to-end narrative. Or, you might wish to complicate the order by interruptions or relocations of normal chronological sequence. In this instance, you could bracket a narrative by beginning near the end, then going back to the beginning and working to the end again. Or you might have some witness—someone "in the know"—start the story, then recede while the characters take over and live their experiences, and finally reappear at the end to remind the reader how it all started.

The narrator may be partially involved or a total outsider, and in either case may impart a sense of perspective or detachment. Either way, the author creates a **persona**, an invented speaker, who masks the writer's own point of view and permits him to remain more or less in the wings.[1] If the narrator is a principal actor, his account of things may be colored by his personal involvement or be sufficiently one-sided as to create ironic discrepancies with what contrastingly emerges as nearer to the truth. Finally, several characters with conflicting viewpoints and differing attitudes toward the events may offer successive versions of the story. Or these different sides of the story may mesh together, compli-

---

[1]Joseph Conrad's "Heart of Darkness" is a famous example. A more complex one would be William Faulkner's *Absalom, Absalom!*

cating an otherwise simple course of events. The reader will be left to make his own comparisons and to exercise his own judgments. He will use the data selected by the author to survey the field and—to borrow geometry's term—determine unknown dimensions by "triangulation."[2]

Out of these possibilities, the raconteur, the dramatist, or the poet manages to enhance a mere chronicle of events by engaging his listener's own resources, forcing him to participate in art's imitation of life. Most authors will intensify this process by all the literary devices at hand. These may be called the *representational* or *narrative modes*: the logistics of conveying ideas, situations, and characters toward an end. In poetry, they exist in patterns formulated from direct feelings, projected feelings, and indirect representations of feelings in word association, motifs, and ideas—all employed toward some artistic effect. The modes may at times be those of narrative or drama, making use of description of a state or of an action, or by dialogue or monologue. Or they may be an evocation of psychic and physical conflict, personal and structural tension—all of which enhance the reader's involvement and, ultimately, reflect the thrusts and balances evident in the world that poetry tries to communicate.

The Idea of a Speaker

While poetry has its own peculiar means for intensifying itself (that is, by aural and linguistic means), it also employs the innumerable expressive modes we generally associate with such communicative arts as fiction and drama. The narrative strategies mentioned in the preceding section are but a few. Certain novelists since Conrad's time (for example, James Joyce and Virginia Woolf in England and Thomas Wolfe and William Faulkner in America) built their rhetoric on an imagery almost as dense as any poet's. They were able to concentrate their narratives and intensify their emotional

---

[2] The technique is as old as Homer, but it has come into its own in modern times. Browning's *The Ring and the Book* is an example of the many-sided truth, as are such 20th century works as Masters's *Spoon River Anthology* in verse, and Faulkner's *The Sound and the Fury* in fiction.

charge to a higher pitch than ordinarily attained in novels. Poetry, on the other hand, began—especially in the latter part of the 19th century—to acquire more of the dramatic techniques of a play or the tight structural tensions of a short story. Monologue and dialogue were found to express a type of indirect poetry more kinetic and vivid than that expressed directly by the poet's voice. The idea of the poet's mask, the *persona,* had existed from antiquity; but it was revived with particular effectiveness by Browning and, subsequently, became one of the most distinctive qualities of modern poetry.

Actually, since poetry and drama were frequently inseparable in Greek and Roman times—and well up into the verse drama of Renaissance England—Robert Browning's use of dramatic viewpoints in his psychological poems was merely a variance of the older traditions. The method has been implicit as early as some of the popular ballads, such as "Lord Randal," "The Demon Lover," and "Edward." An implied "speaker," as we have already noted, permitted a more sophisticated approach in some of Spenser's and Michael Drayton's sonnets (as in "Since There's No Help"), while John Donne, and later Andrew Marvell, evolved semi-monologues of even richer ironic overtones. Browning simply concentrated on one speaker's characterization, with his self-revealed nature forming the whole point of the poem.

In this dramatic milieu, pure lyricism gave way to a verbal and psychological poignancy largely dependent on the inner dialectic of the poem. Readers were soon educated to look for the subtler implications rather than the direct emotion conveyed by the poet. In Wordsworth's sonnet, "The World Is Too Much with Us" (p. 21), the poet is speaking to himself, a monologue which is, of course, intended for the reader. His view, to be sure, is ordered in the prosodic pattern of a sonnet; but as far as the mode of representation goes, there is nothing between us and Wordsworth. We also saw that Matthew Arnold, in "Dover Beach" (p. 26), provided a spokesman—a stand-in for himself, however faintly dramatized—and a particularized setting or circumstantial frame. Thus the poet has made use of a mask through which he presents a personality apart from his own. This—and the rudimentary dialogue it makes possible—makes the poem structurally more complex and, for some, more interesting. We have in it, then, a "mode of representation" in action.

In Tichborne's "Elegy" (p. 103) the poet declares his hopeless condition to himself only, but formalizes it into a prayerlike confession, with only a series of slightly varying metonyms between himself and his reader. (One can, of course, consider confession as a mode of representation.) With a powerful and obsessive sort of redundancy, Tichborne details his list of disappointments, an object lesson, surely, and a spectacle for pity. There is no mask other than that incident upon the "confessional" as a traditional posture. The impact of his approaching doom is emphasized by all the aural means of recurrence and expectancy. Unrelieved as they are, the succession of plaints builds up an impressive charge, certainly with more immediacy than those of Wordsworth's sonnet. With the meagerest evidence, we can still visualize the scene and the *persona*. In the eloquence of his despair, this "speaker" has little need for further representational devices.

Both Wordsworth and Tichborne gain immediacy from the personal "I," as opposed to a more remote account from a third person. Had Wordsworth generalized his declaration in the sonnet's sestet to "Great God, *a man* would rather be" (and so forth), he would have blunted the effect of projection in his outburst. In "Elegy," change the "My" and "I" to "His" and "He," and our identification with the speaker would be similarly blunted. With the lines changed, as below, a vague "somebody" suffers—

> *His* prime of youth is but a frost of cares . . .
> And now *he* lives, and now *his* life is done . . .

—but without the self-dramatization of Tichborne's style.[3]

---

[3]Aside from the personal mood of "Elegy," the almost overwhelming use of verbal repetition intensifies the mode of representation. These recurrences come both at the beginning and the end of lines:

> 1 The day is past, and yet I saw no sun,
>   And now I live, and now my life is done.

146

The sometimes oppressive recurrences in "Elegy" of metonymy in antithetical, or parallel, structure provide part of the expressive mode of the poem. They complement the speaker's obsessive point of view. The poem can be thought of as several correlated modal effects working toward a final effect. In a similar way, in Henry Reed's "Naming of Parts" (p. 107), the pun of the rifle mechanism with the sex motif becomes the theme itself (not entirely dissimilar to Tichborne's lament for his aborted youth).

But images, rhetoric, and a carefully posed dramatic situation are not enough, in themselves, for any poem, unless there is interaction of the parts with the whole. Poems in which images are merely strung together without organic relationship lack artistic integrity. An example of how mere repetition can fall short—minus the balance or interaction of theme in Reed's or Tichborne's poem—are the lines of "God's Will," a popular favorite of calendar verse:

> Just to be tender, just to be true,
> Just to be glad the whole day through,
> Just to be merciful, just to be mild,
> Just to be trustful as a child,
> Just to be gentle and kind and sweet,
> Just to be helpful with willing feet,
> Just to be cheery when things go wrong,
> Just to drive sadness away with a song,
> Whether the hour is dark or bright,
> Just to be loyal to God and right,
> Just to believe that God knows best,

---

2 My thread is cut and yet it is not spun,
   And now I live, and now my life is done.
3 My glass is full, and now my glass is run,
   And now I live, and now my life is done.

Only when we have examined the arrangement of these compelling sounds—counterbalanced as they are for harmonic purposes—can we appreciate how the effect of monotony is not accidental but skillfully contrived to express the central fact—premature death. The speaker's stance is nearly as vivid as that of Hamlet soliloquizing from the battlements of Elsinore.

> Just in his promises ever to rest—
> Just to let love be our daily key,
> That is God's will for you and me.[4]

The parallelism of beginning phrases is a meritorious attempt at modal form, and superficially suggests Reed's or Tichborne's recurrences; the difference is the organic integrity with which the metaphorical element becomes part of a whole. "God's Will" merely strings together pious admonitions, tritely expressed, and united only by the parallelism and metronomic rhyme and meter.

Again, in the little poem by Vincent Ferrini, "A Dog Ran down the Night" (p. 127), the *persona* intensifies the sense of guilt, including the reader much in the same way as Baudelaire does in his "Au Lecteur" (see discussion p. 149). However shadowy this "I" remains, we are subtly drawn into his traumatic experience. As his alter ego, we are forced—dreamlike—into sharing responsibility for the dog's behavior. This identification, plus the familiar yet striking imagery, raises the poem above what might have become mere sentiment over a dog.

In "Blue Girls," a fine poem by John Crowe Ransom, there is a speaking presence even though the identity barely emerges (and then only ambiguously) at the end. The monologue may or may not be spoken to listening persons, but the poet has provided a definite setting and charged the poem with inherent tension:

> Twirling your blue skirts, traveling the sward
> Under the towers of your seminary,
> Go listen to your teachers old and contrary
> Without believing a word.
>
> Tie the white fillets then about your lustrous hair
> And think no more of what will come to pass
> Than bluebirds that go walking on the grass
> And chattering on the air.

---

[4] Charles E. Guthrie, "God's Will," *Best Loved Religious Lyrics.*

Practice your beauty, blue girls, before it fail;
And I will cry with my loud lips and publish
Beauty which all our power shall never establish
It is so frail.

For I could tell you a story which is true:
I know a lady with a terrible tongue,
Blear eyes fallen from blue,
All her perfections tarnished—and yet it is not long
Since she was lovelier than any of you.

Whoever the speaker (an aging professor? a lady dean? or perhaps even the "lady with a terrible tongue" herself?), he or she looks at the insouciant girls from a viewpoint both wise and bitter in the discrepancies of time. The audible meditation spans the speaker-listener gap. It is less distinct than the *persona* of Tichborne's complaint (so repetitively pronounced), but it evokes a richer mode because it is ambiguous. The poet gains perspective by invoking the listener throughout, and the resulting poem is more kinetic and vivid than it might have been with a generalized voice speaking to a generalized reader.

Is this liaison between speaker and listener always desirable? It depends, of course, on the ultimate intent of the poet and the degree to which the implied or varying presence furthers the living sense of the poem. In Baudelaire's "Au Lecteur," already mentioned, the conspiratorial tone helps to excite the reader through complicity:

How well you know this fastidious monster, reader,
—Hypocrite reader, you!—my double! my brother![5]

Thus invoked, the reader is no longer a bystander and must accept the uneasy role of guilty participant.

In Robert Horan's "Suppose We Kill a King" (p. 65–66), this complicity is suggested by the "we" rather than the more general "one" or "they." It might, of course, have been

---

[5]Tu le connais, lecteur, ce monstre délicat,
—Hypocrite lecteur,—mon semblable,—mon frère!

"you," but the tone would then have been suppositious. As it is, the reader becomes an accessory before and after the fact in the cycle of dynastic intrigue. In Andrew Marvell's "To His Coy Mistress," on the other hand, the mode of address is reduced from "we" to "I" and "you," individualizing the speaker and his lady within the intimacies of the boudoir. The speaker is alone with his fashionable mistress, and Marvell's remarkable blend of sincere lover with worldly courtier makes his voice ironically ambiguous. The reader may be either an amused eavesdropper or a concerned participant as the speaker's underlying seriousness breaks through the mocking hyperbole in such lines as

> But at my back I always hear
> Time's winged chariot hurrying near.

Henry Reed's "Naming of Parts" (p. 107) conveys a more immediate irony from the rifle drill by letting the speaker become "we." The pronoun, of course, stands for all the rookies engaged in this elementary arms exercise. The "we" assumes a passive majority accepting this ritual of war. Yet actually, only the speaker seems to stand as nature's misfit. Unlike the potential soldiers with whom he drills, this one emerges as an unwarlike maverick in a warlike age. He alone registers the irony of this grotesque drill against the counterpoint of nature's more seminal ritual of spring.

Dramatic Monologue

Coming closer to the realm of drama itself, lyric poets at various times have experimented with **dramatic irony**, a condition of unawareness in the actor, a situation early developed by the ancient Greek playwrights. Essentially the principle was to let the spectator in on a character's fate before the character became aware of it.[6] As a poetic device, it

---

[6]In the plays of 5th century Greece, the characters and plot were derived from a known myth. In *Oedipus Rex*, for example, the king's true identity, and the complications arising from it, remain hidden to all except Tiresias and the play's audience.

served admirably for subtle indirection and ambiguity of tone. In the most familiar examples, a central character is allowed to speak without realizing what self-revelation he affords his listener. He testifies, as it were, against himself, and the implications are more and more damaging.

Robert Browning seems to have perfected this psychological device for poetic purposes, giving it the name **dramatic monologue**. In his best known example, "My Last Duchess," the Duke of Ferrara entertains a visiting envoy with accounts of the lady whose portrait they are admiring among the duke's art treasures. It seems the duchess was too spirited a lady, too open in her enjoyment of what pleased her, to suit the duke. His explanation of her reprehensible conduct is intended to edify the envoy. Only near the end do we learn that the object of the envoy's visit was to negotiate with the Duke of Ferrara about a second wife. The duke's offhand words as they finish viewing the portrait—"There she stands /As if alive"—leaves her fate ambiguous to the listener. Beyond the self-revelation of a very cold nature, we glimpse the deeper irony in the discrepancy between Ferrara's vanity and the wasted humanity of a woman he had intended to own.

Browning pursued the techniques of the dramatic monologue in nearly a dozen poems, among others "Fra Lippo Lippi," "The Bishop Orders His Tomb at Saint Praxed's Church," "Andrea Del Sarto," and "Soliloquy in a Spanish Cloister."[7] In "Andrea Del Sarto" the successful, though unfulfilled, painter tries to explain to his beautiful and unfaithful wife, Lucrezia, how he had at first looked to her for inspiration. As he talks, it becomes clear that she has cared little for him or his work—except insofar as his sales pay for her

---

[7]His most ambitious poem, *The Ring and the Book,* is actually nine extended dramatic monologues providing nine different versions of an old murder. It is both a meticulous study of character and an admirably sustained poetic achievement. It also set a pattern for subsequent experiments in multiple-view narrative, such as Master's *Spoon River Anthology,* Robinson's *Captain Craig,* and Steven Vincent Benét's *John Brown's Body.* Modern fiction has adapted multiple-view more extensively than poetry, with such examples as William March's *Company K,* Virginia Woolf's *Jacob's Room,* John Dos Passos's *Manhattan Transfer,* and William Faulkner's *As I Lay Dying.*

frivolities. Here—as in all the monologues—only one voice is heard, but by skillfull suggestion the poet transcends the limitation. The self-imposed boundary of narrative scope gains for an artist a certain psychological advantage comparable to the prosodic boundaries of, say, the sonnet form. In "Andrea" the final nuance comes when the painter pauses —perhaps imagining some gesture of contrition on her part —and, from below, her latest lover whistles discreetly. Lucrezia has become restless as Andrea goes on in the settling dusk describing his vanishing hopes of rivaling Rafael, Leonardo, and others. But, he confesses, "there's still Lucrezia,— as I choose." Apparently there is no response, and the poem ends as he says, "Again the Cousin's whistle! Go, my Love."

"Soliloquy in a Spanish Cloister" and "The Bishop Orders His Tomb" vary the dramatic monologue in certain respects. In the former, the speaking monk has no audience except the reader, permitting him to reveal hatred that might not otherwise ever have been shared. The technique, exploited later by T. S. Eliot in "The Love Song of J. Alfred Prufrock," invites the listener to share in motives and desires that, according to the epigraph heading the poem, no speaker would willingly reveal to anyone alive. Brother Lawrence, the object of Browning's monk's un-Christian envy and malice, emerges in spite of the speaker's bitter meditation as relatively human and warm-blooded. Again, the ironic reversal becomes the kinetic force of this dramatic mode.

In "The Bishop Orders His Tomb," we listen to the deathbed maunderings of a Roman bishop. Even in extremis, his fevered mind hovers around the worldly assets of his prelacy. It glances back and forth, from visions of past mistresses to the tricks on his rivals that helped to get him ahead. The grotesque ramblings—reducing him to a caricature of the holy man—are only interrupted by chance reminders of his high office, extracting at best a pious phrase or two. As in "Soliloquy in a Spanish Cloister," the irony is compounded by the dying bishop's half-humorous confusion between the spiritual office and the frequent venalities of a very worldly life.

Direct and Indirect Discourse

Since the latter part of the 19th century, few poets have capitalized on the potentialities of direct discourse as Browning did. Tennyson left a few good specimens ("St. Simon Stylites," "Ulysses," and "Lucretius") and Matthew Arnold and William Morris practiced their own modifications, a mixture usually of traditional narrator and a more developed *persona*. One of Morris's best known narratives, "The Haystack in the Floods," seems in recollection to be a monologue, but is actually a projection of the consciousness of the central character, Jehane, through the narrator's view. We are let inside her mind so skillfully, and her inner loyalties are so thoroughly searched, that one's impression in retrospect is that she has been her own spokesman. The opening eight lines below, followed by six lines near the middle of the poem, illustrate Morris's art of interior projection:

> Had she come all the way for this,
> To part at last without a kiss?
> Yea, had she borne the dirt and rain
> That her own eyes might see him slain
> Beside the haystack in the floods?
>
> Along the dripping leafless woods,
> The stirrup touching either shoe,
> She rode astride as troopers do....
>
> .   .   .   .
>
> She laid her hand upon her brow,
> Then gazed upon the palm, as though
> She thought her forehead bled, and "No,"
> She said, and turn'd her head away,
> As there were nothing else to say,
> And everything were settled....

The mode here was to bring detailed psychological narrative back to the service of lyric poetry. Of course, modern fiction—especially in the art of the short story over the last fifty years—has made this blend of narrative and interior projection quite familiar. But Morris's technique here, as in "The Defense of Guinevere" and "The Eve of Crecy," was part of the revival, already begun by Browning, of a sharpened historical realism. Their harsh, down-to-earth interpretations of the past were a timely corrective to the romanticized chivalry of Tennyson's *Idylls of the King*. In America, Edwin Arlington Robinson was to attempt this psychological realism in his reconstruction of the Malorian legends of Lancelot, Merlin, and Tristram. But by this time—the 1920s—poetic narrative was competing for about the last time with prose fiction; it was not to have so good a run again as with his brief revival of a languishing art.[8]

The 20th century saw many variations on the pure dramatic monologue, as in the posthumous meditations of the people in Edgar Lee Masters's *Spoon River Anthology* or the monologues of Robert Frost's strangely restless country folk in the *North of Boston* poems. By the mid-twenties, Robinson Jeffers was attempting semidramatic narratives on a Greek tragic scale in *Roan Stallion*, *Tamar*, and *Cawdor*. Somewhat earlier, among the Imagists, Amy Lowell's "Patterns" could be considered a modification of dramatic monologue into the kind of incantatory style she and Eliot were developing, as in these lines:

> In Summer and in Winter I shall walk
> Up and down
> The patterned garden-paths
> In my stiff, brocaded gown....
> Christ! What are patterns for?

Following Lowell's method (though borrowing his tone mostly from Jules Laforgue), Eliot gave his Prufrock poem the benefit of dramatic monologue and certain lyric refrains and

---

[8]There were a few individual successes in narrative verse, such as Masefield's *Dauber*, Jeffer's *Roan Stallion*, and Benét's *John Brown's Body*, but they may be considered as "sports" of the prevailing species of poetry.

sound effects. As with Browning's Spanish monk or dying bishop, Prufrock's meditations are a confessional that he never intended should be brought to light. Eliot, however, achieves a kind of counterpoint between psychological analysis and lyric overtones. Against the speaker's agonized craving for transfiguration into something primitive or elemental, we hear the stereotyped voices that surround Prufrock:

> In the room the women come and go
> Talking of Michelangelo.

By creating two attention levels, Eliot manages to give his dramatic monologue the extra richness of contrast.

Perhaps what "The Love Song of J. Alfred Prufrock" most reflects is the special tone or **voice** of the effete milieu Eliot wants to hold up to view. He seems to have modeled this tone very closely on the **vers de société** (poetry about society) of Jules Laforgue. As early as the 1880s, the young Laforgue, fresh from Argentina, perfected an insouciant, self-mocking *persona* called Pierrot, whose monologue is sometimes mixed with dialogue. In the "Lament" below ("Autre Complainte de Lord Pierrot") a distinct tone emerges, progressing through an inconsequential and mocking dialogue to its ironic conclusion:

> She is the one who started me on women!
> Let's begin by saying in my coolest way:
> "The sum of the angles of a triangle, dear girl,
>   Is equal to two rights."
>
> And if she should cry: "O my God I love you so!"
> I: "God will claim his own." Or, in her hurt tone:
> —"On the keyboard of my heart, you're my sole
>   theme."
>   I: "Everything is relative."

Both eyes on me then! with feelings so trite:
"Ah! You don't love me, while plenty are jealous!"
And I, an eye turned toward the Subconscious:
    "Thanks, not bad; and you?"

—"Let's play at being faithful!"—"To what use, in
    all sense?"
"Whichever one loses, wins!" Then, one more
       round:
—"Ah! you'll be weary first, that I'm sure of..."
    —"After you, if you please."

At last if, some evening, she expires softly among
My books; feigning not to believe my eyes,
I'll come up with: "Ah then, but we had so much to
    live for!
    Was she really that serious?"[9]

---

[9]Translated by the author. The French text follows:
    Celle qui doit me mettre au courant de la Femme!
    Nous lui dirons d'abord, de mon air le moins froid:
    "La somme des angles d'un triangle, chè âme,
        Est égale à deus droits."

    Et si ce cri lui part: "Dieu de Dieu! que je t'aime!"
    —"Dieu rereconnaîtra les siens." Ou piquée au vif:
    —"Mes claviers ont du coeur, tu seras mon seul thème."
        Moi: "Tout est relatif."

    De tous ses yeux, alors! se sentant trop banale:
    "Ah! tu ne m'aimes pas; tant d'autres sont jalous!"
    Et moi, d'un oeil qui vers l'Inconscient s'emballe:
        "Merci, pas mal; et vous?"

    —"Jouons au plus fidèle!" —"A quoi bon, ô Nature!"
    "Autant a qui perd gagne!" Alors, autre couplet:
    —"Ah! tu te lasseras le premier, j'en suis sure ..."
        —"Après vous, s'il vous plait."

    Enfin, si, par un soir, elle meurt dans mes livres,
    Douce; feignant de n'en pas croire encor mes yeux,
    J'aurai un: "Ah çà, mais, nous avions De Quoi vivre!
        C'était donc sérieux?"

Anyone familiar with Eliot's "Portrait of a Lady" or "La Figlia Che Piange" (pp. 182–83) will detect the faintly contrite, gently supercilious tone carried over from Laforgue—for example, the effete confessional of this final paragraph of "Portrait":

> Well! and what if she should die some afternoon,
> Afternoon grey and smoky, evening yellow and
>   rose;
> Should die and leave me sitting pen in hand
> With the smoke coming down above housetops;
> Doubtful for awhile....

It was chiefly in this strain that Cummings and Stevens (and after them, Theodore Roethke, Randall Jarrell, W. H. Auden, and George Barker) managed the monologue or direct discourse, seeing its subtler nuances rather than Browning's more rugged and clear-cut characterizations.

Direct discourse and the imaginary dialogue (that is, with the silent listener) have been traditional enough—from Chaucer's "Complaint" to his empty purse ("to you, my purse, and to non other wight /Compleyne I") through the sonnets of the 16th century addressed to wayward friends or recalcitrant mistresses (for example, Drayton's "Since there's no help, come let us kiss and part!"—see p. 178) to Milton's "Lycidas" or Wordsworth's "Tintern Abbey." Such one-way discourse or soliloquy may be addressed to a muse, an alter ego, some silent presence, or a personification of nature. A more modern poet, A. E. Housman, without practicing what could be called Browning's type of monologue, adapted the one-way discourse in The Shropshire Lad. Toward his "doomed" and youthful Shropshiremen he wears the masks of boon companion, melancholy seer, and rugby fan. The result, always bittersweet, is a kind of fond master-pupil tone that can be hauntingly beautiful (as the longtime popularity of his book testifies). Through imaginary discourses or monologues, Housman managed to link together poems as personal and ironic as "Is My Team Ploughing" and as humorous and relaxed as "Terence, This Is Stupid Stuff."

Since those Edwardian and Georgian decades, other devices have been evolved in which the author's surrogate is more an attitude than an identifiable *persona*. Wallace Stevens, for instance, manages in poems like "Peter Quince at the Clavier" or "Le Monocle de Mon Oncle" to project his voice as the personification of an abstraction. In Stevens's "Bethou Me, Said Sparrow"[10] the poem may be thought of as consisting of many voices (the stylized chirping of ceaseless birds), carrying no specific message except their metaphor of persistent self-assertion:

> Bethou me, said sparrow, to the crackled blade.
> And you, and you, bethou me as you blow,
> When in my coppice you behold me be.

Similarly, Auden limits his own voice in "Law Like Love" by sardonically submitting the contradictory aspects of law by an abstract set of *personae*. Each voice asserts its personal or professional idiosyncrasy. Pretending no authoritative viewpoint of his own, the poet assumes a mocking detachment until the final section (here omitted), letting the derisive symposium of voices reflect the irony of law's supposed infallibility:

> Law, say the gardeners, is the sun,
> Law is the one
> All gardeners obey
> Tomorrow, yesterday, today.
>
> Law is the wisdom of the old
> The impotent grandfathers shrilly scold;
> The grandchildren put out a treble tongue.
> Law is the senses of the young.
>
> Law, says the priest with a priestly look,
> Expounding to an unpriestly people;
> Law is the words in my priestly book,
> Law is my pulpit and my steeple.

---

[10]From "It Must Change," *Notes toward a Supreme Fiction.*

Law, says the judge, as he looks down his nose,
Speaking clearly and most severely,
Law is as I've told you before,
Law is as you know I suppose,
Law is but let me explain it once more,
Law is The Law....

And so the voices go on. The poem's amusing sharpness comes largely from the caricatures that are self-revealed by the tone of the successive speakers.

A final example of these permutations of speaker might be the use of allusion to help color an entire poem. Archibald MacLeish, for example, achieves through his title "You, Andrew Marvell" a voice distinct from his own. The echoes of that cavalier courtier's preoccupation with "time's winged chariot" create richer associations for the theme of ever-moving time. MacLeish's contemplation of the receding sunlight, country by country, becomes an indirect salute to the dead poet:

And here face down beneath the sun
And here upon earth's noonward height
To feel the always coming on
The always rising of the night.

Broken Discourse

Stream of consciousness, brought into the service of fiction during the last half century, is really a modification of the monologue. Since James Joyce gave it psychological credence as a narrative device in *Ulysses,* it has undoubtedly interested a number of recent poets. As a literary mode, it would be untenable if it were what some assume it to be—a direct transcription of undirected mental impressions. What a writer using it does, of course, is to select out of the assumed fragments a sufficient representation to be intelligible yet still appear uncontrolled. He then fits these into a "stream" toward some narrative pattern or purpose. What is set down on the printed page can merely be the token for uninhibited mental process. Psychologically, the stylistic result is simply an illusion of naturalism and only a few degrees below the stylization of controlled narrative.

In one sense, the "stream" method affords much the same means of revelation as the grammatically conventional dramatic monologue. This is quite apparent, for example, in Browning's "Soliloquy in a Spanish Cloister." The psychological dynamics of free association are meant to prevail. A lyric poem, because of its traditional requirement of compression, would naturally be more selective in exploiting the way stations of rambling thought than a book like *Ulysses*, running as it does to nearly a thousand pages.

Eliot found this fragmented discourse a suitable means for expressing the memories and associations of Gerontion, as well as those of his counterpart, Tiresias, in *The Waste Land*. The poem "Gerontion" is a qualified success to many readers because what lyricism they find in it depends on their apprehension of the kaleidoscopic shifts in the old exile's far-flung memories. This is an aspect of Eliot's allusiveness (see pp. 101–2) that excited many readers and critics as part of the experimentalism of the early 20th century. The opening twelve lines of "Gerontion" seem a conventional enough monologue, but disconnected elements soon force our attention:

> Here I am, an old man in a dry month,
> Being read to by a boy, waiting for rain.
> I was neither at the hot gates
> Nor fought in the warm rain
> Nor knee deep in the salt march, heaving a cutlass,
> Bitten by flies, fought.
> My house is a decayed house,
> And the Jew squats on the window sill, the owner,
> Spawned in some estaminet of Antwerp,
> Blistered in Brussels, patched and peeled in London.
> The goat coughs at night in the field overhead;
> Rocks, moss, stonecrop, iron, merds.

Because Eliot intends many of the speaker's references to carry symbolic overtones ("old man," "in a dry month," "waiting for rain," "house," "Jew"), the disjointed mode ("Rocks, moss, stonecrop, iron, merds") requires double recognition on the reader's part. The difficulty is compounded because some of the allusions ("hot gates" and "Antwerp... Brussels,") and later on "The Titians," "Straits of Belle Isle," "The Horn," and "Christ the tiger") exist factually, while others (such as "the goat coughs at night," "Hakagawa," "Madame de Tornquist," and "Mrs. Cammel") are invented by him to convey the jaded atmosphere of postwar disenchantment and cultural decay. The combination of historical with fanciful and random scraps appear in these final lines:

> What will the spider do,
> Suspend its operations, will the weevil
> Delay? De Bailhache, Fresca, Mrs. Cammel, whirled
> Beyond the circuit of the shuddering Bear
> In fractured atoms. Gull against the wind, in the
>   windy straits
> Of Belle Isle, or running on the Horn,
> White feathers in the snow, the Gulf claims,
> And an old man driven by the Trades
> To a sleepy corner.
>   Tenants of the house,
> Thoughts of a dry brain in a dry season.

By these combinations of fractured images, Eliot had hoped to reflect the troubled meditations of Gerontion, the perennial survivor. They also reflect the incongruities of postwar Europe. To express that mood, the conventional mode would not serve Eliot's purpose as distinctly as the artful arrangement of the old man's proliferating associations— "Tenants of the house...." The devices within this fragmentational mode drew from all conceivable sources—from subtly chosen names, a concomitant jargon, and flashes of contrasting lyricism ("Gulls against the wind in the windy straits / Of Belle Isle...."). The obscurity of allusion is similar to that of Gerard de Nerval's "El Desdichado" (see pp. 119–20), although it is pushed further by the drama of direct discourse, not to mention the relaxation of traditional form. For Nerval, the sonnet imposed conventional restraints of meter and rhyme, a narrow confinement to which Eliot never subjected himself.

Eliot's experiment in the poetry of fragmentation resulted in one of the most influential poems of this century, *The Waste Land*, published in 1922. This collage of selected scraps expanded his "Gerontion" and required a set of footnotes to guide the reader. Today, after two generations, scholars accept the difficulties of reading it with something of the deference accorded to a Dante or a Spinoza. Explicatory aids have spoiled some of the fun, though one may still elect, if he chooses, to do his own digging of sources.

There is no set speaker in *The Waste Land;* rather, a shifting *persona* through whom we see the paradoxical death-in-life, old-and-new, sweet-and-bitter duplicity of postwar Europe. What is seen and said is always in terms of an overlay from other times and places.

> What are the roots that clutch, what branches grow
> Out of this stony rubbish?   (lines 19–20)

—asks this Gerontion-like presence, this shadowy *persona*, at one point a jaded aristocrat, at another, an eavesdropper on the Thames-side London pubs. And the answer, from an equally shadowy presence (sometimes Tiresias, sometimes the preacher of Ecclesiastes, sometimes the Fisher King out of Celtic myth):

> Son of man,
> You cannot say, or guess, for you know only
> A heap of broken images, where the sun beats
> And the dead tree gives no shelter, the crickets no
>   relief,
> And the dry stone no sound of water.   (lines 20–24)

No single mode conveys the whole poem. No single theme

expresses the complex attitudes that Eliot hopes to project. No single style of verse dominates the 433-line poem. The excerpt just quoted gives, for instance, an illusion of incantatory smoothness in a more or less hexamater line; but immediately before and after these lines, the rhythms differ, varying between direct discourse in tetrameter and in free verse. Transitions from one tempo to another are abrupt, as in the two passages below (the first ending Part I, the second near the end of Part II):

> I 60 Unreal City
> Under the brown fog of a winter dawn,
> A crowd flowed over London Bridge, so many
> I had not thought death had undone so many. . . .

> I 69 There I saw one I knew, and stopped him, crying: "Stetson!
> "You who were with me in the ships at Mylae!
> "That corpse you planted last year in your garden,
> "Has it begun to sprout? Will it bloom this year?
> "Or has the sudden frost disturbed its bed?
> "O keep the Dog far hence, that's friend to men,
> "Or with his nails he'll dig it up again!
> "You! hypocrite lecteur!—mon semblable,—mon frere!"

> II 139 When Lil's husband got demobbed, I said—
> I didn't mince my words, I said to her myself,
> HURRY UP PLEASE ITS TIME
> Now Albert's coming back, make yourself a bit smart.

The last passage is a composite in itself, combining stream of consciousness, monologue, and the mechanical phrases of the pubkeeper. The earlier passage is a mixture of ingredients: first, the opening phrase of Baudelaire's "The Seven Old Men," next his own phrases concerning the London fog, balanced by Dante's speech about the dead lovers in *Inferno* (Circle Two), then a transposition of a World War I comrade to a battle of the First Punic War, then fragments from John Webster's play, *The White Devil*, and finally the concluding line of Baudelaire's prefatory poem of *Les Fleurs du Mal*.

Through such literary marquetry Eliot offered readers of the twenties the effect of an ultramodern poem with fashionable concepts of myth and anthropology, yet made up of scraps from venerable sources. To this day the work is viewed in different lights with differing degrees of appreciation. To some, it is still clumsy and pretentious. Others have come around to it, respecting its complex conception. Far-fetched as these motley ingredients may seem—myths and medieval chivalry against Sanskrit utterances from one of the Upanishads—Eliot's intensity of vision somehow justifies their rather shocking juxtaposition. He accomplishes this partly by letting certain motifs recur, much as more conventional poets used repetends and aural recurrences (which Eliot, of course, also used). For example, the passage above (beginning "Unreal City..." is echoed in sardonic form 150 lines further along (III, 207ff.):

> Unreal City
> Under the brown fog of a winter noon
> Mr. Eugenides, the Smyrna merchant
> Unshaven, with a pocket full of currants
> C.i.f. London . . . .

Toward the end of the section (lines 259–260) there is a further shift, echoing the despairing Oedipus ("O City city"...), to the seamy side of the modern counterpart:

> O City city, I can sometimes hear
> Beside a public bar in lower Thames Street,

> The pleasant whining of a mandoline
> And a clatter and a chatter from within.

These motifs in broken discourse are a sort of popular vehicle for the interruptive, retrospective lyricism Eliot wanted
for this idea of the modern waste land. They expressed the
fragmentation of secularized existence. The shifts of tone
and movement, of time and place, result from the superimposition of one period of London's life on another, with
resulting ironic disharmony and decline. These are furthered
by the shifting person of the speaker himself—now a
Gerontion-like refugee; later an ubiquitous *persona* brooding over the "unreal city"; later still, voices from the
dead (figures transmogrified like the Phoenician sailor);
then the war-weary Londoners in the pub—collectively or
singly symbolized by the Fisher King, Tiresias, the Rhine-
daughters (also Thames-daughters), St. Augustine, and Christ
Himself joining two companions toward Emmaus. Throughout, the associative identities of these *personae*, of this time,
that time, and of this place, that place, are very much part
of the expressive mode of the poem.

There have been any number of comparable examples of
the technique of broken discourse—from Cummings's "Next
to of Course God" to MacLeish's *The Hamlet of A. MacLeish*
and parts of *Conquistador*, or from Carl Sandburg's *The
People, Yes* to William Carlos Williams's *Paterson* and Ramon
Guthri's *Maximum Security Ward*. In most cases, the object,
if not the method of the work, was comparable to Eliot's—
namely, to convey the multiplicity of values and shifts
of modern life, the anachronism of prevailing forms and institutions, and the persistence of our feelings and responses
to a holdover rhetoric and manner. Cummings's stripped-
down sonnet expresses that mode in this way:

> "Next to of course god america i
> love you land of the pilgrims' and so forth oh
> say can you see by the dawn's early my
> country 'tis of centuries come and go
> and are no more what of it we should worry

in every language even deaf and dumb
thy sons acclaim your glorious name by gorry
by jingo by gee by gosh by gum
why talk of beauty what could be more beautiful than these heroic happy dead
who rushed like lions to the roaring slaughter
they did not stop to think they died instead
then shall the voice of liberty be mute?"

He spoke. And drank rapidly a glass of water.

Modes of Representation: Tradition and Experimentation

In the wake of successive movements to renovate or vary the idiom of poetry, it might appear that only current experimentation is viable. But a careful review of a few major undulations of English poetical history shows that some of the most far-reaching revolutionary movements went on quietly. Chaucer, for example, borrowed themes and prosody from Italy and France, adapting them to the medieval allegories and always improving upon them. He set the direction of narrative verse toward the mainstream of realism from which sophisticated poetry and fiction continue to flow. Yet this tremendous legacy took quite a while to have its effect.

The Elizabethans channeled a newly flowered learning and rhetoric into a dramatic poetry that came to express the national imagination. Any medium but poetry for the vital world of London's playhouses would scarcely have served. Even their prose emanated it. The results were among the most brilliant the world had known since the public drama of Athens. Invention? Imitation? Experimentation? Even if these poets thought themselves to be following older traditions—an elegance redisclosed—their poetry made it all new again. So, too, poets of the Jacobean and Stuart periods carried the Elizabethan penchant for **conceits** a bit further, popularizing the cerebral and metaphysical quality of their images. Experiment? Invention? In the era of Ezra Pound and T. S. Eliot, the "experiments" of Donne, Vaughan, Herbert, Marvell, and others were reintroduced as a new norm. In the half century of Wordsworth and Coleridge, the wave of reaction to the strong conventions of the Augustans and mid-18th century literary climate took the revolutionary line. In theory—and usually in practice—the new poets rode this wave of Romanticism until the end of the 19th century. After mid-century, Browning, along with a few contemporaries influenced by the ironic tradition in France, reacted with a new critical, anti-romantic sensibility. Only then could one say that the romantic "revolution" had become the middle-class "tradition."

The French Symbolists began as a countermovement to what they considered the inevitably lagging perceptions of a bourgeois public. Others, like Browning and, at times, William Morris, sought for poetry a psychological realism in keeping with similar tendencies in drama and fiction. The French experimenters meanwhile withdrew from the effort to please their public, preferring to write for a limited and sophisticated audience. The era of a segregated culture had arrived.

This final phase became the phenomenon sometimes called the "dissociation of sensibility."[11] When the "renaissance" of pre- and post-World War I was still fresh to America, the average literate citizen was indeed likely to be dissociated from the poet—and vice versa. The imagistic, semi-elliptical, sometimes complex, frequently free-form verse of poets like Amy Lowell, Ezra Pound, T. S. Eliot, E. E. Cummings, Edith Sitwell, Wallace Stevens, and Williams Carlos Williams proved a formidable dose to readers educated to the familiar prosody of their 19th century favorites.

Prevailing tastes had been conditioned largely on poetry of the Romantics—both in England and America—and Tennysonian lyricism. The new poets thus seemed to have left tradition behind. Curiously enough, most of them—like Pound, Eliot, and Cummings—were reviving an earlier poetics than the one reigning through much of the 19th century. Technically, all three harked back to Elizabethan, 17th century,

---

[11]A term used by T. S. Eliot in his essay, "The Metaphysical Poets" (1929). Further discussion in Glossary.

and earlier European traditions. Yet, like the non-Parnassians in late 19th century France, the American reformers managed to alienate those inheriting these "prevailing tastes." Most of the critics of the time were hardly trained, either, for the new look and sound. By ridiculing or scolding these upstarts, they increased the segregation of the *cognoscenti* and those still contented with what had been around since Longfellow's and Tennyson's time.

Recent counter-tendencies, like Beat poetry,[12] or "Pop Art," may have worked in the opposite way—to desegregate the fine arts once more, rendering them first ridiculous then broadly tolerated because of their heavy adulteration with the commonplace. In contrast to this trend (so often thought of as grass roots, and therefore democratic), the best poetry in past eras (that of the Elizabethans, for instance, or the 5th and 6th centuries of Greece) was aristocratic in its standards, yet public in its scope. It was a literature that had not been forced to stoop for the new, representing instead an excellence to which all might rise.

As we noted in Chapter 1, experiment in modern times tends to be equated with asperations of political or of social progress. This view assumes that the arts are progressive, an assumption that is neither historically nor philosophically sound. This is not to say that within the all-enveloping forces of current mass media, the discipline and quality of the arts are not undergoing change. Indeed, they are. But it may be some time before the best critics will be in a position to evaluate such change.

---

[12]The "Beatnicks" were thought of by some readers in the fifties as *avant-garde* ("ahead of the procession"). An examination of selected specimens in Thomas Parkinson's *A Casebook on the Beat* (1961) may leave some doubts as to why their work was taken seriously at all—unless as a phenomenon of the revival of oral recitation. The celebrated "Howl," by Alan Ginsberg, cries for craftsmanlike control, however fervid its proclamation of wrongs. This lack of discipline illustrates a popular fallacy that form wilts spontaneity.

Some of the poems in Lawrence Ferlinghetti's *A Coney Island of the Mind* occasionally offer memorable vignettes of city types and places. At their best (when not overextended), they have a sardonic, often surreal vividness.

Practical Criticism

Expressive Devices

1. In the following anonymous poem, "The Cutty Wren," note the degree to which set phraseology is repeated throughout (except in stanzas 4, 7, and 10, omitted here). Why do you suppose these "expressive devices" were attached to the recitation?

> O, where are you going, says Milder to Malder,
> O, I cannot tell, says Festel to Fose,
> We're going to the woods, says John the Red Nose,
> We're going to the woods, says John the Red Nose.
>
> O, what will you do there, says Milder to Malder,
> O, I cannot tell, says Festel to Fose,
> We'll shoot the Cutty Wren, says John the Red Nose,
> We'll shoot the Cutty Wren, says John the Red Nose.
>
> O, how will you shoot her, says Milder to Malder,
> O, I cannot tell you, says Festel to Fose,
> With arrows and bows, says John the Red Nose,
> With arrows and bows, says John the Red Nose.
>
> O, how will you bring her home, says Milder to Malder,
> O, I cannot tell, says Festel to Fose,
> On four strong men's shoulders, says John the Red Nose,
> On four strong men's shoulders, says John the Red Nose.
>
> O, that will not do, says Milder to Malder,
> O, what will do then, says Festel to Fose,
> Big carts and waggons, says John the Red Nose,
> Big carts and waggons, says John the Red Nose.
>
> O, that will not do, says Milder to Malder,
> O, I cannot tell, says Festel to Fose,
> Hatchets and cleavers, says John the Red Nose,
> Hatchets and cleavers, says John the Red Nose.
>
> O, how will you boil her, says Milder to Malder,
> O, I cannot tell, says Festel to Fose,
> In pots and in kettles, says John the Red Nose,
> In pots and in kettles, says John the Red Nose.

O, who'll have the spare ribs, says Milder to Malder,
O, I cannot tell, says Festel to Fose,
We'll give them to the poor, says John the Red Nose,
We'll give them to the poor, says John the Red Nose.

2. Consider the effect of the following abridgment of the first
three stanzas. Proceed in the same manner and assess the
relative merits of the ritualistic first version (at the same time
speculating on the possible origin and composition of "The
Cutty Wren").

> O, where are you going?
> O, I cannot tell, save that
> We'll be going to the woods.
>
> What'll you do there?
> O, I cannot tell, save that
> We'll shoot the Cutty Wren.
>
> And how'll you shoot her?
> O, I cannot tell, save that
> It'll be arrows and bows.

Repetitive Exposition

1. Poe's "Annabel Lee" (the fifth stanza omitted) is made up of
considerable repetitive exposition. Does the kind of lyrical
form Poe was susceptible to justify this repetition?

> It was many and many a year ago,
>   In a kingdom by the sea,
> That a maiden there lived whom you may know
>   By the name of Annabel Lee;—
> And this maiden she lived with no other thought
>   Than to love and be loved by me.
>
> *I* was a child and *she* was a child,
>   In this kingdom by the sea,
> But we loved with a love that was more than love—
>   I and my Annabel Lee—
> With a love that the winged seraphs in Heaven
>   Coveted her and me.

And this was the reason that, long ago,
    In this kingdom by the sea,
A wind blew out of a cloud, chilling
    My beautiful Annabel Lee;
So that her high-born kinsmen came
    And bore her away from me,
To shut her up in a sepulcher
    In this kingdom by the sea.

The angels, not half so happy in Heaven,
    Went envying her and me:—
Yes!—that was the reason (as all men know,
    In this kingdom by the sea)
That the wind came out of the cloud, by night,
    Chilling and killing my Annabel Lee.

For the moon never beams without bringing me dreams
    Of the beautiful Annabel Lee;
And the stars never rise but I feel the bright eyes
    Of the beautiful Annabel Lee;
And so, all the night-tide, I lie down by the side
Of my darling,—my darling,—my life and my bride,
    In her sepulcher there by the sea—
    In her tomb by the sounding sea.

2. Consider the effect of reducing "Annabel Lee" to actual dialogue. Does this tend to focus the emotion better or is too much of the lyricism lost? If you find the variations on the first two stanzas interesting, proceed with your own revision in a similar manner:

"It was many a year ago," he said to me,
    "In a kingdom by the sea
I knew this maiden—you knew her too—
    Her name was Annabel Lee."
Loath I felt, yet answered him, "She was true
    And loved you enough, did your Annabel Lee."

"We were but children," he said again,
    "In this Kingdom by the sea—
Yet even then love bound us as one—
    I and my girl, Annabel Lee."
"Ah there was the rub," I turned to him then,
    "The envy of Heaven falls on such love."

Point of View and Variations

1. Explain how the point of view in T. S. Eliot's "La Figlia Che Piange" (p. 183) functions as an expressive mode.

2. Check a few of the following poems (three are in this text, the others will be available in most anthologies) and note how (a) the use of a *persona*, and (b) the variation of the form of discourse enlivens the expressive mode of the poem:

   a. Anonymous, "Edward"
   b. Michael Drayton, "Love's Farewell" (p. 178)
   c. John Donne, "The Canonization"
   d. Andrew Marvell, "To His Coy Mistress" (portions on pp. 109 and 114).
   e. Robert Burns, "To a Field Mouse"
   f. William Blake, "The Lamb"
   g. Tennyson, "The Lotus Eaters"
   h. Thomas Hardy, "Waiting Both"
   i. Robert Frost, "Two Tramps in Mud-Time"
   j. Robert Graves, "I Wonder What It Feels Like to be Drowned?"
   k. Edith Sitwell, "Aubade"
   l. W. H. Auden, "Musee des Beaux Arts"
   m. Wallace Stevens, "Peter Quince at the Clavier"
   n. Henry Reed, "Naming of Parts" (p. 107)

SEVEN

Meaning and Substance;
Direction and Indirection

Connotation of Words and Ideas

We have been tracing the poet's *means*, his use of language and expressive modes, toward some total meaning. The inseparability of means and meaning has come to be accepted as the natural state of much lyric poetry. Such acceptance is evidence of the organic nature of lyric poetry in which the parts—whether aural, imagistic, expressive, or moral—form integral elements of the whole. When content or "message" seems merely *added* to these elements—rather than integrated with them—the poem lacks the subtlety that distinguishes it from the logical structure of expository prose. In those examples of didactic verse by Henley (discussed on p. 18), we expect the message to be quite obvious. The poem is a vehicle for a fairly direct transmittal of the moral values of the poem. One may think of its images, meter, point of view, and so on, as separable from "what the poem has to say." In this kind of poetry, the words are more likely to be *denotative* (having the relatively specific meaning of dictionary definition) and the ideas to be conveyed correspondingly accessible.

Meaning is something we always want to confine. It is as automatic for us to go after the main idea as it is for a trained dog to retrieve a stick. Our increasing experience might show, however, that we cannot always bring back these "meanings" in portable form. They will be entangled with various qualifying conditions: the poet's presumed intention, a *double entendre,* a subjective interpretation, or a universal projection (in which a specific sense becomes one of timeless or abstract dimension).

Any serious poet eventually becomes aware of these conditions, for they are the result of the mysterious power of words. From the most frivolous to the most savage, words function practically as much by connotation, or by the user's tone and gesture, as by the usages of explicit communication. These conditions disturb the "scientific" mind, but they become an enrichment for the poet.

In comparison to a language based on verbal denotation, the language of imagery is oblique. Images themselves (as we found in Chapter 5) contain the elements of metamorphosis, always transforming one form of reality to another. The words that make up a metaphor ("O bird of time!") are usually commonplace in themselves yet gather a peculiar charge by the connotations of special arrangement. ("Bird" has acquired an array of associations, not the least of them being a symbol for flight and seasonal change; so, the word is a transforming component in this metaphor for "time.") Aside from the differing usage in different parts of speech, many of our everyday words function in a rainbow of contexts—from concrete to abstract, physical to intellectual, substantial to ethereal. There are, for example, at least a dozen ways in which our word for "world" varies as we shift its context: (1) "out of this world," (2) the finest car in the world." (3) "an underworld character," (4) "a new map of the world," (5) "the war of the worlds," (6) "the world is too much with us," (7) "the animal world," (8) "what in the world!" (9) "world finance," (10) "the World as Will and Idea," (11) "in the afterworld," (12) "O World, O Life, O Time!" (13) "He came to save the world."

It is interesting that the everyday words—of pre-Norman or preclassical influence—although the shortest, often carry in varying context the widest connotations. For instance, such words as "spit," "hold," "drum," or "fix," suggest more usages and more connotations than their Latinate synonyms. Thus, *fix* may connote "repair," "stabilize," "establish," "limit," "arrange," "attach," "solidify," "form," "make certain," "determine," "prepare," "take revenge," "bribe," "find a navigational position," and so forth. Our everyday "word," from Old English, would seem to have many more connotations that later acquisitions of limited meaning, such as "communication." There are, for example, the simple household, literary, rare, linguistic, folksy ("What's the word, Mac?"), religious, and many other connotations. The early English word "spit" has by now acquired usages that extend it far beyond the neoclassical importation, "expectorate," which means only one thing. The more complicated linguistic imports are likely to have a special and, therefore, limited meaning; consequently they tend to have limited connotations and, thus, limited depth as words for poetry.

"Basic English" consists of words most closely associated with our first learning in childhood, and each has acquired many facets to make up for a limited number of words. Those later constructed from Greco-Latin stems and attachments were assumed necessary to a more systematic vocabulary. They were in great demand during the 18th and early 19th centuries when new sciences called with ever-increasing zeal for new terminology. Since a basic desire of science was to be precise, scientists tended to shun ambiguous words—thus the made-to-order vocabulary to serve the world of technology. Since a basic desire of poets is to play with words that carry overtones and suggestions of other meaning, poets search for the most evocative words, those with associations both in historical and personal time.

Here are twenty-one words from the first five lines of a famous sonnet: "time," "year," "yellow," "leaves," "none," "few," "hang," "boughs," "shake," "against," "cold," "bare," "ruined," "choirs," "late," "sweet," "birds," "sang," "see," "twilight," and "day." All but four of these are monosyllabic; most are from the "continuum" vocabulary of Old English origin; all are in basic, everyday use. They are, by analogy, capsules of one culture's stored energy. Probably the words came as naturally to the poet as they would to one speaking simply about his deepest feelings. And, if the poet has great feelings for his language, the energy so stored in the words would be released for the reader by the verbal interaction.

We might assume that this preference for words of national heritage would be more normal for the Elizabethans than for us. But not so, as can be discovered by glancing over the hardier lyrics in any anthology. The vocabulary of Donne, Milton, Dryden, and others was often heavy, learned, and polysyllabic. That of the Romantic poets—Blake and Wordsworth, not to mention quite recent poets such as Frost, Sandburg, MacLeish, Roethke, and Bishop—is selectively meager. MacLeish's "You, Andrew Marvell" begins,

> And here face down beneath the sun
> And here upon earth's noonward height
> To feel the always coming on
> The always rising of the night—

In this example, the key words "face," "beneath," "sun," "earth's," "height," "feel," "always," "coming," "rising," and "night" are commonplace. Generally, the English poems we return to most often are made up mainly of a vocabulary of familiar usage. This may seem to contradict the popular urge to widen one's vocabulary, but the magic of the best poems lies in the unique arrangement of words, always with the right word in the right place. The "right" one may seemingly be the most familiar, yet quite affecting and strange as the linkage of words within the poem disturbs the semantic connotations.[1]

Let us take a final example from the contemporary poem by Vincent Ferrini (discussed earlier, p. 127). The five key words of the first stanza—"dog," "ran," "night," "left," and "hand"—are not startling in terms of "poetic" vocabulary, syntactical order, or poetic "color":

> A dog ran
> down the night
> with my left hand.

The words are as simple as those from a child's tale. Possibly for that reason, a word such as "dog" is haunted with

---

[1]This explains in part the dynamism of some of E. E. Cummings's poems, in which he disturbs clichés, wrenching new meanings from them by the shock of rearrangement.

more than casual memories. "Ran," by itself, may be less evocative, but as predicate to "dog," it gives characteristic action to the noun. Then "night" (a dog running "down the night") and "with my left hand" suggests both a primary act and a curious involvement with the speaker. Why "my left hand"? In any case, these five simple words, strung together in what seems a simple declarative, contain in their subject, verb, and predicate modifier, an evocative, if not overly complex, image.

Of course, any emotional overlay those words possess depends largely on the context of the rest of the poem. This relationship, by which a certain part of a poem may be energized from the tone of the poem as a whole, contributes to the verbal connotations (discussed earlier, pp. 13–14). Thus "left" as a qualifier of "hand"—at first glance a mere oddity —makes the "dog–hand" relationship more portentous, suggesting for the poem as a whole a sense of guilt between master and dog. We find in the Romance origins of certain words associated with our "left" (Latin, *sinistra*; French, *gauche)* the persistence of some idea of wrong—*sinister* (baleful, hurtful) and *gauche* (left-handed, clumsy). We can see then how the connotations of one word add to the overtones of the now less-than-casual three-line stanza. We may also begin to see possible symbolic extension in the two final tercets (see earlier discussion, pp. 127–28):

> And on a hill
> I saw the dog
> burying the
>
> bone of my
> left hand
> in the moon.

Confession and Insinuation

As one plays with words—these ever-shifting ingredients of meaning— so he may play with ideas on the borderline of fact and imagination. When the Jacobean sonneteer, Michael

Drayton, announces that he has had enough of love, if his lover has, he balances the ultimatum by leaving the door open to some last-minute reconciliation:

> Since there's no help, come let us kiss and part
> Nay, I have done, you get no more of me;
> And I am glad, yea, glad with all my heart,
> That thus so cleanly I myself can free.
> Shake hands for ever, cancel all our vows,
> And when we meet at any time again,
> Be it not seen in either of our brows
> That we one jot of former love retain.
> Now at the last gasp of Love's latest breath,
> When, his pulse failing, Passion speechless lies,
> When Faith is kneeling by his bed of death,
> And Innocence is closing up his eyes,
> Now, if thou would'st, when all have given him
>   over,
> From death to life thou might'st him yet recover.

Using the personification of "Love" as his central image, the poet discusses "Love's" moribund condition with his mistress. All is settled now; there must be no messy aftermath of their former mutual concern for the patient. The underlying denotation of the sonnet's octave is unmistakable: "We're through, and it's better that way." But even though the speaker maintains the pretense of disinterestedness, he leads up (in a subtly executed "turn" beginning the sestet) to a final proposal for reconciliation. Some last minute remedy might—just might—be arranged. And so, in the delayed reversal of the final couplet, it is the *thou* behind the disguise of personification who is charged with this final cure. By implication, the speaker has insinuated his wish to carry on. It is a kind of joke on himself, for he reveals indirectly his real feeling while so transparently juggling the extended simile of their love's imminent demise.

The "meaning" or "idea"? That love is hard to kill? That

love can raise the nearly defunct? That lovers' wiles are not proof against the truth of love itself? Any, or all, of these, of course, are part of what the poem lets us surmise but never goes so far as to tell us. The meaning is in the means by which the sonnet works itself out, progressively revealing (against the speaker's opening defiance) his real wishes. There probably are contemporary connotations to the figurative idea of love "dying," since the word often carried a double entendre for sexual consummation. While intercourse may have left the lovers satiated—"dead"—the power of the other's presence and ministrations ("Now, if thou would'st, when all have given him over") may bring about the miracle of resurrection. The punning analogy adds an extra dimension to a poem on an old subject.

With less wit, but with a strong measure of self-commiseration, the late Victorian Ernest Dowson invoked the dark shadow of Cynara in a farewell to wine and roses. Unlike Drayton, he confesses to the evil effects of earlier incontinence to Cynara (from Latin *cynararia,* possibly an urn for crematorial ashes) who doubles as all his old loves rolled in one:

NON SUM QUALIS ERAM BONAE REGNO CYNARAE

Last night, ah, yesternight, betwixt her lips and
    mine
There fell thy shadow, Cynara! thy breath was shed
Upon my soul between the kisses and the wine;
And I was desolate and sick of an old passion,
    Yea, I was desolate and bowed my head:
I have been faithful to thee, Cynara! in my fashion.

All night upon mine heart I felt her warm heart
    beat,
Night-long within mine arms in love and sleep she
    lay;
Surely the kisses of her bought red mouth were
    sweet;

But I was desolate and sick of an old passion,
    When I awoke and found the dawn was gray:
I have been faithful to thee, Cynara! in my fashion.

I have forgot much, Cynara! gone with the wind,
Flung roses, roses riotously with the throng,
Dancing, to put thy pale, lost lilies out of mind;
But I was desolate and sick of an old passion,
    Yea all the time, because the dance was long:
I have been faithful to thee, Cynara! in my fashion.

I cried for madder music and stronger wine,
But when the feast is finished and the lamps expire,
Then falls thy shadow, Cynara! the night is thine;
And I am desolate and sick of an old passion,
    Yea, hungry for the lips of my desire:
I have been faithful to thee, Cynara! in my fashion.

While Drayton addressed the other partner in attendance on expiring love, Dowson addresses the personification of lost innocence, a sort of ghost of a purer lost love.[2] It is a type of the confessional poem in which the early Romantic poets sought to exorcize their guilts. The inheritors of the Romantic movement avidly turned to variations featuring the remorse-of-love theme. Baudelaire had been quite clinical about the awful aftermath of sexual incontinence (for example, "A Voyage to Cythera," pp. 133–34). Poe gave it a more middle-class idealization, as in "Annabel Lee" (see pp. 170–71), where the physical aspect of romance is vague or ethereal. Dowson, in keeping with the late Victorian proprieties, might illustrate the requirement that poetry may only insinuate shameful

---

[2]An amusing possibility (and, indeed, probably coincidental) is that Dowson was parodying the purplish type of elegy for lost love that characterized the poetic efforts of many Fin du Siecle poets. The word cynara means artichoke in Latin. Had Dowson been suffering from an overindulgence of this vegetable when he went out on a night of wenching? Or, again, did the probable meaning of "burial urn" disguise Dowson's mementos of love: the ashes of a venereal ailment, in those days love's too prevalent accompaniment?

things—suggesting as agonies of the soul what may too often have been unpoetic decreptitude.

Between Drayton and Dowson, the confessional poem had a long run. John Donne, in "The Canonization," "A Valediction: Forbidding Mourning," and others, found the confessional attitude well adapted to his tormented anatomization of the love relationship—a point of interest considering his later rejection of secular loves for that of the church. The Romanticists of the 19th century turned almost compulsively to confessional poetry. Wordsworth, Coleridge, Byron, and Shelley (along with Chateaubriand, Lamartine, and Alfred de Mussey in France) seemed to find little neutral ground between their audiences and the emotions straight from their hearts. Poetry in this vein was autobiographical, even when fitted out in the somewhat objective narrative of "The Rime of the Ancient Mariner." By symbols, Coleridge may have hoped to transfigure his guilt feelings toward wife and child.[3] Although there was sufficient creative intensity in Coleridge's poetic imagination to do the trick, not all confessional poems have had sufficient form and objectification.

The artist of the confessional, acting as confessor, priest, and sometimes redeemer to himself, must be resourceful in creating the actors, the masks, and other properties for the drama. Baudelaire, Nerval, Poe, and Laforgue were skilled in this shadow show, refining it with almost masochistic cruelty, dissimulating and insinuating with matter-of-fact dryness. Hawthorne and Melville brought the skill to fiction and drama in works like "The Minister's Black Veil," *The Scarlet Letter*, *Billy Budd*, and *Moby-Dick*. Browning invented his special dramatic monologue which provided readers with a grim glimpse of the self-revelations of his artists, aristrocrats, and men of God. Two generations later, Eliot explored behind the memories and inhibitions of his more abstracted characters (sometimes a blend of Browning's self-revealing monologue and Laforgue's faintly sadistic ironists). "The Love Song of J. Alfred Prufrock" is a true classic of this category. It has been a favorite in college classrooms, perhaps because

---

[3]Kenneth Burke has convincingly discussed this in a chapter of *The Philosophy of Literary Form* (See Anchor Books edition).

the overcultivated, self-conscious Prufrock has his likenesses on any campus. In a more nebulous way, the speakers in "Gerontion," *The Waste Land,* "The Hollow Men," and "Ash Wednesday" are confessing their spiritual death within (or alienation from) a disintegrating modern society. The fastidious aesthete of "La Figlia Che Piange" ("the weeping girl") confesses to more interest in recalling the young lady's gesture and attitude than in any real sorrow he might have caused her. Like Browning's Duke of Ferrara, he has the connoisseur's interest in women, and is only incidentally concerned for their real feelings. Some of the phraseology (as shown below) betrays Eliot's early fascination with the phrases and tones of Laforgue, particularly his "Moon Solo"[4] and his "Lament" (translated on pp. 155–56):

> Stand on the highest pavement of the stair—
> Lean on a garden urn—
> Weave, weave the sunlight in your hair—
> Clasp your flowers to you with a pained surprise—
> Fling them to the ground and turn
> With a fugitive resentment in your eyes:
> But weave, weave the sunlight in your hair.
>
> So I would have had him leave,
> So I would have had her stand and grieve,
> So he would have left
> As the soul leaves the body torn and bruised,
> As the mind deserts the body it has used.

---

[4]"Solo de Lune" (from *Derniers Vers*). Some of the last lines (translated by the author) suggest the connection:
> Here it is fresh, fresh and cool,
> Ah, at this very moment
> She too threads the forest edge,
> Baptizing her misfortune
> In a wedding with the moon. . . .
> Ah, if only I had fallen to my knees!
> If only you had fainted there with me!
> I would have been the ideal mate for you
> Just as the sweep of your dress is a model too.

I should find
Some way incomparably light and deft,
Some way we both should understand,
Simple and faithless as a smile and shake of the
    hand.

She turned away, but with the autumn weather
Compelled my imagination many days,
Many days and many hours:
Her hair over her arms and her arms full of flowers.
And I wonder how they should have been together!
I should have lost a gesture and a pose.
Sometimes these cognitations still amaze
The troubled midnight and the noon's repose.

In the third section, admitting some twinge of guilt about
la figlia, the speaker lets his imagination speculate on what
it would have been like had "they" stayed together. There is
ambiguity as to whether the speaker himself is the source of
her disappointment, or whether he is only a third party
observing the lady's relationship with another man. In any
case, he reminds himself that had there not been this parting,
he (the speaker) would not have had this exquisite specimen
among his souvenirs. The last two lines compound the earlier
ambiguity: we do not know whether these "cogitations" are
of remorse (for his midnight *is* "troubled") or a lingering
after-image of the weeping girl. Whatever ambivalence of
point of view Eliot may have intended, the essence of the
poem lies inextricably in the means, the character revelation
in the confession, and the mood of the reverie as such, rather
than in any separable meaning.

Intentional and Subliminal Meaning

The complexity with which meaning is involved with
means is reflected by the creative process itself. Many writers
testify that the conscious aims and directions of composition

may undergo surprising modifications before fulfillment.[5] Our consideration of poetry—at least with reference to that which is organic in its development—might be illuminated by Sigmund Freud's psychological theory of how the *unconscious* affects our dreams, and how the devious means by which the pressures seek release transform the inhibited images into disguises, or symbols.

It was Freud's theory that dreams consist of imagistic distortion which disguise inadmissable or normally inhibited impulses. These images are the disguises of repressed desires released from the *id* (Freud's term for the unconscious) when the conscious part of the mind is asleep. The odd performances and composite actors of our dreams represent fragments of waking experience. By appearing incognito, they evade the supposed restrictions imposed by that part of the *superego* which Freud called the *censor*. It was the psychoanalyst's job to unmask these performers and reveal their "latent" import. The manifest or outward images of things in dreams are symbols of their real significance. When properly interpreted, and their components recombined and related to the actual experiences of the dreamer's waking past, latent causes and effects of behavior can be assessed.

Whether all this is psychologically valid or not,[6] we still might find the hypothesis useful as an analogy for the dynamics of various stages of artistic composition. A poet, for instance, hides behind images while seeming to set down things as true. He wants to confess himself through his art; his experiences seek outlet. Yet social inhibitions (like Freud's socially constituted censor) impede his free expression, imposing seemingly inherited reticence. The poet then often resorts to his own language of innuendo, intensifying the principle of likeness in difference. So, art has its indirection,

---

[5]See *The Creative Process* (ed. by Brewster Ghiselin), a symposium of poets, musicians, painters, scientists, and others, on their personal experiences while writing, composing, and formulating or solving problems. (Mentor edition available.)

[6]Freudian dream interpretation remains controversial among psychologists today. Ironically, its symbology caught and held the imagination of writers and artists even when Freud's clinical methods were scouted.

its disguises of means. From Homer's *in medias res* (the contrivance of structural order) and his ambiguity about the gods and their control of human passions, to Eliot's disclosures of the buried life and his subtle refinements of motive and conflict, it would seem that the author's job is, as Emily Dickinson says, to tell all the truth, but tell it slant."

Without assuming the doubtful authority of the psychologists (Freudian or post-Freudian), we can still appreciate the subliminal or psychically buried part of poetic composition. This might be called the *dynamic* of literary creativity (that is, the power to "change"). In an illuminating little book called *Poetic Unreason*, published in 1925, Robert Graves was one of the first to consider this "dynamic" effect of the unconscious on poetry. With intentional reduction of terms, he says that there is "good" poetry and "bad" poetry. The "good" stems from those unconscious roots of emotional experience that tend to feed the poet with the most reliably artistic images—because they are presumably irresistible. The "bad" stems from the merely conscious levels of thought in which true emotion can be garbled by the expedient tampering of the "socialized" mind. It is not that the intellect is taboo; rather, that in poetic creation, dependence on the rational gets in the way of the primitive and, presumably, more authentic springs of inspiration.[7]

As we observed in Chapter 2, there is no permanent critical basis for arbitrary values in literature. Graves's doctrine is imbued with the climate of the times—as to his equally ebullient anthropological interpretation of early Greek culture. To accept such a one-sided value judgment of literature would be to dismiss all but an organic conception of verse and, presumably, drama and fiction (since the same virtues of subliminal composition that the theory claims for poetry would hold for the rest of literature). Let it suffice for us that we recognize the complexity of poetic creation, includ-

---

[7]The "good" poetry, Graves goes on to say, serves a real need of poet and reader; "bad" poetry serves no need at all (unless perhaps the vanity of the poet). The key to the value latent in "good" poetry is in secondary elaboration, the conscious attempt to expand or mimick the real thing. "As in dreams," he concludes, "so also in poetry."

ing the duality[8] of conditions to all creative effort. The cerebral part we accept as the *critical* adjunct of poetry, and the subliminal or unconscious part the energy and inspiration of it. One without the other—as the Greeks knew 2,500 years ago—would result in a lack of harmony and would be rejected.

In her essay "How Are Poems Made," Amy Lowell recognizes the dynamic aspect of the "Muse," but avoids Graves's assumption of an eccentric "spell" upon the author. She admits—though quite matter-of-factly—to the roundabout process by which one of her poems gets written:

> Whether poetry is the fusion of contradictory ideas, as Mr. Graves believes, or the result and relief of emotional irritation and tension, as Sara Teasdale puts it, or the yielding to a psychical state verging on day-dream, as Professor Prescott has written a whole book to prove, it is impossible for anyone to state definitely. All I can confidently assert from my own experience is that it is not a day-dream, but an entirely different psychic state and one peculiar to itself.
>
> . . . It would seem that a scientific definition of a poet might put it something like this: a man of an extraordinarily sensitive and active subconscious personality, fed by, and feeding, a non-resistant consciousness. A common phrase among poets is "It came to me." So hackneyed has this become that one learns to suppress the expression with care, but really it is the best description I know of the conscious arrival of a poem.
>
> Sometimes the external stimulus which has produced a poem is known or can be traced. It may be a sight, a sound, a thought, or an emotion. Sometimes the consciousness has no record of the initial impulse, which has either been forgotten or springs from a deep unrealized memory. But whatever it is, emotion, apprehended or hidden, is a part of it, for only emotion can rouse the subconscious into action. How carefully and precisely the subconscious mind functions, I have often been a witness to in my own work. An idea will come into my head for no particular reason; "The Bronze

---

[8]This duality was reflected in what Nietzsche (in *The Birth of Tragedy*) called "the Dionysian" and "the Apollonian" in art, even before 5th century Greece. Psychologically, the principle was dramatized in Euripides' last play, *The Bacchae*, where the two are in fatal conflict.

Horses," for instance. I registered the horses as a good subject for a poem; and, having so registered them, I consciously thought no more about the matter. But what I had really done was to drop my subject into the subconscious, much as one drops a letter into the mail box. Six months later, the words of the poem began to come into my head, the poem —to use my own private vocabulary—was "there."

The subconscious is, however, a most temperamental ally. Often he will strike work at some critical point and not another word is to be got out of him. Here is where the conscious training of the poet comes in, for he must fill in what the subconscious has left, and fill it in as much in the key of the rest as possible. Every long poem is sprinkled with these *lacunae*; hence the innumerable rewriting which most poems undergo. Sometimes the sly subconscious partner will take pity on the struggling poet and return to his assistance; sometimes he will have nothing to do with that particular passage again. This is the reason why a poet must be both born and made.

Evidence from many other sources has supported Amy Lowell's testimony. The "Muse," whom the ancients invented to inspirit artists and writers, were thought to "enter" the poet when properly invoked and to guide him by supernatural means. It is tempting to think that the power of the unconscious still serves the artist in some such capacity as the Muses did. The most exacting poets admit uncertainty as to how particular words or images came to them, or why certain lines seemed to shape themselves without their own forethought or recollection. Afterward, a poet may remain unaware that his images had fallen into the patterns he later detects. Indeed, the critical reader has often been the first to call attention to the poetic unity such patterns have given his poem.[9] Robert Browning, Robert Frost, and others some-

---

[9]My own experience in being shown an interpretation of one of my published poems was enlightening. When "Mon Frere et Mon Semblable" appeared in the Rutger's literary magazine, *Anthologist*, a Korean student and former member of my course in modern literature undertook a rather detailed analysis. When he rather shyly submitted it for my comment, I was startled at the interconnection which he found among the images, and the unity which they gave the poem. I had been aware of patterns, but had not been conscious of marshaling the parts into the "meaningful" order which Mr. Wanna Joe found for me.

times expressed amazement and amusement at the ingenious-
ness of their interpreters. As poets, they have realized that
a perceptive reader might see things that they themselves
might overlook in the heat of composition. At the same time,
a Frost could find irony in some of the more exhibitionist
efforts to expand poems as self-contained as "The Road Not
Taken" or "Stopping by the Woods on a Snowy Evening."
Frost did not specifically deny some of the ramifications so
zealously pointed out; what caused him to shake his head
was the tedious length of the articles as they appeared in
well-known literary journals. It seemed to embarrass him
that a simple lyric, functioning modestly and efficiently,
should have spawned such pedantry.

There has scarcely been a time when the *double entendre*
set up by the unconscious has not lent a kind of split level
to poetry of a certain subjective type. Certainly Donne, or
Marvell, or Blake were aware of the subliminal echoes
of some of their associations in such images as "Get with
child a mandrake root," or "My dream thou brok'st not,
but continued'st it," or "My vegetable love should grow/
Vaster than empires," or "How the youthful harlot's curse/
... blights with plagues the marriage hearse." By the
time of Robinson Jeffers or Dylan Thomas there was more
conscious effort to find subliminal depth through Freudian or Jung-inspired imagery. Thomas's early poems, for this
very reason, suffer from overly contrived symbols that tend
to obscure the primary level of communication. The first of
his so-called religious sonnets (already discussed in Chapter 5) is a montage of allusive metaphor reflecting Freud,
Jung, ancient Greek, and Biblical myth, and serving as fanciful archetypes depicting Creation:

> Altarwise by owl-light in the half-way house
> The gentleman lay graveward with his furies;
> Abaddon in the hang-nail cracked from Adam,
> And, from his fork, a dog among the fairies,
> The atlas-eater with a jaw for news,
> Bit out the mandrake with tomorrow's scream.
> Then penny-eyed, that gentleman of wounds,

Old cock from nowheres and heaven's egg,

With bones unbuttoned to the half-way winds,

Hatched from the windy salvage on one leg. . . .

Archaic associations here are impudently linked with a slightly disreputable contemporary figure—the God-Adam-Christ lineage rolled into a Finnegan-like antihero.

By the early thirties, Freud's psychoanalytical criteria had become almost compulsive with certain American writers (though more likely to be spoofed by the British). Sherwood Anderson, James Branch Cabell, and Eugene O'Neill had made much of the psychic patterns of behavior (by then fairly standardized), while poets like Graves, William Empson, Jeffers, Eliot, and Thomas tried with varying success to employ the symbology for their poetic imagery.[10] But it was Freud's early associate (and later revisionist) Karl Jung whose broader idea of the *collective unconscious* came to appeal most strongly to the poetic imagination. Jung discounted the personal origin of the most prevalent symbols emerging from dream experience, postulating instead "archetypal" forms inherited from man's racial past. Jung's archetypes had the virtue of connecting with many of the anthropological figures from other cultures, both ancient and modern (the Fire-bringer and the Savior-God, the Father-God, and the Son-God—and the perennial sacrifice of one for the other). But in a more general sense, Jung's archetypes were simply the repetitive aspects of racial history: the old man (any long-lived wise man), the queen-mother (the nurturing female, the mother earth), the *persona* (the mask of self, the chosen social role), the *anima* and *animus* (the secret and primitive self), and so forth.[11] One convenience

---

[10]Freud's *The Interpretation of Dreams, The Pleasure Principle,* and *Moses and Monotheism* were particularly influential, the first providing many of the explanations of recurrent dream symbols (turrets and spires, caves and tunnels, ladders and falling, water and the uterus, or houses and running), as well as explanation of dominant drives (sex, hunger, ego-expression, the hero complex, anxiety, and the death wish).

[11]See *Modern Man in Search of a Soul,* 1933. The classic study of Jung's symbols in relation to literature is Maud Bodkin's *Archetypal Patterns in Poetry* (available in Anchor editions).

of the hypothesis of collective unconscious for literary study was that it accounted for persistent parallels and recurrences of myth figures in literature since the earliest times, explaining a kind of inherited imagery from the time of 5th century Greek drama to the compulsive symbols of Ibsen's and Strindberg's plays, or to stories like Henry James's "Turn of the Screw."

The dual influence on a poet's labors of intentional meaning and subliminal stimuli, as expressed by Amy Lowell (pp. 186–87) has become acceptable to most people, although psychoanalysis itself is still viewed by some as baseless because of its largely theoretical criteria. By the time of the "new critics," it had become an article of faith that what a poet means to say and what is contained in the record are not necessarily the same. In H. L. Mencken's time, a critic asked "What does the author intend to say?" as the starting point in his critical analysis.[12] This approach now became naive to many psychologically oriented academicians. One of these tagged the intentional approach as the "intentional fallacy."[13] On the other hand, to assume that a given work contained several "layers" of significance, each of which must be examined, was a job almost psychoanalytic in itself. More assiduous scholars scrutinized the works of proper Victorians for subliminal revelations. Since biographers were rediscovering the human fallibilities of great figures from Queen Victoria down,[14] it was probably inevitable that poets

---

[12]Joel Spingarn's Creative Criticism, 1926, suggested that a critic approach any literary work to be considered with the questions: (1) what does the author try to do? (2) How does he go about doing what he intended? (3) How well has he done it? (4) Was it worth doing? Mencken reviewed it in an essay, "Criticism of Criticism of Criticism," using it as the best antidote to date against the more absolute criteria of the "Neohumanists."

[13]Quite a few "fallacies" were exposed during the ascendancy of the "new critics," who included in one capacity or another I. A. Richards, William Empson, Allen Tate, Kenneth Burke, and John Crowe Ransom. Besides the "intentional" there were the "paraphrastic fallacy" (to dispel the idea that one may sum up a poem's meaning by paraphrasing it), and the "affective fallacy" (which deplores the evaluation of a poem in terms of its effect on the reader).

[14]Lytton Strachey's Queen Victoria and Those Earnest Victorians made popular the debunking approach in the contemporary biography.

like Hopkins, Emily Dickinson, Tennyson, and the gentle Charles Dodgson ("Lewis Carroll")—all of whose images permitted a certain amount of psychological ambiguity— would be found fit subjects for the literary couch.

Practical Criticism

1. Which words in the parallel lists below evoke the widest associations? Can you explain why?

a. rain	a. precipitation
b. death	b. decease
c. kinsmen	c. relative
d. grass	d. herbage
e. memory	e. retrospection
f. foretell	f. prognosticate
g. graveyard	g. cemetery
h. face	h. countenance
i. work	i. employment
j. candy	j. confection
k. think	k. cogitate
l. fire	l. conflagration
m. foreshadow	m. adumbrate
n. eater	n. consumer

2. Consider whether A. E. Housman is direct enough in presenting the human situation in his poem "Is My Team Ploughing?" If the dialogue seems at cross-purposes, what poetic effect do you think is gained by the indirection?

> "Is my team ploughing,
>   That I was used to drive
> And hear the harness jingle
>   When I was man alive?"
>
> Ay, the horses trample,
>   The harness jingles now;
> No change though you lie under
>   The land you used to plough.

"Is football playing
    Along the river shore,
With lads to chase the leather,
    Now I stand up no more?"

Ay, the ball is flying,
    The lads play heart and soul;
The goal stands up, the keeper
    Stands up to keep the goal.

"Is my girl happy,
    That I thought hard to leave,
And has she tired of weeping
    As she lies down at eve?"

Ay, she lies down lightly,
    She lies not down to weep:
Your girl is well contented.
    Be still, my lad, and sleep.

"Is my friend hearty,
    Now I am thin and pine,
And has he found to sleep in
    A better bed than mine?"

Yes, lad, I lie easy,
    I lie as lads would choose;
I cheer a dead man's sweetheart—
    Never ask me whose.

3. Many English folk ballads, like "Lord Randal" and "Edward,"
   played up a pattern of query and response, with frequently
   macabre implications. Can you see any connections between
   the semidramatic mode above and the popular audiences to
   which ballads were delivered?

   Is there a latter day connection between the response to these
   folk ballads and the tone and modes of current popular journalism?

4. Check the passages below with respect to their comparative

degree of statement or of implication. Would any of these examples benefit from more or less of either?

a. Western wind, when wilt thou blow,
    The small rain down can rain?
 Christ, if my love were in my arms
    And I in my bed again!
          (Anonymous)

b. Come live with me and be my love,
    And we will all the pleasures prove
              (From the first stanza of Marlowe's
                "The Passionate Shepherd to his Love")

c. O Rose, thou art sick:
 The invisible worm
 That flies in the night
 In the howling storm,
 Has found out thy bed
 Of crimson joy,
 And his dark secret love
 Does thy life destroy.
          ("The Sick Rose," by Blake)

d. Fear Death?—to feel the fog in my throat,
    The mist in my face
 When the snows begin, and the blasts denote
    I am nearing the place
          (From "Prospice," by Browning)

e. I caught this morning morning's minion, kingdom of
        daylight's dauphin, dapple-dawn-drawn
          Falcon in his riding
              (Opening lines of Hopkins's
                "The Windhover")

f. And Richard Cory, one calm summer night,
    Went home and put a bullet through his head.
              (Last lines of Robinson's
                "Richard Cory")

193

g. But never met this fellow,
   Attended or alone,
   Without a tighter breathing,
   And zero at the bone.
                    (Last stanza of Emily Dickinson's
                    "A Narrow Fellow in the Grass")

h. Altarwise by owl-light in the halfway-house
   The gentleman lay graveward with his furies
                    (Opening lines of Thomas's *Sonnet*)

EIGHT

The Poem in Its Context

Additive Factors

Up to this point we have dealt with poetry as a completed phenomenon—the work of art on a printed page. Whether we first heard or read the poem, we met the written word at its face value. No doubt concurrently—though with more and more attention as we went on—we became aware of the order and interconnection of images, the sequence of ideas, and the structural tensions that made up the totality of the poem's meaning. As we have seen, these devices more often than not were indirect, the words and ideas connotative rather than denotative, and the ultimate meaning deliberately suspended. But, everything has been texually contained: a matter of the poem in itself.

Our final problem of poetic analysis is the poem in context. We have noted in passing only a few of the external factors affecting a poem. For some poems, questions arise about the conditions surrounding an author and the fortuities affecting his compositions. This part of the analysis is frequently dismissed as incidental to a true appreciation of poetry, yet it has direct bearing on our interpretation of certain poems—especially those conceived in a highly subjective way. For this reason we shall devote this final chapter to a brief consideration of these "peripheral" matters and try to see how they affect a true reading of a given piece of poetry.

For convenience, let us divide them into two groups: (1) external data (biographical facts about the author, cultural and social influences, and bibliographical matters related to his work, and (2) subjective data (letters, notebooks, diaries, reported conversations, and between-the-line deductions of psychological interest). At its best, this sort of scholarly exercise adds to the total comprehension of any work of art; at its worst, it distracts from the primary evidence of art in the text of the poem itself.

External Data: The Poet as His Own Editor

In reading the poetry of our own time, we might expect to do without headnotes, footnotes, or incidental glosses on details of background. We may encounter some obscurities, probably from the refinements of a deeper mind than ours, or the ellipses and twists from timely experiment in form— but presumably we would be spared the accumulation of biographical and bibliographical data from the oncoming generation of scholars. The poets writing within the last score of years are people whom we may have heard or met. They speak our language, or so we would like to think. Yet, ironically, the reverse of this is often the case. A later generation may have developed its own idiom, finding an imagery and phraseology quite innocent of the emotional or intellectual tones we want. We can understand those of our grandparents' generation better now—a Robinson, a Frost, or even a Jeffers—more readily than a John Berryman, a Howard Nemerov, or a Thom Gunn.

Up to a certain point the perspective toward the receding figures improves with distance. The less we see or hear them in the flesh, the more they speak to us. This seeming paradox depends on two circumstances: (1) all good poems contain a core of absolute value transmitable to readers at any time, and (2) the more a poem devolves into a permanent canon, the more it will be the subject for scholarship and its context explored. Even so, at the near end, aids to context must often be provided. When Eliot's *The Waste Land* appeared in 1922, it was (and has been ever since) published with the author's notes to guide the reader. In the fifty years since then, these skeletal references have been augmented by hundreds of essays and book-length commentaries. By capturing the elusive images, explaining the milieu, and connecting the more obscure references, scholars have added a dimension to the understanding of that kind of poetry. So, between a studious author and devoted investigators, few poems in English are graced with so rich a context.

Compared to many other periods, the last sixty years has been one of industrious and problem-conditioned readers—not only readers of Eliot, but of his difficult contemporaries —Yeats, Pound, Hart Crane, Cummings, Jeffers, Auden, Stevens, Marianne Moore, Conrad Aiken, and MacLeish. Some of Eliot's successors took his cue, like Randall Jarrel, who, as recently as 1964, deemed it practicable to supply explanatory notes to his *Selected Poems*. Even his best-known and most-anthologized piece, "The Death of the Ball Turret Gunner," had this explanation:

> A ball turret was a plexiglass sphere set into the belly of a B-17 or B-24, and inhabited by two .50 caliber machine-guns and one man, a short small man. When this gunner tracked with his machine-guns a fighter attacking his bomber from below, he revolved with the turret; hunched upside down in his little sphere, he looked like the foetus in the womb. The fighters which attacked him were armed with canon firing explosive shells. The hose was a steam hose.

He has provided the technical background just in case—but we note that he has (as Eliot and others had) studiously avoided any explication of the metaphorical relationships by which the short piece achieves its surprising unity of effect:

> From my mother's sleep I fell into the State,
> And I hunched in its belly till my wet fur froze.
> Six miles from earth, loosed from its dream of life,
> I woke to black flak and the nightmare fighters.
> When I died they washed me out of the turret with
>   a hose.

The image of falling into "the State" (ironic reference to the boyless youth of those drafted in their late teens and doomed to die in a second fetal servitude of death) is continued in the image of his "wet fur" freezing (metonymy for the just-born cub, in these circumstances dressed in the airman's fleece-lined jacket). In a pitifully abortive existence, he has in his brief exchange of wombs been awakened in time to die, high over the earth—another mother—he'd barely come to know.

Essential, if laconically brief, context was provided by Theodore Roethke for his poem, "Elegy for Jane." The poem, without its superscription, goes as follows:

> I remember the neckcurls, limp and damp as
> > tendrils;
> And her quick look, a sidelong pickerel smile;
> And how, once started into talk, the light syllables
> > leaped for her,
> And she balanced in the delight of her thought,
> A wren, happy, tail into the wind,
> Her song trembling the twigs and small branches.
>
> The shade sang with her;
> The leaves, their whispers turned to kissing;
> And the mold sang in the bleached valleys under
> > the rose.
>
> Oh, when she was sad, she cast herself down into
> > such a pure depth,
> Even a father could not find her:
> Scraping her cheek against straw;
> Stirring the clearest water.
>
> My sparrow, you are not here,
> Waiting like a fern, making a spiny shadow.
> The sides of wet stones cannot console me,
> Nor the moss, wound with the last light.
>
> If only I could nudge you from this sleep,
> My maimed darling, my skittery pigeon.
> Over this damp grave I speak the words of my love:

I, with no rights in this matter,
Neither father nor lover.

As the poem stands, we can grasp the idea all right—the speaker's deep, sensitive, and avuncular regret for a girl's apparently fatal injury. But given the six-word headnote, we find tones of subtler ambivalence coming into focus:—"My Student, Thrown by a Horse."

In a similar way, Gerard Manley Hopkins places the two stanzas of "Heaven-Haven" within a personal frame by an explanatory superscription. The text reads:

I have desired to go
    Where springs not fail,
To fields where flies no sharp and sided hail
    And a few lilies blow.

And I have asked to be
    Where no storms come,
Where the green swell is in the havens dumb,
    And out of the swing of the sea.

The eight lines would remain general and vague, but are given point by the brief directive: "A Nun Takes the Veil."

Some poets have been more susceptible to headnotes, subtitles, and epigraphs than others—Wordsworth and T. S. Eliot being two worth noting. Wordsworth's subtitles frequently become as explicit as labels to items in a museum. To the restrained heading "Lines," he adds the information: "Composed a Few Miles above Tintern Abbey, on Revisiting the Banks of the Wye during a Tour, July 13, 1798"; to "Elegiac Stanzas," the headnote: "Suggested by a Picture of Peele Castle, in a Storm, Painted by Sir George Beaumont"; and to his celebrated "Ode," the supplement: "Intimations of Immortality from Recollections of Early Childhood." Wordsworth believed in an early and ample enlightenment of the reader.

Eliot's supplemental information tended toward epigraphical quotations selected to provide oblique commentary on what was to follow. For "The Love Song of J. Alfred Prufrock," he prefixes six lines from Dante's *Inferno*; *The Waste Land* has but one short epigraph and one dedicatory line to Pound—but his extended "Notes" make up for this comparative reticence; "The Hollow Men" has two epigraphs; and all but three or four of his early poems carry at least one. What such devices provided was, of course, a tie-in to another world and its traditions, remote yet comparable. Certainly the laconic "Mistah Kurtz—he dead," from Conrad's "Heart of Darkness," remains one of the more tenuous in its connection to what follows in "The Hollow Men."[1]

---

[1]The assumption has often been made that a poem properly written does not need epigraphs, notes, or any other ancillary matter. Emily Dickinson, E. E. Cummings, and A. E. Housman (for many of his poems) went so far as to omit titles. Among the sonneteers of the 16th century, poems in a sequence were merely numbered. Thereafter, posterity had to borrow the poem's first line in lieu of title. It might be considered that such a poem was a self-contained unit, and that its charm was enhanced through the resultant quality of reserve. The poem must say only what it has to say without any hems and haws from the author or anybody else.

On the other hand, a cross section of a few titled poems will suggest the degree to which titles not only identify but provide extra dimension to the idea of the poem. George Herbert's method was to make his title suggest a physical object, calling attention to its complicated metaphysical idea (for example, "The Pulley," "The Collar," "The Window"). Blake, in "The Sick Rose," "The Lamb," "The Poison Tree," used many titles as analogues to what the poem was about, sharpening his sometimes abstract conception. Browning liked slightly racy headings—something that might have popped into his head on a horseback ride—"How It Strikes a Contemporary," "One Word More," "A Toccata of Galuppi's," "My Last Duchess," "Childe Roland to the Dark Tower Came," and "Sibrandus Schafnaburgensis" (from "Garden Fancies"). E. A. Robinson's "Mr. Flood's Party," "Miniver Cheevy," and "Eros Turannos" strike a note in their titles of ironic discord with the textual substance. The same, to a lesser degree, would be true of certain of Hardy's pieces ("In Time of 'Breaking of Nations,'" "The Meeting of the Twain," "The Man He Killed," "And There Was a Great Calm"). Mockery and oblique irony are implied in Wallace Stevens's "The Emperor of Ice-Cream," "Memoirs of a Magnifico," or "Connoisseur of Chaos." The same would be true of Marvell's "To His Coy Mistress," and Frost's "Out, Out—." Yeats's "The Second Coming" and "The Long-Legged Fly" fix on a motif or feature of history, and then put it through a kind of mystical paradigm in the poem. The allusiveness of MacLeish's "You, Andrew Marvell" works to the same advantage for the poem, borrowing a central metaphor from the older poet as a starting point.

One way or another, whether by title, subtitle, epigraph, or omission of title, a poet reveals a particular attitude toward what he has written. He is inviting the reader to partake of his labeled work of art, expressing an oblique comment (or noncomment, when he offers no title at all), or availing himself of some external comment, however, tangential, in using an epigraph or headnote. During Eliot's generation, the titling of poems often reflected an "anti-poetic" posture, a playing down or low-key approach by the poet. "The Love Song of J. Alfred Prufrock" or "Sweeney among the Nightingales" and Wallace Stevens's "Le Monocle de Mon Oncle" or "An Ordinary Evening in New Haven" carry this suggestion. Frost's "Happiness Makes Up in Height for What It Lacks in Length" or Horace Gregory's "The Woman Who Disapproved of Music at the Bar" are titles intended presumably to be antipoetic. Of course they are often deceptive, heightening in the long run the poetic impact by their ironic obliquity. This is demonstrated in Jarrell's "The Woman at the Washington Zoo" and Elizabeth Bishop's "Large Bad Picture" (see pp. 214–15), each title bringing in its prosaism the piquancy of ambiguity.

Subjective Data: The Poet's View of the World

So far, then, the poet speaks for himself. To stop here would be, for the most part, to take the poem at face value. Poets are—with a few voluble exceptions—reticent as to their intentions or fulfillment. They seem to say, "There it is—the way it should be. Just concentrate on what's there." But the critic or scholar has more in mind. Major literature, the critic would say, is never mere communication. It is a job of verbal craftsmanship—a floating iceberg in which the floating superstructure is but a portion of the mass of hidden evidence. Poems, individually, may be part of a wider intellectual puzzle. They must be put together, both as parts of an author's whole work and as a literary manifestation of their times. The scholar-critic's graduate training prepares him to conduct autopsies on the corpus of a literary work.

Most work that has a sound constitution can stand the dissection.

For a later generation the world in which the poet has lived, or which he must invent for himself, slips quickly from the grasp. Without some reconstruction, premises and sidelights related to the vital habits of the author are misted over or ignored. Or, a certain poet may have a philosophy that has provided a scaffold or framework for his poems, a set of principles based on his philosophy that may be turned into the key metaphors of his poem. Let us take the example of Yeats's "The Second Coming," a work of medium length, accessible enough in one reading for comprehension at the surface level:

Turning and turning in the widening gyre
The falcon cannot hear the falconer;
Things fall apart; the center cannot hold;
Mere anarchy is loosed upon the world,
The blood-dimmed tide is loosed, and everywhere
The ceremony of innocence is drowned;
The best lack all conviction, while the worst
Are full of passionate intensity.

Surely some revelation is at hand;
Surely the Second Coming is at hand.
The Second Coming! Hardly are those words out
When a vast image out of *Spiritus Mundi*
Troubles my sight: somewhere in sands of the
    desert
A shape with lion body and head of a man,
A gaze blank and pitiless as the sun,
Is moving its slow thighs, while all about it
Reel shadows of the indignant desert birds,
The darkness drops again; but now I know
That twenty centuries of stony sleep
Were vexed to nightmare by a rocking cradle,

And what rough beast, its hour come round at last,
Slouches towards Bethlehem to be born?

The apocalyptic vision is comparable to George Meredith's "Lucifer in Starlight" (see p. 88) and clear enough in its primary terms. Yet one suspects that considerably more lies behind its images and allusions than the simple denotation.

What is the relation between the "widening gyre" and the "vast image out of *Spiritus Mundi*," or the "twenty centuries of stony sleep" and the "rough beast, its hour come round at last"? What special thought lies behind such ominous assertions as "things fall apart; the center cannot hold"? What is the connection between "The best lack all conviction ... the worst ... full of passionate intensity" and "A shape with lion body and head of a man"? Evidently, to order these widely ranging images beyond their primary denotation, one needs a definitive context.

And this was precisely what Yeats himself provided, constructing over many years a theory of diametrical relationship with the dualities and oppositions he saw in the microcosm and the macrocosm of human existence. The finished book, called *A Vision*, is a difficult one to describe. But in it he tried to classify the related truths that his intuitions and rationalizations about experience seemed to have taught him: a rationale of mystic dualities, opposing geography and seasons, complementary personalities, alternating celestial phrases, diametric causes and results, second comings, the rise and fall of civilizations, and the shifting phenomena of the present, past, and future. The figures and allusions, not only of "The Second Coming" but recurrent as well in more than half of Yeats's later poems, are projections of *A Vision*. Without reference to it a reader must remain a literalist in his interpretation, enjoying without doubt surface texture and statement, but guessing at the rich allusiveness, the ordered paradigm of time's rotating ages into which Yeats fits his powerful metaphor of the beast.

The "plain spoken" poem, pleasant enough at first reading, requires a conventional comprehension; and it is a justifiable irritation when a poet's "special" world is not

orderly and systematic, as Yeats's was. One feels that when
a poet requires an elaborate context for his work, that context should be the result of a viable philosophy or world
view. But, above all, the poetry itself should be of sufficient
intensity to justify and sustain this contextual scaffolding.
Two poets of recent years, Robinson Jeffers and Wallace
Stevens, premised the entire range of their work on their
respective philosophical or aesthetic beliefs. As a result, the
poems of both possess the kind of thematic unity which,
formidable at first, ultimately provides their work with integrity. We have to enter into Jeffers's world by a tentative
adoption of his peculiar life perspective. We have to transcend the shock of poems like "Roan Stallion" or "Original
Sin" because they are the particulars of his bleak view
of mankind. Above all, we can realize the sincerity of
his disgust with man and his repudiation of man's social
self-consciousness in the knowledge that his views *are*
his world context. When he speaks out from the brooding
lines of "Roan Stallion" (humanity is "the mold to break
away from") or from "Hurt Hawks" ("I would sooner, except
[for] the penalties, kill a man than a hawk"), we know this is
not bravado but the classical pessimism of the Roman Lucretius, supplemented by Jeffers's own primitivistic images.

Only out of a familiarity with Jeffers's classical background will readers today see the appropriateness of this
pessimism in *Cawdor*, in *The Cretan Woman*, or in his adaptation of Aeschylus's *Oresteia*. The issue is rationalized in his
little poem, "To the Stone-Cutters":

> Stone-cutters fighting time with marble, you fore-
>   defeated
> Challengers of oblivion,
> Eat cynical earnings, knowing rock splits, records
>   fall down,
> The square-limbed Roman letters
> Scale in the thaws, wear in the rain. The poet as
>   well
> Builds his monument mockingly;

For man will be blotted out, the blithe earth die,
    the brave sun
Die blind and blacken to the heart:
Yet stones have stood for a thousand years, and
    pained thoughts found
The honey of peace in old poems.

An awful beauty, external to himself, is the basis for the verses that he writes. Yet in nearly every poem, Jeffers finds man the only inharmonious element in a universe greater than man. The attitude has been oppressive and misleading to those who are constitutionally incapable of looking beyond the humanistic. Not to grasp the deeper roots of the poet's conditioning, or to sense the gentleness of the man even as he repudiates the worst of man, would be a typical illustration of a fatal ignorance where context is essential.

Working from an attitude as subjectively conditioned as that of either Yeats or Jeffers, Wallace Stevens created a world of tensions from which nearly all his images could be drawn. It required of the reader a response more philosophically sensitive than Jeffers's, and an imaginative projection quite as special, if somewhat more limited, as that of Yeats. There is an equal admiration and respect for the natural world, though Stevens's approach is more sensuously involved. Stevens is aesthetically more discriminating of the textures of experience; Jeffers has more the naturalist's detached respect, a more passionate regard for an almost monolithic aspect of all worlds. All three poets savored the beauty of an environment, with Jeffers and Stevens sharing the unsentimental values of the true Epicurean. Critics of his earlier career often labeled this quality in Stevens as "hedonism," and their mistake is an example of insufficient grasp of a total context. For, far from a random celebration of pleasure, the parts of Stevens's work fit together—much as did Yeats's under the symmetry of *A Vision*—in a harmony of interrelated values. As befitted an early admirer of French symbolism, Stevens evolved a pattern of recurrent polarities by which his imagery must be interpreted.

A poet's poet, appealing to but a few in his own lifetime, Stevens's work now attracts a wider circle of readers. His singularly homogeneous images repay the same intensive analysis as those in Yeats's paradigms of history. One may trace the inflections of leading concepts from poem to poem. Yet Stevens drew up no formal system or set of keys; the pattern of recurrences merely reflect the "grooves" of his thought, capable of being traced by any careful reading. Many of the correspondences are of colors, seasons, geography, occupations, flora, and fauna. Most are metaphorical of the polarities of our existence: mind versus imagination, raw nature versus order, south versus north, sea versus land, music versus business, green versus red, tropics versus snow—elements in the relativity of our fixed condition.[2] His poem "Domination of Black" may illustrate how some of these controlling images are played over like notes in a musical composition, in this case turning the varying qualities of blackness into a harmony of associated concepts. The poem is metaphysical in the way that physical, sensate things become symbols for attitudes of the imagination and the mind. One might expect the result to be pedantic, but instead there is a fluid, swirling effect of words constantly recurring in a ghostly duel between reality and imagination:

> At night, by the fire,
> The colors of the bushes
> And of the fallen leaves,
> Repeating themselves
> Turned in the room,
> Like the leaves themselves
> Turning in the wind.
> Yes: but the color of the heavy hemlocks
> Came striding.
> And I remembered the cry of the peacocks.

---

[2] See the discussion of "Thirteen Ways of Looking at a Blackbird," pp. 121–23.

The colors of their tails
Were like the leaves themselves
Turning in the wind,
In the twilight wind.
They swept over the room,
Just as they flew from the boughs of the hemlocks
Down to the ground.
I heard them cry—the peacocks.
Was it a cry against the leaves themselves
Turning in the wind,
Turning as the flames
Turned in the fire,
Turning as the tails of the peacocks
Turned in the loud fire,
Loud as the hemlocks
Full of the cry of the peacocks?
Or was it a cry against the hemlocks?

Out of the window,
I saw how the planets gathered
Like the leaves themselves
Turning in the wind.
I saw how the night came,
Came striding like the color of the heavy hemlocks.
I felt afraid
And I remembered the cry of the peacocks.

Here Stevens conjures with his favorite question: the relation between the creative imagination and the assumed reality of the physical universe. Students may recognize this as a theme of recurring interest to the Romantic poets. Wordsworth and Coleridge had followed it in poem and in essay. It had bemused Keats in his odes—particularly those to a "Grecian urn," to the "nightingale," and to "melancholy." Yeats returned to it with the Byzantium poems and "Lapis Lazuli." It is the constant by which we begin to fix the shifting correspondences of Stevens's central fund of imagery. Each poem may seem to be an isolated problem until we discover interconnections of these dominant images. Once we understand Stevens's fascination with the duality of the sensuous world (the natural elements, color, seasons, and so forth) and the indispensible, if illusory, play of the imagination, we understand his world. Then, with image and idea potentially unifiable in our minds, we discover a very rewarding freedom within the whole of his poetry.

Critical scholars will go on examining authors in historical context, very often making definitive assessments too late for many of us. Prevalent tastes within a writer's lifetime are notoriously fickle; only later does a higher kind of judgment seem to be exerted. About all that we know of a given man's reputation is that it will probably change, undergoing cycles comparable to those of dress, abode, religion, and other aspects of our varying life styles. The true arbiters are time and the scholars' persistence. Historically, there is sometimes an inverse ratio between the stature of certain authors and the learning accumulated about them. Those of remote times, about whom little factual knowledge has survived, are often widely acclaimed (for example, Euripides and Shakespeare, whose known biographies could be stated in a short paragraph, but whose work still receives voluminous study and commentary). Works of those of relatively modern times, about whom the life records are abundant, frequently remain in critical limbo, partly because such works have not found their permanent rank: for example, *Tristram*, by Robinson; *The Dynasts*, by Hardy; *Testament of Beauty*, by Robert Bridges; *The Bridge*, by Hart Crane; *Fatal Interview*, by Edna St. Vincent Millay; *The People, Yes*, by Sandburg; *Paterson*, by William Carlos Williams; and *Brother to Dragons*, by Robert Penn Warren.

Unearthing the Poet's Psyche

Two poems that intelligent scholarship did help to fix in magnitude and rank are Coleridge's *The Rime of the Ancient Mariner* and "Kubla Khan." The suggestion of complicated association in the imagery of both poems led the late John

Livingston Lowes on a long and roundabout trail of reading and investigation. His suspicions had been aroused when he first read Coleridge's note to "Kubla Khan" in the 1816 edition of his *Poems*:

In the summer of 1797, the Author, then in ill health, had retired to a lonely farm-house between Porlock and Linton, on the Exmoor confines of Somerset and Devonshire. In consequence of a slight indisposition, an anodyne had been prescribed, from the effects of which he fell asleep in his chair at the moment that he was reading the following sentence, or words of the same substance, in "Purchas's Pilgrimage": "Here the Khan Kubla commanded a palace to be built, and a stately garden thereunto. And thus ten miles of fertile ground were enclosed with a wall." The Author continued for about three hours in a profound sleep, at least of the external senses, during which time he has the most vivid confidence, that he could not have composed less than from two to three hundred lines; if that indeed can be called composition in which all the images rose up before him as *things*, with a parallel production of the correspondent expressions, without any sensation of consciousness of effort. On awakening he appeared to himself to have a distinct recollection of the whole, and taking his pen, ink, and paper, instantly and eagerly wrote down the lines that are here preserved. At this moment he was unfortunately called out by a person on business from Porlock, and detained by him above an hour, and on his return to his room, found, to his no small surprise and mortification, that though he still retained some vague and dim recollection of the general purport of the vision, yet, with the exception of some eight or ten scattered lines and images, all the rest had passed away like the images on the surface of a stream into which a stone has been cast, but, alas! without the after restoration of the latter!

What had Coleridge been reading besides Purchas to have fed his active imagination in the conceptions of his two most famous poems? What extended absorption in such remote things had led up to the passage in *Purchas's Pilgrimage*? It seemed to Professor Lowes that if the author was able to recall the immediate stimulus of the opening of the shorter poem, there might well have been more hidden sources behind not only "Kubla Khan" but also the exotic allusions and metaphors of *The Rime of the Ancient Mariner*. Piece by piece, Lowes examined the collection of 16th and 17th century voyages by Purchas, Haklyut, Churchill, and many others that he suspected the poet of reading in the months prior to that singular dream and to the composition of the two poems. Some passages could be directly related, as in the excerpt below from *Purchas His Pilgrimage, or Relations of the World and the Religions Observed in All Ages* (1613); others required detective work of such intricacy that the resulting account seems full of the suspense of fiction. Here is just one short passage from Purchas in which Lowes has italicized words echoed later by Coleridge in the poem:

> *In Xanadu did Cublai Can* build a *stately* Palace, encompassing sixteene *miles of* Plaine *ground with a wall*, wherein are *fertile* Meddowes, pleasant springs delightfull Streames, and all sorts of beasts of chase and game, and in the middest thereof a sumptuous house of *pleasure*, which may be removed from place to place.

These are the first eleven lines of "Kubla Khan":

> In Xanadu did Kubla Khan
>   A stately pleasure-dome decree:
> Where Alph, the sacred river, ran
> Through caverns measureless to man
>   Down to a sunless sea.
> So twice five miles of fertile ground
> With walls and towers were girdled round:
> And there were gardens bright with sinuous rills
> Where blossomed many an incense-bearing tree;
> And here were forests ancient as the hills,
> Enfolding sunny spots of greenery.

Other accounts suggestive of the wording of "Kubla Khan" or parallel to the seascapes and flora and fauna of *The Ancient Mariner* had also been absorbed into Coleridge's free-floating associations (as the later references to "And on a dulcimer she played,/ Singing of Mount Abora," in which key words are specifically used). These and the unexpected links in a chain of poetic images innocently imbedded in the longer poem proved to have been made without any apparent conscious volition on Coleridge's part.

The composition behind "Kubla Khan" and *The Rime of the Ancient Mariner* is but one instance of a poem's complex origin. Without the scholary illumination, the vital context in which we are now able to read both poems might never have come to light. One would like to know similar things about Milton, Donne, Blake, Tennyson, or Hopkins. Or, with our increased sophistication about psychological motivations, we might want to assess how *conscious* art may have attempted to guide the *unconscious* faculty in the work of Poe, Baudelaire, Yeats, Paul Valery, Amy Lowell, De La Mare, Graves, Thomas, Theodore Roethke, Muriel Rukeyser, and many others. Poe wrote his own essay, "The Philosophy of Composition," exploring what he purports to be his method for writing "The Raven." Browning, in *The Ring and the Book*, was sufficiently fascinated by the psychological context in the origins of his work to magnify his roundabout approach in the finished work. Such theorizing went on more intensely in the 20th century—such as Robert Graves's stress on the dark side of poetic activity, Eliot's essays in *The Sacred Wood*, Valery's *Poetics*, Stevens's *The Necessary Angel*, Kenneth Burke's *The Philosophy of Literary Form*, or, finally, Howard Nemerov's recent *Journal of the Fictive Life*.

Poetical Perspectives Since 1920

Our reading of a poem, which began with the rallying to its sound and prosody, has now gone beyond the text to the author himself. Broadly speaking, one is always involved with the poet's background; but in the psychological temper of our time even the poet's thought process has become part of a creative context. As a final consideration of poetic context in recent times, we need to see what kinds of criticism prodded new poets or increased our understanding of the old.

Across the conditions we have discussed lie the permutations of a millenium of English poetry—its experiments, realignments, and reversions to half-forgotten tradition. In almost every generation the canons of poetic art are altered —not necessarily for the better, as many may have felt while looking at the anti-art of today. In time, as the products of a computer society, we may need no poetry. Or, we may, in turn, revert to the rhymed couplets of the Augustan age. We never know. To the Imagists of that rousing period before World War I to the end of the twenties, the neatly surveyed territory of the 19th century looked very old-fashioned. The rebel tendency from age to age is to wipe out what is thought to have outrun its attraction. Even when the substitutes prove nourishing, it takes a long time for the news to make sense for the great bulk of readers, much as they may wish to be in the vanguard. Fads spread like grass fire; the understanding that gives permanent pleasure moves as imperceptibly as a change of climate.

The climatic change which became the "poetic renaissance" we have already mentioned was more conservative than it appeared on the surface. Poets like Yeats, Pound, Eliot, Cummings, Frost, Graves, Jeffers, Millay, Stevens, or Auden, went further back or wider afield into world literature for the materials and models of a renovation, rather than performing an extermination. There is the example of Eliot, whose influence on a later generation was profound, who borrowed from both revolutionary sources (LaForgue and others) and reverted to the literary traditions of Jacobean England. Innovative artist as well as self-conscious scholar, Eliot represents (from his early imitative lampoons of society to the patchwork of The Waste Land) a realignment of separate forces, national and foreign alike.

What the renovators substituted for those 19th century attributes (the syntactical completeness and formal prosody) was not limited merely to free verse. All but a few of them accentuated the nominal outward forms with new spirit: the offbeat sonnets of Cummings; the epical suggestion in the spacious, rolling lines of Jeffers; the cosmopolitan assortment of poetic finery in Pound's elliptical style; the quasi-academic touches and personae of Stevens; the reconstituted ideas of Yeats in a set of new images—all seemed more piquant because tradition was never far beneath the surface. It was a time to disguise one's literary forebears as well as one's more obvious meanings. A Prufrock's agonized reveries were intended to keep action in ironic suspension. The sonnet form of Cummings's "Cambridge ladies" was deliberately roughed up to seem colloquial, Jeffers's "bloody sires" were a primitive invention to drive home a wrath that the bemused poet could feel only in the abstract, Stevens's "connoisseurs of chaos" opted for the imagination over the studied veleities of continental intellectuals.

This renaissance, this "New Poetry" (as its loyal editor, Harriet Monroe, was to call it), has taken several hitches in its aesthetic belt since those remarkable leaders fell silent. While some of the more superficial attributes are still pursued for the wrong reasons, the real inheritors used the new emphasis as a starting point for an even tighter imagism. Some, like John Crowe Ransom, William Empson, Allen Tate, and Robert Penn Warren, were both poets and teacher-critics. Theirs became an intellectualized product in which form prevailed over content, and subtleties of expression over primary emotion. The end of poetry of this sort was in the means, or as expressed by MacLeish, "A poem should not mean/ But be." There are, said Ransom, seconding the ideas of I. A. Richards in England—and supported by his younger friends Tate and Cleanth Brooks—controlling factors to help determine what a poem shall "be." Accordingly, a set of disciplines was formulated by which good poetry could be tested. In any case, to interpret a poem properly, one stuck to the text, explicating it. In this major respect, they were nearly back to Matthew Arnold and his judgment by "touchstones." By about 1941, these poets and critics had established a formula for reading a poem or story, and their method had come to be called "the New Criticism."[3]

In England (with the exception of the styles of C. Day Lewis and Louis MacNeice), the traditional psychological-romantic tendency still prevailed. In a countermovement to the harder, drier styles described above, long-standing lyrical values were reasserted in the poems of Edith Sitwell, John Betjeman, Stephen Spender, George Barker, and Dylan

[3]More fully discussed on pp. 217–18.

213

Thomas. A younger group, in America, carried the reductive process of Pound's, and then Ransom's, contemporaries to an almost formalized understatement. W. H. Auden, Theodore Roethke, Randall Jarrell, and Elizabeth Bishop (to mention only four) are quite different in their final product, yet they share a common devotion to almost simplistic statement, characterized by fear of poetic diction or triteness of emotion. Jarrell's "The Death of the Ball Turret Gunner" (see p. 197) illustrates this attitude. Its noncommittal reportage is the result of drastic compression, mocking the melodramatized thrills of air-combat. From such caustic comment, the step would not be great to the irritable social and political denunciations of Robert Lowell, James Dickey, Howard Nemerov, or the Beatniks.

A last poem, Elizabeth Bishop's "Large Bad Picture," must serve to emblemize the qualities first introduced in the New Poetry. Here are some of Eliot's early *vers de societé*, Pound's sense of the *outré* or exotic, and Wallace Stevens's elegant sparring with aesthetic ghosts. Note that the almost prim poetic form encourages the viewer's eye to linger on the childish minutiae of the scene:

Remembering the Strait of Belle Isle or
some northerly harbor of Labrador,
before he became a schoolteacher
a great-uncle painted a big picture.

Receding for miles on either side
into a flushed, still sky
are overhanging pale-blue cliffs
hundreds of feet high,

their bases fretted by little arches,
the entrances to caves
running in along the level of a bay
masked by perfect waves.

On the middle of that quiet floor
sits a fleet of small black ships,

square-rigged, sails furled, motionless,
their spars like burned matchsticks.

And high above them, over the tall cliffs'
semitranslucent ranks,
are scribbled hundreds of fine black birds
hanging in "n"s, in banks.

One can hear their crying, crying,
the only sound there is
except for occasional sighing
as a large aquatic animal breathes.

In the pink light
the small red sun goes rolling, rolling,
round and round and round at the same height
in perpetual sunset, comprehensive, consoling,
while the ships consider it.
Apparently they have reached their destination.
It would be hard to say what brought them there,
Commerce or contemplation.

Among the shifting values we have discussed, the reforma-
tion and counter-reformation of what was considered aesthetically moribund appear to bring the style full circle. In
"Large Bad Picture" (the title itself a faintly antisentimental,
almost antipoetic touch), we have a psychologically real,
tenderly disparaging poem. The emotion has been carefully
refined to a sort of third-hand state, yet still subtly conveys
the primary values with which a little girl must once have
looked at the picture.

Poetical Criticism Since 1915

A brief outline of the intellectual milieu of World War I
and after will complete this chapter on poems in context.
Herein may be seen some of the shifting values brought to
modern poetics and how contemporary attitudes have in-

directly influenced the writing of poetry, while directly affecting the interpretations and judgment of it.

Since the late 19th century, "historical" criticism prevailed; that is, poetic evaluation was conducted within the guidelines of literary tradition and historical fact. The criteria (many of them reflecting the kinds of contextual approach discussed in our last few sections) were relatively fixed. It was no accident that the most authoritative judgments emanated from universities and established literary reviews. Since the second decade of this century, however, criticism has undergone considerable soul-searching and consequent discord within its ranks. In America the revelations matched the revival of an experimental poetry, such as Imagism, or the broader subject matter and relaxed approach of mid-western poets like Masters, Lindsay, and Sandburg. By the middle of the twenties, groups of critics adopted favored approaches, some quite specialized or tangential to the literary mode in question. Thus, in addition to the historical critics (many of whom had taken the label "new humanism"), there were the "psychological critics" (some of whose approaches we encountered in Chapter 7), the "impressionists," the "semanticists," the "anthropologists," the "sociological critics," the "naturalists" (or would-be literary scientists), and the "new (or analytical) critics."

Most of these attempted to apply a particular set of premises or conditions of inquiry in interpreting the literary effort. In all but the last—the New Critics—the process of interpretation usually brought into play the tools of the respective discipline involved: the New Humanists, the conditions and standards of a classical tradition; the semanticists, the verbal refinements of poetic meaning through language and usage; the social activists, the evaluation of literature in terms of its political-economical awareness, and augmentation of civil responsibility; the anthropologists, the relationship between literature and racial-cultural origins and customs, with special emphasis on myths and rituals; the naturalists, the determination of an author's sensibilities by social, biological, and economic forces. Each of these "schools" used its singular convictions to explain how a poem is generated, how it exists, and how it is understood.

Some of these methods of interpretation and evaluation corresponded to the intellectual climate that engendered them. Literary interpreters with militant social awareness, for example, thrived in the economic hardship of the depressed thirties. They tended to be impatient with the "ivory tower," that is, with literature that did not concern itself with aiding the underprivileged or improving social conditions.[4] Earlier, the New Humanist criticism (with its passion for tradition and form based on classical models) had urged the larger perspectives of the historical approach (see p. 216). In the first and second decades, it largely dominated the universities. The professor-critics, who claimed to uphold the values of a vanishing humanism, were reacting against: (1) the impressionism of art for art's sake, and (2) the rising menace of naturalism (with its reductive portrayal of man as a creature determined largely by natural forces). Both tendencies were regarded by the New Humanists as, respectively, formless or decadent, mechanistic, antihumanist, and pessimistic.

In the forties and fifties the New Critics, like the Neo-Humanists before them, were opposed to the haphazard directions of existing criticism (especially of the impressionists, who, both agreed, had no real critical standards). But their particular target was the very historical emphasis that the tradition-dominated colleges and graduate schools had made the basis of much of the literary study required in their courses. The New Critics urged a return to the literary text itself (a practice they had noted as the long-established method in French schools). Readers should concentrate on explication of the text, rather than on distracting secondary matters. Their aesthetic attitudes ranged from the "pure poetry of form" (reminiscent of the elevation of the "means" of art for art's sake) of John Crowe Ransom and his Kenyon school, to the metaphysical-semantical-psychological approach of I. A. Richards, William Empson, Richard Blackmur, and Kenneth Burke. In between were the professor-critics

---

[4]First enunciated by Tolstoi in *What is Art?* Good art, he said, must have uplifting value; otherwise it degenerates into the enfeebling diversion of art for art's sake.

Cleanth Brooks and Robert Penn Warren,[5] who organized the principles of close textual analysis into handbooks for class study. The universal ingredients of good poetry, they claimed, were resolvable into these principles.

Many expedients have been pressed into the service of poetical criticism. No single theory or program can be counted on by itself as the "key" to enduring poetry. With their ingenious analyses, the New Critics made attentive readers more aware of specified imagistic and structural elements by which the eligible poems succeeded. They demonstrated the efficacy of "ambiguity," "paradox," "irony," "tension," and the rest of their favored criteria. On the other hand, they were often blind to the relationship of the minimal essentials of a text to an available background or foreground.[6] But the New Critics had no monopoly on single-mindedness. Critics representing the sometimes brilliant psychological or anthropological school too often left the *corpus delecti* of the poem where it lay and went off after tangential, if fascinating, clues—ones that might or might not concern the reality of the poem in question.

So, text and context: how should each be given its due? The poem itself must always be foremost; but, as we have seen in the preceding chapters, no single element of a poem, no separate approach, can bring us all we want to know. A reader will be cutting off his resources if he finds nothing in the background of a poem or its author that is essential to some fuller interpretation.

---

[5]Along with Allen Tate and Ransom, they were called the "southern agrarians." Brooks's *The Well Wrought Urn* affords a sample of their methodology. The object was to show that a poem as eminent as one by John Milton or as newly minted as one by Dylan Thomas could be evaluated on the same scale.

[6]For the most part, the analytical approach favored in literary courses today is a consequence of such influential texts as Cleanth Brooks's and Robert Penn Warren's *Understanding Poetry*, widely used in the '40s and '50s. Even graduate instruction, which sets patterns for future teachers, began to accept the method—with its borrowed French name —"explication de texte." Now it seems widespread enough. Much of the bogus scientism of traditional graduate study has given way to this preference for critical and interpretive studies.

Conclusion

We have covered three main divisions in this study: (1) the aural-phonetic values of a poem, (2) the language and discourse as central to a poem's means, and (3) the ways in which both means and meaning are served by context.[7] These are the basic values to which we believe a reader responds; they are also the areas in which a poem achieves likeness in difference. The tensions within poems are built from the recurrences and correspondences of sound and orthography, or of image-forming words (connections or oppositions), or from the ratio between the speaker, what he says, and the person to whom he speaks. Themes or ideas become poetic as a result of the interrelation of these tensions.

Tension is generated by every aspect of the connection and the opposing of meanings (direction and indirection), or of the likeness and difference between an author's objectives in his art and the emotions of his generating impulse. There are also the tensions in the disparity between what a poet intentionally puts into his poem and what transpires from his images and formal treatment. Finally, a certain tension may be said to exist between a poem's independence in time and the relative impact that a poet's circumstances, his world, and his age might have on it.

These psychological checks and balances, operating both in the composition of a poem and in the transmission of it to the reader, are part of the condition in which a poem lives. They are the circles within circles by which we measure an organic growth. Form is what the poet achieves when he has caged many diverse and sometimes contrary aspects of words so that they will sing for us.

Practical Criticism

Two groups of projects for exploring the theoretical and historical context of poetry are listed below. They are suggested as topics for

---

[7]This has been our general outline, and its diagramatic form can be found in the Appendix.

219

independent study leading to a class report or formal written paper.

Poetics in a Shifting Milieu

1. The emergence of a narrative poetry of manners in Chaucer's *The Canterbury Tales*
2. Medieval romance as adapted in Chaucer's narrative verse
3. Chaucer and the evolution of realistic portraiture
4. The "romantic" and the "everyday" in Shakespeare's verse
5. An analysis of Shakespeare's sonnets in the light of baroque tradition
6. The range of images in Shakespeare's *Hamlet* (or *Macbeth, Othello, Richard II, Henry V*, or other plays)
7. Shakespeare's soliloquy as a forerunner of dramatic monologue (See Houston Peterson's *The Lonely Debate*)
8. The reasons for the term "metaphysical" as applied to some 17th century poets
9. Have there been successful experiments in English quantitative verse?
10. The prevalence in English verse of forms of syllabic recurrence other than rhyme
11. A comparison between accentual, syllabic, and quantitative meter in selected English poems
12. Free verse: cadence versus meters; a look at the development of free verse in English poetry
13. Historical experiments in prose style: Euphuism and Gongorism
14. Parallelism in Hebrew poetry: the influence on American poetry (Whitman, Eliot, and others)
15. Recent experiments toward varying our system of scanning verse (for example, audiometrical comparisons, micrometer impulses, and so forth)
16. Requirements of an epic poetry: some modern attempts at the epic (Hardy, *The Dynasts*; Steven Vincent Benét, *John Brown's Body*; and others)
17. Attempts at free-form poetry: spatial verse and tmesis (Cummings, Mallarmé, Apollonaire), prose poetry (John Gould Fletcher and "orthophonic prose"), eye poetry or shaped poetry (currently "concrete poetry"), beginning rhyme, incantation, and so forth.

18. Verse drama in modern times: W. B. Yeats, Maxwell Anderson, Robinson Jeffers, Archibald MacLeish, Christopher Fry, Eliot, or Edna Millay

19. The revivals of narrative poetry: Tennyson, William Morris, E. A. Robinson, Benét, Jeffers, or Robert Penn Warren

20. Browning's dramatic monologues: origins and influences

21. Evolution of the *persona* ("speaker") as a representation in lyric poetry

22. The Japanese *haiku* and *tanka*: characteristics and their effects on English poetry (Pound, "H. D." (Hilda Doolittle), Wallace Stevens, and others)

23. A comparison of the medievalism of Tennyson, William Morris, and E. A. Robinson

24. Some origins of 19th century American ballads; or, origins and influence of English ballads (See Clark and Clark, *Introduction to Folklore*)

25. Some techniques of Beat verse (Ferlinghetti, Ginsberg, Corso, and others); the relative literary merits

Poetry and the Poet

1. Donne: secular to sacred

2. Blake: poet, illustrator, reformer?

3. Blake as a spokesman of his times

4. Coleridge's ideas on the poetic imagination

5. Keats and the "negative capability"

6. The range of imagery in selected poems of Keats

7. Poe's influence on Baudelaire. Were Baudelaire's critical conclusions sound?

8. Whitman and pluralism: catalogue and themes of multiplicity

9. Whitman and the use of parallelism as verse technique

10. The force and variety of Hopkins's imagery

11. Poetry and the unconscious with Hopkins

12. E. A. Robinson and the personal factor: evidence of a philosophy

13. Housman and environment: the background and mood of his poems

14. How to understand *A Vision*, by Yeats

15. How Yeats utilized the images of *A Vision* in his later poems

16. Jung and the "archetypes": a study of Maud Bodkin's *Archetypal Patterns in Poetry*
17. The evolution of Eliot's *The Waste Land*; some influences of Pound on Eliot
18. The emergence of "Imagism": Pound, "H. D.," Amy Lowell, and others
19. A-humanism: an investigation into Jeffers's philosophy
20. Virginia Woolf: poetic lyricism and the prose medium
21. Thomas Wolfe: the poetic medium in the work of prose
22. I. A. Richards and "practical criticism"
23. Ideas from William Empson's *Seven Types of Ambiguity*
24. E. E. Cummings and disguise of form in poetry
25. Eliot and the critics: contemporary reaction to his poetry
26. Influential ideas from Eliot as a literary critic
27. Cleanth Brooks's presentation of the new criticism: *The Well Wrought Urn*
28. The particular poetic style and form of Dylan Thomas (or of Elizabeth Bishop; Jarrell; Theodore Roethke; or others)
29. The controlling symbols of Wallace Stevens
30. Influences of certain French Symbolists on Eliot or on Stevens.
31. The Beat poets: a study of oral rhetoric in relation to written verse
32. A study of a contemporary poet and his relation to tradition

Foreign Influences

Problems and exercises in the work of a selected French poet, or of a German poet, and so forth. The influence of a European poet on an English or American poet. (This division can be expanded according to the background and linguistic range of members of the class. Normally, there are a fair proportion of students who are taking, or have completed, a course in a modern European language and its literature.)

APPENDIX

The Relation of Poetic Values

Notes:

1. The divisions merge into each other. The values function concurrently rather than successively or in strictly isolated form.
2. Readings differ; each poem calls for a separate kind of emphasis.
3. Characteristics of some poems may be grasped at the unconscious as well as the conscious level.
4. True criticism begins with the awareness of all the values below as they work correlatively in a given poem.

VALUE A—AURAL/PHONETIC

1. *Aural* (heard effects)

(Recurrence and expectancy)
—stress; rhythm; meter;
mutations of meter; quantity
or duration; pitch; phonemic
effects (orchestration);
onomatopoeia

2. *Imagined Sound* (the
inner ear)—aural/verbal synthesis in silent reading; tone
projection; pause

3. *Phonetic* (orthographic
effects

(Likeness in difference)—
syllabic and orthographic recurrence: rhyme (end; internal); parallelism (beginning rhyme); alliteration;
assonance; consonance; slant
rhyme; visual effects of
phonemic orthography

4. *Eye Appeal* (shaped
verse)—verbal and lineal
arrangement; "eye poetry"
(alias "concrete")

VALUE B—MEANS AND MEANING

1. Vivification of Language

a. Images that connect (likeness in difference): simile; personification; metaphor

b. Images of ambivalence: allusion; synecdoche; metonymy

c. Images that oppose (likeness in contradiction): pun; *double entendre;* hyperbole; litotes (understatment); paradox; oxymoron; symbol; allegory

2. Concept and Mode: Expressing the Substance

a. Narrative modes: the idea of the speaker; dramatic monologue; direct/indirect discourse; broken discourse; forms of irony

b. Disguising the substance: direction and indirection; connotation of words and ideas; confession; insinuation

c. Intentional and subliminal meaning: the creative and the unconscious; traditional symbols

3. Tension: likeness and opposition; expression and reticence; relative versus absolute denotation; substance and means; psychological conflict

VALUE C—THE POEM IN ITS CONTEXT

1. Subjective Data

a. Additive factors: the poet as his own editor—titles, epigraphs, notes

b. Autobiographical revelation: textual evidence; letters; diaries

2. External Data

a. Psychological factors: interpretations from text; life records; interpretations of data

b. Historical facts: contemporary social, religious, philosophical

3. Critical Perspectives—Contemporary views of the poet and his work; the kinds of criticism (historical viewpoints and theory; impressionistic; psychological; semantic; sociological; anthropological; analytic or "New")

A GLOSSARY OF TERMS

Some of the terms briefly explained here are more fully illustrated in the main text. A few additional terms (not specifically mentioned in the text) are included here to make the list useful for general reference.[1]

ACATALECTIC—See **catalectic**.

ACCENT—See also **stress** (which refers strictly to metrical beat). Accent has to do with the intensity of emphasis in the pronunciation of the syllables of a word. It is a feature of language in general rather than of metrics in particular. Distinction is normally made between primary accent (the strongest) and secondary or tertiary accents (of successively decreasing strength). Symbols used vary according to dictionaries. **Accentual meter** is distinguished from syllabic meter. (See **syllabic verse**.)

AESTHETIC DISTANCE—The perspective that distance imparts to a work of art. In poetry, drama, or fiction the term has been applied by the "New Critics" to indicate the degree to which a *reader* achieves the necessary separation between the material of raw life and the literary representation of it. As applied to the *writer*, it means his ability (largely through form) of removing himself far enough from a personal experience or emotion to deal with it objectively and in perspective.

ALEXANDRINE—A line of verse with six **iambic** feet, borrowed from the conventional meter of French classical drama (which had a uniform twelve syllables to the line). It was first developed in the French verse of the 12th and 13th centuries.

ALLEGORY—An elaborate and extended variety of metaphor, developed normally as narrative, with **personification** of abstract ideas or qualities. Allegory seems to have reached its greatest popularity in the 16th and early 17th centuries,

---

[1]Terms in boldface are explained elsewhere in the Glossary.

although poetic narratives as early as *Beowulf* or *Sir Gawain and the Green Knight* are assumed to have allegorical bases. Important later examples are (in drama) *Everyman*, (in poetry) *The Fairie Queene*, and (in prose tale) *The Pilgrim's Progress*.

ALLITERATION (or *head rhyme* or *initial rhyme*)—The repetition of (usually) initial syllabic sounds within a line of verse. Swineburne ("Where the weeds that grew green from the graves of its roses") and Hopkins (see poem, p. 60) had a powerful predilection for alliteration. It was one of the earliest prosodic devices in our poetry, being widely used in Old English verse. Hopkins tended to favor **internal rhyme** ("How a lush-kept plush-capped sloe . . ./ Gush!—flush the man, the being with it, sour or sweet"), which is frequently confused with alliteration, but—as can be seen—rhymes the final syllable or the whole word, rather than the first syllable alone.

ALLUSION—A reference, direct or indirect, to a person, place, or thing with which the poet wants to make associations— speare's plays, Greek and Roman classics, mythology, and literature. In classical literature, allusions were most often to speare's plays, Greek and Roman classics, mythology, and literature. In classical literature, allusions were most often to Homer, Hesiod, and the myths. Distinctions in this text have been made between direct allusion ("Or like stout Cortez when with eagle eyes/He star'd at the Pacific. . . .") and a connotative or implied allusion, as in Eliot's *The Waste Land*, with such associative references as,

> After the torchlight red on sweaty faces
> After the frosty silence in the gardens
> After the agony in stony places,

which are oblique references to Christ's fast and temptation.

AMBIGUITY—The quality of being understood two or more ways. This is often desirable in poetry where the connotative implications and overtones of words are considered an enrichment of the language used. The quality of irony, for instance, is intensified in Marvell's "To His Coy Mistress" (see discussion, p. 114) because the speaker plays intentionally on double meanings. An influential modern analysis of this aspect of poetry is William Empson's *Seven Types of Ambiguity*.

226

AMPHIBRACH—A metrical foot of three syllables (applicable chiefly to classical prosody) in which the unstressed (or, quantitatively, two *short*) syllables flank one stressed (or, quantitatively, *long*) syllables, as in un *kind* ly and re *ceiv* ing.

AMPHIMACER—The reverse of **amphibrach**. It has two stressed (or *long*) syllables flanking one unstressed (or *short*) syllable, as in con tra dict.

ANACREONTIC VERSE—A form named after the Greek poet Anacreon (6th century B.C.) that celebrates wine, woman, dance, and other joys that will pass.

ANACRUSIS—An extra unstressed syllable (or syllables) at the beginning of a line that normally would not need it.

ANAPEST—A metrical foot of three syllables, the first two unstressed, the last stressed (in tĕr pōse). Browning's "Saul" is predominantly anapestic ("Ănd Ĭ paúsed, | hĕld mў bréath | in sŭch sí | lĕnce, ănd líst | enĕd ăpárt").

ANAPHORA—See also **parallelism** and **repetend**. A repetition of words or phrases, especially at the beginning of lines, or **hemistitches**, affording within lines, or from line to line, desirable prosodic effect. It is a common device of Hebrew poetry, as in these lines from the Song of Deborah (Judges 5:27), "At her feet he bowed, he fell, he lay down: at her feet he bowed, he fell: where he bowed, there he fell down dead." Walt Whitman, echoing biblical style, used anaphora probably more than any other prosodic device, as in this sample from "Crossing Brooklyn Ferry":

> It avails not, neither time or place—distance avails
>   not;
> I am with you, you men and women of a
>   generation, or ever so many generations hence;
> I project myself—also I return—I am with you,
>   and I know how it is.
> Just as you feel when you look on the river and
>   sky, so I felt;
> Just as any of you is one of a living crowd, I was
>   one of a crowd;
> Just as you are refreshed by the gladness of the
>   river and the bright flow, I was refreshed....

ANASTROPHE—Deliberate inversion of the normal or logical order of words or sentence parts. (See also **inversion**.)

ANTEPENULT(IMATE)—See **penult(imate)**.

ANTISTROPHE—The second of three stanzas that make up the triad of the Pindaric or choric ode. (See **ode**.)

ANTITHESIS—A deliberate balancing of one term, clause, or sentence against another for rhetorical effect, as in the aphoristic style of Francis Bacon ("Discourse maketh a ready man; writing maketh an exact man; reading maketh a full man").

APHORISM—A condensed, neatly (sometimes antithetically) phrased statement, usually reflecting proverbial or folk wisdom. (*Cf.* "proverb" and "maxim.") Some verse may be called aphoristic. Pope gives an aphoristic sentiment the status of a maxim in his line, "To err is human; to forgive divine."

APOCRYPHA—Referring to Holy Scripture, those books not regarded as divinely inspired, and therefore excluded from the sacred **canon**. Of literature in general, works that have not received attribution by authoritative judgment.

APOSTROPHE—An address to someone, or an invocation to something personified or abstract. A rhetorical device common both in prose and in poetry, as in Shelley's

"O World! O Life! O Time!
On whose last steps I climb"

APPROXIMATE RHYME—See **near rhyme** (also called *slant rhyme*, *imperfect rhyme*, and *off rhyme*).

ARCHAISM—In both poetry and prose, words and dictions no longer in common use, employed to convey a tone of solemnity or remoteness in time. Archaic parts of speech or inflections are commonly associated with biblical literature and prayer, as in the verb endings and pronouns "thou," "ye," "wilt he?" "Go ye," "hast thou?" and "believeth." Archaic usage was associated with poetry well into the 19th century but seems universally eschewed among the best modern poets.

ARCHETYPE—A generic term for any of a group of long-standing symbols connected with man's racial development. The psychologist Jung identified certain of these—such as "old man," "*anima*," "*persona*," and so forth—as having a permanent place in man's imagination and serving as a continuing set of symbols. Drama and poetry, from Homer on, have offered successive versions of these, supplying modern artists with access to what has often been called the "racial" or "collective unconscious." Thus, in Eliot's *The Waste Land*, Tiresias appears as a voice connecting the modern events described with dim parallels in the past. (See Maud Bodkin, *Archetypal Patterns in Poetry*.)

ASSONANCE—The recurrence of similar vowel sounds within successive words in a line of poetry ("scream—beach," or "fail—paid"). It is distinct from **internal rhyme** and **alliteration**, in which, respectively, final syllables of words within a line and beginning syllables of words in the line have matching sounds. (*Cf.* **consonance**, for the similar recurrence of consonantal sounds.)

AUBADE—A term (borrowed originally from music) for a **lyric** poem composed to celebrate the dawn, and more specifically, a parting of lovers at the break of day.

AUCTORIAL VOICE (or *authorial voice*)—The direct injection by the author of his control or viewpoint, as opposed to expressing himself through a character's voice or **persona**. In poetry the *persona*, or **speaker**, is often a surrogate through whom the author expresses himself. (This relationship between poet, *persona*, and reader is discussed in Chapter 6.)

BACCHIC FOOT (or *bacchius*)—A trisyllabic foot of one unstressed syllable followed by two stressed syllables ("and strode high on light feet"). The reverse of this (ᴗ∕ᴗ) is called an antibacchic foot. When bacchics occur in the prevailing iambic line, the result is sometimes called a spondaic effect (see **spondee**). The tendency to call deviations from a prevailing meter **substitution** sometimes obscures the existence of spondaic effect or bacchic feet. Their occurrence, however, usually marks special effects and a more deliberate purpose on the poet's part than the term "substitution" implies, as in the special rhythm Masefield achieves with alternating **pyrrhics** and spondees of each fourth line of the stanzas of "Sea-Fever."

BALLAD—A form of short narrative verse marked by a definite rhythm and intended originally for oral recitation; sometimes set to music.

BALLADE—A verse form that originated in France, usually having three stanzas, in each of which the same rhymes occur in the same order. Each stanza ends with a refrain, and the poem ends with an **envoy**, or postscript. Chaucer's "Balade de Bon Conseyl" (c. 1390), has three seven-line stanzas, each with the refrain "And trouthe shal delivere, hit is no drede," with an envoy of seven lines, also ending with that refrain.

BALLAD STANZA—The traditional form of the ballad was a series of quatrains of alternating tetrameter and trimeter, rhyming a b c d.

BAR—See **virgule**.

BAROQUE—Originally an architectural term to designate the ornate designs of the late 16th and the 17th centuries, with their heavy adornments, molding, and Romanesque influence. In poetry the term has come to be applied to a comparable quality sometimes associated with Elizabethan sonneteers, sometimes with Shakespeare, and generally with Milton, Edward Waller, Richard Crashaw, and others by whom nature was deemed improvable by artifice. (*Cf.* "rococo.")

BEAT—Another term for **stress** in a metrical line.

BEGINNING RHYME—See **rhyme**.

BLANK VERSE—Unrhymed iambic pentameter verse, the usual vehicle of English epic and dramatic poetry. Generally, any metrical but unrhymed verse.

BRACKET RHYME—In quatrains, rhymes of the first and fourth and of the second and third lines: a b b a (as used by Tennyson in his *In Memoriam*).

BREVE—A curved mark ($\smile$) used to indicate a short vowel in the pronunciation of a word. In verse **scansion** the breve is used to indicate the unstressed syllable in accentual meter, or the short syllable ("bĕ gīn," "tō tăl") in quantitative meter (see **quantity**). The long mark (–) is called a **macron**. See **ictus** (the name for the stressed syllable in accentual scansion).

BURDEN—See **refrain**.

CACOPHONY—The aural effect of harshness or discord in the choice and arrangement of words; in poetry, usually a deliberate discordance to correspond to an intended harshness or ugliness in the sense. The exaggerated **consonance** in

Browning's line from "Rabbi Ben Ezra" suggests an intended jolt to the reader:

> Irks care the crop-filled bird? Frets doubt
> the maw-crammed beast?

CADENCE—The rhythm natural to a language (especially as used orally), which arises from the normal stresses of speech. **Free verse** tends to be based on these cadences of speech rather than on a regular syllabic meter.

CAESURA—A break in a line of verse (usually in the middle), permitting a pause, sometimes to set off an internal rhyme (see **leonine rhyme**). It is indicated by a space in Old English poetry, and in scansion by a double **virgule** or *bar* (‖). A segment of a line formed by a caesura is called a **hemistich**. Originally caesurae may have been prompted—especially when occurring in long lines like hexameter or heptameter— by breath pauses, by the striking of musical strings, or by an attempt to regularize the rhythms as a mnemonic aid to the reciter.

CANON—In sacred literature, the scriptural books that officially have been declared as divinely inspired; those not so declared would fall into the **apocrypha**. In secular terms, works authenticated as attributable to an author (for example, "those plays admitted to the Shakespeare *canon*") or included by reason of on-going acceptance in anthologies or as representative of major writers of a period (for example, "our established *canon* of English poetry").

CANTO—A major section of a long poem. From Italian meaning "song," and exemplified in the *canti* of Dante's *Comedia*, Byron's *Childe Harold*, or Ezra Pound's *Cantos*.

CANZONE—Short poems of equal stanzas (with variation possible in the number of lines per stanza, plus an *envoy* of fewer lines). Originally a song or ballad in Italian and Provençal, the form was influential on Edmund Spenser and other poets of the English Renaissance.

CARPE DIEM—A thematic poem (Latin for "seize the day") that celebrates the enjoyment of the momentary aspects of life.

CATALEXIS (or *catalectic*)—A line having a final incomplete foot, usually by the omission of one or more syllables otherwise required by the meter. Also, the **truncation** of an initial unstressed syllable, resulting in what is called a "headless" line. In Emily Dickinson's "There's a Certain Slant of Light," the final foot of the second and last lines of the stanza below are most plausibly read as catalectic:

> None may teach it—Any—
> 'Tis the Seal Despair—
> An imperial affliction
> Sent us of the Air—

In this couplet by Housman, the first part of the second line is truncated:

> And if | my ways | are not | as theirs
> Let | them mind | their own | affairs.

A line of verse that is not deficient in its unstressed syllables is *acatalectic*. A line that has one or more syllables in excess of normal is *hypercatalectic*.

CHAIN VERSE—Lines or stanzas interlinked throughout by the same rhymes, as in the **villanelle**, whose six stanzas have but two rhymes recurrent throughout.

CHANTEY (also *chanty* and *shanty*.)—A song with very strong rhythm and refrain, sung by sailors at work.

CHAUCERIAN STANZA—See **rhyme royal**.

COMMON MEASURE (or *common meter, hymnal stanza,* or sometimes just *CM*)—A regular iambic meter with usually alternating tetrameter and trimeter lines, used traditionally in church hymns.

COMPENSATION—Generally, the means of adjusting for deficiencies in an otherwise regular metrical line. This is done on an *accentual* basis by replacement of syllables (usually one or more unstressed) in one foot to compensate for those omitted elsewhere. When such adjustment is made in *quantitative* meter, the compensation is dependent on **equivalence**, whereby the **duration** can be increased for some syllables to make up for those whose duration has been shortened.

Accentual compensation may be illustrated in the two lines from Coleridge's *Christabel* below, which are really trimeter (having but three stresses), while the rest of the section is predominantly iambic tetrameter (with four stresses):

Ĭs thĕ níght | chíllў | ănd dárk?
Thĕ níght | ĭs chíl | lў, bŭt nŏt dárk.

The first foot of the first line has an extra unstressed syllable, and the last foot of the second line has two extra unstressed syllables. The effect is to compensate for the deficient number of stresses by extending the syllabication. Coleridge continues the process in the next couplet, having a compensated line follow the regular iambic tetrameter line:

Thĕ thín | grĕy clóud | ĭs spréad | ŏn hígh
Ĭt có | vĕrs bŭt nŏt hídes | thĕ skў.

The second foot in the second line is not actual **substitution**, which calls for a different kind of foot to replace one in the predominant meter, but compensation for stresses deficient in that foot.

Quantitative compensation, more commonly **equivalence**, requires the added duration of syllables where their number is decreased. In actual phonation, the apparent increase of duration (that is, the time required to sound the vowel in a syllable) may be brought about by the pause following pronunciation of syllables of greater quantity. The two lines concluding the second stanza of Cummings's poem "Anyone Lived in a Pretty How Town" illustrate the principle, each of the feet in the tetrameter line consisting of one long syllable (as against the polysyllabic feet of the first line). The quantity—in addition to the stress—is indicated in the second line by a **macron** (–):

thĕy sówed | thĕir ĭs´ | n't thĕy réaped | thĕir sáme
sūn | mōon | stārs | rain

CONCEIT—An ingenious and elaborate metaphor that often becomes the controlling image for an entire poem, as in Drayton's "Love's Farewell," where the idea of love as an ailing patient curable only by the mistress's attentions supports the entire sonnet. Shakespeare's sonnets, Donne's poems, and many of Herbert's poems, to mention three, are often elaborate conceits. Conceits of the 16th century are usually Petrarchan; those of the 17th century, metaphysical. (*Cf.* **baroque.**)

CONNOTATION—The suggestion or associated meaning carried by a word, apart from its denotation or literal signification. (See discussion in Chapter 7.)

CONSONANCE—The recurrence of similar consonant sounds within successive words in a line of verse (distinct from **alliteration** or **internal rhyme**, in which beginning and final syllables, respectively, must have matching sounds). These word pairs are consonantal: "play—poor," "fed—road." E. E. Cummings mingles both consonance and **assonance** in this stanza:

> anyone lived in a pretty how town
> (with up so floating many bells down)
> spring summer autumn winter
> he sang his didn't he danced his did.

CONTEXT—Two applications of this term are common: (1) the surrounding words, lines, and meanings in which a word, line, or meaning must be construed in reading; (2) the general setting, times, and biographical-historical background in which a poem, or any literary work, is read and interpreted.

COUNTERPOINT—A musical term descriptive of plural melody, or of a melody added complementarily to an existing melody; now borrowed for application to the discussion in our text of the aural interaction of rhythm and meter working concurrently in a poem.

COUPLET—Two lines of similar meter, rhyming *a a*. An open couplet is not grammatically completed by the end of the second line, but runs on into a third or succeeding lines. A closed couplet is grammatically completed by the end of the second line, and is punctuated by a period or semicolon, as in the opening couplet of Pope's *Essay on Criticism*,

> 'Tis hard to say, if greater want of skill
> Appear in writing or in judging ill; . . .

DACTYL—A foot of three syllables, the first being stressed (or long in quantitative meter), the other two unstressed (or short quantitatively), and scanned (/⌣⌣). (*Cf.* **triple meter**.)

DECASYLLABIC VERSE—Metrical lines of ten syllables, the notable example being Milton's *Paradise Lost*. The degree of regularity imposed by decasyllabic meter tended to commend it to the orderly minded Augustans. Pope's *Essay on Man* and *Essay on Criticism* are in decasyllabic verse.

DENOTATION—See **connotation**.

DIBRACH—A metrical foot of two short syllables (quantitatively speaking). (*Cf.* **tribrach**.) In accentual meter the dibrach is commonly called a **pyrrhic foot**, and consists of two unstressed syllables.

DIDACTICISM—A tendency to be moralistic. A didactic poem devotes itself primarily to moral instruction or uplift. Modern poetry tends to detach itself from didactic purpose, or at least to disguise it or to let it emerge obliquely. Not so the 17th, 18th, and 19th centuries, in which the greatest works were often didactic (for example, Milton's *Paradise Lost*, Pope's *Essay on Man*, and Tennyson's *In Memoriam*).

DIMETER—Poetic meter of two feet to the line; thus, **iambic** and **trochaic**.

DIRGE—A lyrical poem of lament. (*Cf.* **elegy**.)

DISSOCIATION OF SENSIBILITY—The separation of the artist's and the public's values and tastes in literary or other artistic matters. As first described by T. S. Eliot in 1921 in his essay "The Metaphysical Poets," the phenomenon was a characteristic of the gradual alienation of readers from the more demanding values of art for art's sake and a concomitant experimentalism, in favor of the more generally acceptable forms of literature. The alienation in the 19th century of the Symbolist poets from their bourgeois compatriots, causing the art of these poets more and more to turn in on itself, has been cited as one of the early manifestations of dissociation of sensibility.

DISSONANCE (also *consonantal dissonance*)—A variation of the more common term **consonance**. Interchangeably with the term *half rhyme*, it describes the slight variation of vowel sounds, but with the consonants left more or less intact, in words like "morning—minion," "dauphin—dapples," "riding—rolling," in the three lines of Hopkins' "The Windhover":

> I caught this morning morning's minion,
>> kingdom of daylight's dauphin, dapple-
>> dawn-drawn Falcon, in his riding
> Of the rolling level underneath him steady air....

DOGGEREL—Verse on trivial subjects, written poorly. Often simply bad verse on popular themes—country, motherhood, babyhood, and so forth. The doggerel manner has sometimes been intentionally copied for satirical purposes. Serious poets occasionally slip into doggerel, as Wordsworth in these lines from "Peter Bell":

> Once more the Ass, with motion dull,
> Upon the pivot of his skull
> Turned round his long left ear.

DOUBLE ENTENDRE—A phrase from the French (literally, "to hear twice") with the idea of a double meaning. As used in poetry and drama, it is more involved in context than is the limited word-play of the **pun**. It is often an extended metaphor in which one side of the equation carries erotic, or other, overtones. Donne's "A Valediction: Forbidding Mourning," Campion's "Cherry-Ripe," and Marvell's "To His Coy Mistress" afford examples of double entendre. Reed's "Naming of Parts" (see p. 107) is a modern example of a whole poem structured on *double entendre*.

DOUBLE RHYME—See **feminine rhyme**.

DRAMATIC MONOLOGUE—A form of literature in which a single speaker unwittingly conveys more than he intends. In poetry, the use of this speaker permits considerable irony in providing a reversal of the object or narrative substance the narrator sets out with, thus making the thrust of the poem oblique. Robert Browning developed this poetic technique to a major literary form with such poems as "My Last Duchess," "Fra Lippo Lippi," and "Soliloquy in a Spanish Cloister." Tennyson's "Ulysses" and "Lucretius" are further examples.

DRAMATIC IRONY—The irony arising in a play (originally in Greek drama) when the audience is aware in advance of the imminent fate of the protagonist. In poetry generally, it describes the quality felt by the reader when the **speaker** in a poem misses the truth that the reader sees. This is the psychological interest in the **dramatic monologue**.

DUPLE METER—A line of verse with two syllables to the metrical foot (most commonly iambic or trochaic), as opposed to **triple meter** with three syllables to the foot (as anapestic and dactylic meter).

DURATION or **quantity**—The time required to pronounce the syllables in a line of verse. Quantitative meter bases its measurement of the poetic line on length or shortness of syllables (the prevailing distinction in Latin scansion), as opposed to accentual meter, in which the measure is by stress or nonstress of syllables. In terms of duration, words like "fuse," "sleep," "reason," "pride," "food," "pale," and "thorough" take longer to speak than words with short vowels like "dig," "tap," "hit," "fret," "copper," and "nut."

ECLOGUE—A poem originally intended to represent the songs of shepherds. Vergil's *Eclogues* have served as models for poems following the pastoral tradition. Theocritus (only scraps of whose work remain) is credited with introducing such a style of verse to Rome. Terms related to pastorals are *bucolic* and **idyll**.

ELEGY—A poem memorializing someone dead, as Tennyson's *In Memoriam* or Auden's "In Memory of W. B. Yeats," representing two widely varying approaches. The term is also applied to poems merely retrospective of someone's death (rather than representing an immediate response), as Milton's "Lycidas," Arnold's "Thyrsis," or Allen Tate's "Ode to the Confederate Dead." Death, as such, has seldom inhibited the poet from using the elegy as a means of general religious or social comment.

ELEGAIC METER—A dactylic hexameter line followed by a dactylic pentameter (or hexameter) line.

ELISION—Generally, the omission of unstressed letters or syllables to make a line of verse metrically smooth, as Coleridge's " 'Twas not those souls that fled in pain," in which the presumed "it" is indicated by an apostrophe before the "t." **Syncope**, often associated with elision, and assumed to be the same, is the omission of letters (nearly always vowels) inside a word (as ev'ry" for "every"). By this distinction elision is the running together of words by leaving out either an initial or a final letter or syllable.

ELLIPSIS—The omission of words that are syntactically part of a construction but not considered essential to concise style ("the virtues we admire" instead of "that we admire"). Ellipsis has become one of the more distinctive aspects of modern poetry, and goes much further than omission of one or two words in a grammatical construction. In the poetical practice of Pound, Eliot, "H. D." (Hilda Doolittle), Jeffers, Cummings, Marianne Moore, Stevens, and William Carlos Williams, ellipsis was integral to the desired tightening up of poetic diction. Not only were connecting words freely dispensed with as redundant, sentences themselves were left to a reader's imagination as he leaped from image to image in a poem like Eliot's "Gerontion" or Stevens's "Thirteen Ways of Looking at a Blackbird." Thus in "Gerontion" an effect of stream of consciousness and broken discourse is suggested in the discontinuity of these sentences:

> Signs are taken for wonders. "We would see a sign!"
> The word within a word, unable to speak a word,
> Swaddled with darkness. In the juvenescence of
>   the year
> Came Christ the tiger
> In depraved May, dogwood and chestnut, flowering
>   Judas. . . .

END-STOPPED LINE—A line of verse in which a grammatical and/or logical pause occurs at the line-end, and is normally indicated by a period, colon, or semicolon. (Cf. **run-on line** or enjambment.)

ENJAMBMENT—See **run-on line**.

ENVOY—See **ballade**.

EPIC—A long poem, usually with folk origins, narrating adventures of a national, religious, or ethnic hero and celebrating the traditional qualities of courage, strength, and prowess in arms. This indigenous, folk, or national epic is usually based on distant history or myth. Homer's *Iliad* and the Babylonian epic *Gilgamesh* are examples. Modern or "literary" epics, while following heroic exploits within some organized succession of events, usually attempt a conscious imitation of the qualities of folk epic, while applying the more sophisticated sensibilities of the author's own times. Vergil's *Aeneid*— modeled on Homer's *Iliad* and *Odyssey* combined—is an example of a literary epic in ancient times. Dante's *La Commedia* and Milton's *Paradise Lost* are later examples, both developing religious themes to reflect the sensibilities of the Middle Ages and of the Renaissance. Certain devices associated with epic poems are the Homeric simile, the Homeric epithet, the kenning, and the narrative strategy known as *in medias res* ("in the middle of things"), by which the story is picked up well along in the chronology of events.

EPIGRAM—A short poem treating concisely, pointedly, and often satirically a single thought or event. The Roman poet Martial gave Europe the tradition of condensed wit, a quality good epigrams are meant to have. In modern times many are lured by the seeming simplicity of epigramatic verse. The Augustan poets of England were partial to epigram, as is evident from the number that Pope put into his rhymed couplets. Thus, in *An Essay on Man*:

> Know then thyself, presume not God to scan,
> The proper study of Mankind is Man.

EPIGRAPH—A quotation or motto placed at the head of a poem between title and the beginning of the text. A great many of T. S. Eliot's poems have one or more epigraphs as a means of adding perspectives to the poem. (See discussion in Chapter 8.)

EPODE—The third stanza of a Pindaric ode, derived from the recitation by the chorus of a Greek drama. (See **ode**.) Epodic form refers to the characteristic alternation of long and shorter lines, one of the few traits to survive in recent adaptations.

EQUIVALENCE—The prosodic convention (carried over from quantitative meter) that two short syllables equal one long. In accentual meter the principle of **compensation** sometimes serves the same function, approximating the equivalent of a missing stress by extra unstressed syllables. Equivalence might also be compared to **substitution** in accentual meter, said to be done when a poet uses an untypical foot in a line predominantly of a certain metrical foot (for example, a dactyl for an anapest, where the number of syllables remains the same, but the stressed syllable is in a different sequence; or a spondee for an anapest, where two nonstressed syllables are made up for by the replacement of one stressed syllable).

EUPHONY—The aural effect of pleasing or harmonious tones; the opposite of what is meant by **cacophony**.

EUPHUISM—Elaborate, highly contrived style, popularized by John Lyly in a prose romance of 1579 entitled *Euphues*. A Spanish poet, Luis de Gongora y Argote, developed a similar style of flowery **conceits** not long afterward, giving rise to the term Gongorism.

EXPECTANCY—In a pattern of verbal or sound recurrences in a poem, an expectancy of recurring sounds is set up for the ear and/or eye. (See Chapter 3.)

EXPLICATION—A term derived originally from the pedagogical method in France, *explication de texte*, by which interpretive analysis was concentrated on the poem itself rather than on such tangential matters as biography, historical background, and so forth. The "New Critics" of the 1940s and 1950s made explication their watchword in the critical analysis that they advocated.

EXPRESSIVE FALLACY—A term adopted by the "New Critics" in the 1940s and 1950s to counter the popular impressionistic criticism that advocated the free expression of an artist's emotions and was called "the expressive theory." Poetic feeling as raw emotion, the later critics contended, cannot take the place of accomplished art, that in which the emotions are harnessed and objectified.

EYE RHYME—See **near rhyme** (also known as *slant rhyme*).

FABLIAU—A short, usually humorous or bawdy tale, often in verse, flourishing during the 12th and 13th centuries. Chaucer made use of *fabliaux* as the core for several of his *Canterbury Tales*.

FALLING RHYTHM—The rhythmic effect (opposite of **rising rhythm**) in which the stress comes on the first syllable of a metrical foot. Trochees and dactyls have falling rhythm; iambs and anapests have rising rhythm.

FEMININE RHYME (sometimes *double rhyme*)—Rhyme involving two syllables, one stressed and one unstressed ("action—traction"), rather than one syllable, or **masculine rhyme** ("snow—slow"). See also **triple rhyme**. When there is an unstressed extra-metrical syllable at the end of a line, it is called a **weak** or **feminine ending** (in contrast to **masculine ending**), a commonplace in the line endings of Chaucer's poetry:

Whan that Aprille with his shoures soote
The drought of Marche hath perced to the roote. . . .

FIGURE OF SPEECH—An inclusive term for any kind of phraseology meant to give expressiveness to speech or enhance literary style. The poetic image, metaphor, rhetorical phrase, trope, and so forth, would fall under this heading. Figures of speech are associated with imaginative rather than expository writing.

FOOT—The unit of one or more syllables into which a line of verse is metrically divided. The commonest feet (iamb and trochee) form **duple meter**, while anapests and dactyls form **triple meter**. English metrical feet are scanned (see **scansion**) by putting an ictus (/) over the stressed syllable and a breve (˘) over the one or more unstressed syllables. Beside the four common feet mentioned above are the spondee (//), with two stressed syllables, and the pyrrhic foot (˘˘), with two unstressed syllables. Irregularities of predominant feet in a line of verse—that is, when a different type of foot is mixed in with the prevailing type of foot—are called **substitutions**. Unstressed syllables employed to make up a lack of stress are called **compensation**. Regular substitute feet are the **amphibrach**, the **amphimacer**, and the bacchius (**bacchic foot**).

FORM (or *type* of poem)—The fixed arrangement or pattern of the lines and stanzas of a poem: for example, sonnet, quatrain, rhyme royal, Spenserian stanza, and villanelle.

FOURTEENER—The English equivalent of Homer's and Vergil's quantitative hexameter line (the standard line in rendering epic poetry in the 16th and 17th centuries). Chapman translated the *Iliad* into fourteen-syllable lines, usually of seven iambic feet.

FREE VERSE—Any verse in which regular meter is replaced by the rhythms or cadence of speech. Its patterns may be made up of different line lengths, usually without regular stanzaic form. It may, or may not, use rhyme. Much ancient or oriental poetry is "free" insofar as a constraint such as meter is concerned, although other prosodic recurrences enter in (for example, the **parallelism** in Song of Solomon or Psalms). The modern revival of free verse owed its inspiration largely to the experiment in *vers libre* in France.

GEORGIAN POETRY—A term for the work of British poets writing mostly between 1912 and 1923 (during the reign of George V), and now sometimes considered synonymous with tameness and conventionality. While a proportion of it may have reflected the proprieties of the Georgian era, many admirable poems by such poets as Bridges, Yeats (the middle period), Masefield, Alfred Noyes, and De la Mare will doubtless remain in the canon.

GEORGIC—A poem describing farm life, named after the classic model of Vergil's *Georgics*, and probably invented by Hesiod in his *Works and Days*. A 19th century adaptation—at least of the farm setting—might be Whittier's *Snow Bound*, and in the 20th century, Mark Van Doren's *A Winter Calendar*.

GLOSS—A brief explanation (usually on the margin of a page, sometime between the lines) of textual matter, or definition or qualification of a difficult word or expression. Marginal glosses have been used in some poems in a quasi-explanatory way, as in Coleridge's *The Rime of the Ancient Mariner* or Archibald MacLeish's *The Hamlet of A. MacLeish*.

GONGORISM—See **euphuism**.

HAIKU—A traditional Japanese poem consisting of seventeen characters in a 5–7–5 arrangement (usually rendered into English in three lines, although not necessarily in seventeen words). The chief delight of a good *haiku* is the subtle association set off by the single sharp descriptive impression at the heart of the poem. The revival in England and America of **Imagism** seems to have taken much inspiration from the *haiku*, *tanka*, and other highly imagistic and condensed types of Japanese verse. (See example and discussion in Chapter 1.)

HARMONICS—A term sometimes used interchangeably with **prosody**, describing the simultaneous connection between sounds (as in the recurrences of rhyme, assonance, alliteration, phonemic color, pitch, and so forth). (See also **orchestration**.)

HEAD RHYME—See **alliteration**.

HEAD STRESS—Stresses on opening syllables of metrical feet, where a **falling rhythm** is expected. What Gerard Manley Hopkins called **sprung rhythm** is an adjunct of this effect.

HEMISTICH—The half-line of verse resulting when a full line is divided by a **caesura**. Tennyson's "Battle of Brunnanburh" seems to have been modeled after the Anglo-Saxon original, each hemistich in this case represented as a separate line:

> Athelstan King | Lord among Earls,
> Bracelet bestower and | Baron of Barons. . . .

HEPTAMETER—A seven-foot line; sometimes also called a **septenary** line, from Latin models. Its commonest example in English goes under the name **fourteener**.

HEROIC COUPLET—A rhymed couplet of iambic pentameter, used as early as Chaucer's time, but popularized chiefly by Dryden, Pope, and various verse dramatists of the early 18th century.

HEXAMETER—A six-foot line. The classical hexameter of Homer and Vergil was based on **quantitative meter**. English hexameter is accentual, based on the number of stresses of a line.

HOMERIC EPITHET—A set descriptive phrase used to round out a line in the oral minstrelsy of Homer's time. Epithets were often repetitions of interchangeable tags, such as "resourceful Odysseus," "wrath-bearing Achilles," or "tall-browed Athena."

HOMERIC SIMILE—See **simile**.

HOVERING ACCENT (or *distributed stress*)—An ambivalence in the stress of a syllable between what it takes metrically and what it would be given lexically (that is, in normal speech). In the line from Coleridge's *Christabel*,

> The night | is chil | ly, but | not dark,

it is possible to think of "but" as stressed, to conform to what would seem to be the iambic meter; yet it is *not* stressed in the inflection of ordinary speech. It is thus probable that Coleridge intended "but" and the preceding syllable "-ly" as a pyrrhic foot as a substitution in a predominantly iambic line. The symbol in scansion for a hovering accent is (⌢).

HYPERBOLE—An overstatement for rhetorical effect or emphasis. In commonest terms it is any kind of exaggerated speech. Direct hyperbole is exemplified in many biblical passages, as

[then] all the fountains of the great deep [were]
broken up, and the windows of heaven were opened.

As a poetic image, hyperbole often functions as ironic reversal of what is commonly assumed (see **understatement**). Thus Andrew Marvell comments ironically by intentional negation of what is thought of death and interment:

The grave's a fine and private place,
But none, I think, do there embrace.

HYPERCATALEXIS (or hypercatalectic line)—See **catalexis**.

IAMB(US, IC)—The most common metrical foot in English poetry, consisting of an unstressed and a stressed syllable (˘/). See **foot**.

ICTUS (sometimes confused with **thesis**, a term from quantitative metrics)—The name for the stress (/) in poetic scansion. (*Cf.* **breve**, the mark for the unstressed syllable in poetic scansion.)

IDENTICAL RHYME—The same word used again as a rhyme. (*Cf. rich rhyme.*)

IDYLL—A simple descriptive piece (either in poetry or in prose) that deals with rustic or country life, its pastoral scenes suggesting peace and contentment. (*Cf.* **pastoral**.)

IMAGE–A **figure of speech** that expresses imaginatively the likeness or differences of things observed. In poetry images take various forms, for example, **simile, metaphor, metonymy**. While these and various other images imply comparison between the factual and the imagined, there are images that tend to relate opposites, to *connect* by a kind of reversal of common similarity; see, for example, **hyperbole, pun,** and **oxymoron.** (See Chapter 5.)

IMAGISM—That tendency in poetry to let images express the descriptive matter, or even to stand for certain ideas themselves. As part of the revolution in poetic techniques of the late 19th century—especially as represented by the French Symbolists—images were more and more substituted for overt description and logical explanation. The result of this tendency was an increasing verbal and syntactical ellipsis in the poems of such later experimenters (who by 1912 called themselves Imagists) as Ezra Pound, Hilda Doolittle, Amy Lowell, Richard Aldington, and John Gould Fletcher.

Others whose poetry in this period showed the imagistic style were T. S. Eliot, Carl Sandburg, and William Carlos Williams.

IMITATION—Aristotle's **mimesis** (from the *Poetics*) or poetic reproduction of life, which he said was the prime purpose of dramatic poetry. Although aesthetic viewpoints in modern times tend to reject the *imitative* aspect of this principle, Aristotle's analysis of the general function of the poetic arts remains critically sound. (See Chapter 5.)

INCANTATION—The use of spells or verbal charms to exert influence over a person. In poetry, incantatory qualities have been a basic aspect of the prosody of lyric poets such as Swinburne, Hopkins, Masefield, the early Yeats, Eliot, and Thomas, all of whom used verbal and rhythmic control to exert a hypnotic effect on the reader.

INCREMENTAL REPETITION—The successive repetition—with slight variation each time—of lines or phrases throughout a poem. In the English ballad "Edward" there is incremental repetition in the wording of the first line of the poem— "Why dois your brand sae drap wi bluid, Edward, Edward" —which, somewhat varied, becomes the beginning line of each succeeding stanza. Thus the second stanza opens, "Your haukis bluid was nevir sae red, Edward, Edward," and so on through each first line of five more stanzas.

INDIRECTION—A general term used in this text to designate poetic implication rather than direct statement or explanation. (See **connotation**.)

INFLECTION—The variations in pitch, tone, and timing of one's words in the reading of a poem.

INNER EAR—An expression sometimes used to signify the imagined sound one must achieve in silent reading.

INTENTIONAL MEANING—What the writer is said to have *intended* as he wrote; the avowed purpose with which a poet sets about composing his poem. This avowed intention, it appears, does not necessarily coincide with the unconscious or compulsive direction of a poet's creative impulses. This latter is the view of several recent critics, including that of William Wimsatt, Jr., in his essay "The Intentional Fallacy," which scouts the degree to which critics may safely invoke the poet's intention as a criterion for judging results.

INTERLOCKING RHYME—Rhyme scheme in which the rhymes alternate or occur intermittently (a b a b or a b b a or a b a c b and so forth) rather than in couplets (a a b b, and so forth). The Italian sonnet best illustrates interlocking rhyme, while the **terza rima** used in Dante's La Commedia has a progressive interlocking scheme highly demanding on the availability of rhymes (a b a, b c b, c d c, and so forth).

INTERNAL RHYME—Words rhymed within a line or, as in the example below, within successive lines:

> Suppose by poison or by *water*, kill a queen;
> her *daughter* sits upon the stair.

A highly regularized succession of internal rhymes completing each **hemistich** of lines with a **caesura** is called a **leonine rhyme**. (Cf. also **alliteration** (head rhyme) and *initial rhyme*, the rhyming of the first word of a line with succeeding first words of other lines.)

INVERSION—Deliberate inversion of the normal or logical word order of verse (for example, "Down came the rain" or "Goest thou"—the last being also an **archaism**). See **anastrophe**, a rarer term, but as far as can be determined, the same thing.

IRONY—A reversal of the normal or expected course of things, or an incongruity in what has been purported to be congruous. In certain types of imagery, irony results from the juxtaposition of opposites, as in the paradox of the **oxymoron** "He is killed by thy blind indulgence." Again, irony results from **litotes** or **understatement**, as in

> The grave's a fine and quiet place,
> But none, I think, do there embrace.

ITALIAN SONNET—See **Petrarchan sonnet**.

KENNING—A pairing of words (usually in hyphenate form) to form a metaphor. Kennings originated in ancient epic literature (as in Homer's "Shining-faced Apollo" or "Sea-riding Poseidon") and attained great favor in Anglo-Saxon poetry (as in "wine-joyous hall," "bold-in-battle Scylding," or "craft-begotten evil" from Beowulf).

LAMPOON—A personal satire in written form. Originally applied to the short abusive poems popular in the Rome of Catullus, or in the **vers de société** of succeeding ages.

246

LEONINE RHYME—A regularized form of **internal rhyme** at the end of each **hemistich** of a metrical line divided by a **caesura**. In the lines below from W. S. Gilbert, there is a rhyme terminating each hemistich, with the extra space indicating the caesura:

> When you're lying awake   with a dismal headache,
>   and repose is taboo'd by anx*iety,*
> I conceive you may use   any language you choose
>   to indulge in without impropri*ety.*

LEVEL STRESS (or *even accent*)—This occurs when the accent falls with equal emphasis on both syllables of a two-syllable word ("heartfelt," "forthright," "mankind") or when two succeeding monosyllables are taken as a unit ("cub scout," "first class," "sing-song"). (*Cf.* **hovering accent,** *distributed stress.*)

LIMERICK—A short poem, usually in anapestic meter, rhyming *a a b b a*, with the first, second, and fifth lines in trimeter, and the third and fourth in dimeter:

> There was an old man from Legrange
> Whose habits were thought to be strange;
>   He went out every night
>   In a terrible fright
> Just because he had need of the change.

This form, having lent itself to wide (and sometimes unskilled) exploitation, is easily converted into **doggerel.**

LITERARY BALLAD—A form of narrative verse marked by strong rhythm and usually given a refrain, and modeled after folk or popular balladry. Cowper's "John Gilpin's Ride" is a humorous example, while John Keats' "La Belle Dame Sans Merci" would be a rather subjective one. Coleridge's *The Rime of the Ancient Mariner* is probably the best known example in poetry.

LITOTES—See **understatement.**

LOGICAL STRESS—See **rhetorical stress.**

LYRIC POETRY—Verse of fairly concentrated musical quality, of generally traditional prosody (that is, with various aural and verbal recurrences), and usually of limited length (although Shelley's rather long poem, "Ode to the West Wind," or Wordsworth's equally lengthy "Ode: Intimations of Immortality" are lyrics). The name originated from ancient Greece where it came to be associated with verses sung to the accompaniment of the lyre.

MACRON—In quantitative scansion, a short bar (‒) over the long syllable. In Latin verse the macron equalled two **mora**, indicated by the same sign (ᵕ) as that for the **breve** which, in turn, indicated an unstressed syllable in accentual metrical scansion.

MASCULINE ENDING (or *strong ending*)—When the final syllable in a line of verse gets the stress.

> To bring down on us the judgment of *God.*

An unstressed syllable at the end of a line is called **feminine ending** or **weak ending**. (See **feminine rhyme** for example.)

MASCULINE RHYME—Rhyme that falls on the stressed and concluding syllables (see **masculine ending**) of two successive lines. In **feminine rhyme** the rhyme includes both penult and ultimate syllables, of which the ultimate is unstressed (for example, "eager—beaver").

MEIOSIS—(also **litotes**)—See **understatement**.

METAPHOR—A type of **image** that connects two different things in an imagined likeness: "The Lion of Judah," "My vegetable Love," "the wine-dark sea." When the metaphor is continued as a key to more than one image, it is sometimes called an "extended metaphor," sometimes a "symbol," as in Blake's lines:

> O rose, thou art sick!
> The invisible worm
> That flies in the night,
> In the howling storm,
>
> Has found out thy bed
> Of crimson joy:
> And his dark secret love
> Does thy life destroy.

A metaphor is distinguished from the type of image known as **simile** in which the connection between two different things is made by a grammatical comparison with the preposition "like" or "as."

METER—The division of poetical lines into feet, which are determined by a regular sequence of stresses (accentual meter). While most English verse is in accentual meter, occasional examples occur of quantitative meter, a classical measure in which the feet are determined by the **quantity** or length of each syllable, a device suitable to the pronunciation of ancient Greek, and, to a lesser extent, Latin, which borrowed the system from the Greeks.

Accentual meters range from dimeter (two feet) through trimeter, tetrameter (or quatrameter), pentameter, hexameter, and (rarely) heptameter (in English, "fourteeners"). See **foot** for the kinds of metrical feet.

METRICAL MUTATION—A term sometimes used (as in this text) for the variations within an otherwise regular metrical line of verse. In Frost's line from "Mowing,"

> There was never a sound beside the wood but one

there are two anapestic feet at the head of an otherwise iambic pentameter line. Such shifts may signal the poet's intentional change of pace; they may, on the other hand, be simple mutations resulting from the natural cadence of speech that persists into the formalism of metric.

More traditionally, the prosodic term for a variation from the prevailing metric is **substitution**, in which the poet presumably inserts a different foot by plan. Other mutations of metric are **anacrusis, catalexis, equivalence, compensation,** *distributed stress,* and **truncation.**

METONYMY—A particularized kind of metaphor in which one part becomes emblematic of the larger or more general entity for which it stands: "How many *moons* since she went away?" "The *Crown* must answer to the people," or "this year's champion of the turf." Metonymy enters to some extent into a consideration of the **symbol.**

MOCK EPIC (or *mock-heroic*)—An epical style applied to trivial or unheroic subjects. Pope's *The Rape of the Lock* is a mock epic, the style of which reflects the use of *invocation,* **apostrophe, Homeric simile, Homeric epithet,** *supernatural interference,* and other devices of the traditional epic.

MORA—The sign for short duration (ᵕ) in quantitative metrical scansion. (*Cf.* **breve**, which is the same sign for an unaccented syllable in accentual meter.) In Latin verse, two morae equally a **macron**, indicated as (_).

MUSE—The goddess believed by the ancient Greeks to preside over any of the nine arts and sciences. Of the nine, Erato was the muse of lyric and love poetry; Calliope, that of heroic or epic poetry. Poets in modern times still refer to their "muse," meaning figuratively the special source of their inspiration, or the "One" for whom they write.

NEAR RHYME (or *slant rhyme, half rhyme, approximate rhyme, oblique rhyme, imperfect rhyme*)—An inexact rhyming of words, the sound and, often, the appearance of which suggest but do not duplicate each other. Such approaches to actual resemblance of sounds is usually intended to create subtler aural and verbal recurrences than the unmistakable repetition of regular rhyme. Such a poet as Emily Dickinson offers numerous examples in her poems, such as "up—step," "peer—pare," "while—Hill," and "Star—door" from her piece "I Like to See It Lap the Miles." Later poets like Cummings, Williams, and Marianne Moore have often preferred the piquancy of near rhymes to more clear-cut prosody.

NEOCLASSICAL—A term designating a period in literature and art in which an attempt was made to revive or reproduce many of the values of Greece and Rome. The Augustan age of the 18th century in England saw not only literature, but art and architecture as well, modeled on that of the ancients. Since many of the adopted rules and principles were highly restrictive, the writers of a more romantic imagination who followed later were often in revolt against Neoclassicism.

NEW CRITICISM—A body of criticism advocated by poets and writers in the 1940s and 1950s, the chief thrust of which was greater analysis of the poetical text as a balance to the excessive historical emphasis dominant in much scholarly work. (See Chapter 8.)

NUMBERS—A word, somewhat archaic today, for metric or **prosody**.

OBJECTIVE CORRELATIVE—A phrase (originated by T. S. Eliot in the essay "Hamlet and his Problems") to describe the poetic process that converts primary emotion or attitudes into a more universally realizable action or representation. In his dramatic monologues, Browning seems to have anticipated Eliot in this intent by projecting any feelings he, the poet, may have had into the self-revealed discourse of his characters. Eliot's Prufrock (in "The Love Song of J. Alfred Prufrock") may similarly be thought to act out confessionally his dilemma of personality, rather than the poet describing those feelings in his own voice directly.

OCTAVE (or *octet*)—A poem, or stanza of a poem, of eight lines, as in the **ottava rima**. The eight-line section usually set off as the opening division of a **Petrarchan sonnet** is known as the octave; the concluding six-line division is the **sestet**.

OCTOSYLLABIC—A line of verse containing eight syllables.

ODE—A poem of several sections, probably invented by the ancient Greek poet Pindar and adapted to the chanting recitation of choruses in Greek drama. It consists chiefly of three stanzas of varying length (sometimes twenty or thirty lines), known as the **strophe, antistrophe**, and **epode**. (Upon its entrance to the orchestra, a chorus came to a *stassimon*—stand—then, forming two opposing groups, recited in turn the strophe, or turn, and antistrophe, or counterturn, as they faced one another. Then they came together as one group again and recited the epode, or third part of the ode.)

In modern adaptations (as in Wordsworth's "Ode: Intimations of Immortality"), the three stanzas make up a section, and several sections make up an extended ode. This would be roughly the equivalent of putting several odes from one play into a continuous poem. Normally the choral ode followed each scene—*episodos*—of the drama.

ONOMATOPOEIA—The imitation by a word or arrangement of words of physical sound, as in "buzz," "crack," "*dunder and blitzen*," "rip," and "cock-a-doodle-doo." (*Cf.* **orchestration**.)

OPEN-END—A term sometimes used to describe certain **allusions** and **symbols** and their function, as opposed to those types of allusion or symbol completed (or closed) by the accompanying referent. (See discussion in Chapter 5.)

ORCHESTRATION—See also **harmonics**. A prosodic term of fairly recent origin to indicate the kinds of sound qualities that influence the aural effect of a poem. Rene Wellek and Austin Warren (*Theory of Literature,* 148–49) analyze three aspects of this phenomenon (based largely on the work of

251

recent Russian scholars): (1) sound-patterns, (2) descriptive representation of sound or its associated sound qualities, and (3) actual sound imitation, presumably that which is traditionally known as **onomatopoeia**. (See Chapter 4.)

ORGANIC POETRY—Poetry developing in a manner analogous to a living plant or animal. The organic nature of poetry has been contrasted by Cleanth Brooks and Robert Penn Warren (*Understanding Poetry*) with the mechanical aspects (meter, rhyme, figurative language, and so forth), which they consider often overemphasized in the teaching of poetry. Rather, they say, the relationship among the elements is the essence of a poem's viability. They cite Yeats's distinction between the evocation of emotion in Burns's lines

> The white moon is setting behind the white wave,
> And Time is setting with me, O!

and the altered effect they would have if the "O!" were moved back in the line to read

> The white moon is setting behind the white wave,
> And Time, O! is setting with me.

Yeats's preference for the former wording is based not on any mechanical or purely logical superiority it might have, but on the organic relationship that the "O!" produces on the parts of the poem. (See pp. 18–19.)

OTTAVA RIMA—An eight-line stanza in iambic pentameter, rhyming *a b a b a b c c*; used first in Italy by Ariosto and Tasso. It became a favorite with English poets after its introduction in the early 16th century by Wyatt and Surrey. Byron's *Don Juan* and Yeats's "Sailing to Byzantium" and "Among School Children" are written in *ottava rima*.

OXYMORON—An image in which a seeming contradiction or **paradox** is expressed in sententious or epigrammatic form: "Parting is such *sweet sorrow*," "her *killing kindness*," "free servitude," or "method in his madness."

PARADIGM—A term sometimes applied to literary questions, borrowed from grammatical usage, namely, the changes which words undergo as they are inflected. Thus a poem may come to represent wider and wider meanings as one expands on the interpretations.

PARADOX—A tenet contrary to the general opinion or to common sense. As a rhetorical device, paradox usually generates irony from the seeming contradictions of truth. It has been widely used as an imagistic device. Donne's "Song" is constructed on the ironical overtones resulting from a series of paradoxes, or "impossibles":

> Go and catch a falling star,
>   Get with child a mandrake root,
> Tell me where all past years are,
>   Or who cleft the Devil's foot;
> Teach me to hear mermaids singing,
> Or to keep off envy's stinging,
>   And find
>   What wind
> Serves to advance an honest mind.

Paradox is classified in this text among those images that *oppose*, in distinction from those that *connect* (Chapter 5).

PARALLELISM—A form of poetic structure involving syntactical repetition, found extensively in ancient Hebrew verse and American Indian songs, and a habitual device with Walt Whitman. Parallelism occurs chiefly in the recurrences of sentence structure—as in the opening word or phrases of successive lines of a poem—as opposed to the terminal recurrences characteristic of English prosody dependent on end rhyme. The poetry of Ecclesiastes, Song of Solomon, parts of Job, and the Psalms yield examples, as in this translation from Ecclesiastes:

> A time to be born, and a time to die;
> a time to plant, and a time to pluck up
>   that which is planted;
> a time to kill, and a time to heal,
> a time to break down, and a time to build up.

PARODY—An imitation of an author's form and style, intended to disparage or mock the original. Judging from a number of anthologies of parodic verse, there is a considerable demand for this form of entertainment—especially if it makes fun of the more prestigious writers who may have developed fairly solemn or mannered styles.

PASTORAL—A type of poetry idealizing country life and the company of shepherds. (Cf. **idyll**.) Although there is no set form for pastoral poetry, it has acquired traditional characteristics based on originating models such as those of Theocritus and Vergil.

PATHETIC FALLACY—John Ruskin's critical rejection of the romantic tendency of authors to extend their own feelings to aspects of nature; to pretend in a descriptive passage that nature or the elements weep or laugh with them. The 20th century seems to have formulated its own psychological term "empathy" to take care of the poet's tendency to identify with people and objects.

PENTAMETER—A five-foot line of verse. In accentual meter, the line will have five stresses to a normal total of ten syllables.

PENULT(IMATE)—The next-to-last word (or syllable) in a line of verse or a sentence, in which the ultimate would be the last. An **antepenult** is the word or syllable before the penult.

PERSONA—The mask or "voice" chosen by a writer through which to express himself (the term derived from Karl Jung's archetypal figure, as explained in *Modern Man in Search of a Soul*). *Persona* is interchangeable with the traditional term of **speaker** as the surrogate or stand-in for the **auctorial voice**.

PERSONIFICATION—The process of giving human attributes to nonhuman creatures, inanimate things, or abstractions. Many poetic images start from a degree of personification—**metaphor, simile, apostrophe, allusion, metonymy,** and so forth. The successive metaphor and metonymy in the lines below involve personification:

> The lamppost
> hung its head
> it had no tongue. . . .

PETRARCHAN SONNET (or *Italian sonnet*)—A fourteen-line poem in iambic pentameter with rhymes *a b b a a b b a* (the **octave**) and *c d e c d e* (the **sestet**). There are frequently variations in the order of rhymes in the sestet, although there are always three rhymes. (Cf. **Shakespearean sonnet** or *English sonnet*.)

PHONEME—A term important in structural linguistics, usually referring to the smallest unit of sound in the spelling and pronunciation of words by which distinctions of meaning can be discerned (as in the distinction of "p" sounds in "rapid pup," differentiating the phrase from "rabid pup"). For purposes of phonetic analysis in the **orchestration** of sounds in a poem, phonemes are a main source of the **phonetic color** and affect our aural grasp of the poem.

PHONETIC COLOR (or *phonetic intensive* or *color sounds*)— The orthographic qualities of a word (especially the relation of **phonemes**) that contribute to aural or acoustic variety and richness in poetry. The orthographic qualities combine with etymological and semantical associations in the hands of a skilled poet, who attempts to **orchestrate** these varying linguistic aspects with other prosodic qualities and the overall meaning of the poem. Phonetic color, or color sound, occurs in such words as "swish," "gurgle," "slop," "cuckoo," "crash," and "ding-dong," which actually express the physical sound signified in the word (designated in the traditional term **onomatopoeia**); it also occurs in words that merely suggest or describe what the word betokens, as "murmur," "glide," "whisper," "rub," "dangle," and "rush."

PHONETIC SYMBOLISM—The thesis that speech sounds afford semantical relationships beyond those of an onomatopoeic sort. Thus, the sound and meaning of words like "weary," "water," "doom," "tomb," "blood," and "ocean" may derive their associations in a speaker's mind from some early genesis in the language. Attempts by linguistic scholars are now being made to show that words were often symbols for human experience or state of mind.

PITCH—The vertical range of sound (as opposed to the level range in **duration** or **quantity**) as the human voice moves up and down the scale in reading the words of a poem.

POETIC DICTION—In general, the stylistic qualities by which poetry differs from prose: increased imagery, orchestration of word sounds, inversion of syntax, ellipsis, and various other devices designed to intensify the speech. Since the more recent tendency to a freer style of verse (reflecting more of the rhythms of ordinary speech), the attribution of poetic diction often carries an imputation of the archaic or stilted.

POETIC LICENSE—Liberties traditionally allowed a poet in syntax, rhyme, ellipsis, spelling, and diction in general for the furtherance of prosody or other factors important to the poet.

POLYPHONIC PROSE—Poetry set down in the form of prose, but retaining the rhythms and less obvious prosodic devices of a poem. In the late 19th century, Oscar Wilde and Walter Pater made varying efforts to bring poetry and prose together, as in Wilde's *Prose Poems*; but the name *polyphonic prose* seems to have been given these efforts by John Gould Fletcher. Experimental blends of poetry and prose were made throughout the second decade of this century by both Fletcher and Amy Lowell. The *rapprochement* of poety and proᴆe has existed for centuries, but recent examples seem more in keeping with the general liberalizing of prosody, as in **free verse**. Thomas Wolfe wrote novels in poetic style in the 1930s; James Dickey has written poems in prose style in the 1960s. It is a two-way street.

PROSODY—See also **metrics**. The governing conditions and controlling attributes of poetry, especially the technical aspects of its sounds and meter. The analysis of these factors of a poem is the study of prosody. (*Cf.* **scansion**.)

PROSODIC SYMBOLS (or **scanson** marks)—The sign (ʹ) or **ictus**, and (˘) or **breve**, indicating respectively the stress and the nonstress on the syllables in accentual meter that make up a metrical foot. In *quantitative meter*, the (‒) or **macron**, and the (˘) or **mora** or **breve**, respectively indicate the long and the short syllables in a quantitative foot. The terms *thesis* and *arsis* are also used in designating upbeat and downbeat, but their correspondence to regular stress and nonstress, or to long and short quantity, is not clear, and the explanation in terms of classical meter is somewhat involved.

PUN (or *paranomasis*)—A play on the double meaning of certain words, or the approximate or similar sound of two words whose meanings are different. As a poetic image, the pun has extensive use and is a recurrent source of irony. It may function as two words pronounced the same but with different meaning, as in Donne's line from "A Hymn to God the Father"—"When thou hast done, thou has not done"—the word "done" punning with John Donne's name (pronounced the same); or it may be a word used knowingly (for which there is an intended, though not always respectable, counterpart meaning, as in **double entendre**) as in the use of the word "parts" in Henry Reed's poem, "Naming of Parts." See discussion, 107–8.

PURE POETRY—Poetry that concentrates on prosody, imagery, and other technical aspects more or less to the exclusion of moral or message; a poem read more for its *means* than its *meaning*. Certain of Shakespeare's, Blake's, and Tennyson's "songs" seemed executed more to delight the reader as "pure" poetry than to be **didactic**. Pure poetry probably came into its own with the French Symbolists, the art-for-art's-sake movement in England, the simplistic extremities of Mallarmé, and the French poets who practice what they call *lettrisme*. A certain amount of pure poetry seems to have been intended by such members of the Southern agrarian circle as John Crowe Ransom and Randall Jarrell, as well as the accomplished independent, Elizabeth Bishop.

PYRRHIC FOOT (or **dibrach**)—A metrical foot of two unstressed syllables (◡ ◡). (*Cf.* **tribach**.)

QUANTITY (or **duration**)—Quantitative meter (the normal metrical basis of Greek and Roman poetry) is determined by the length or the brevity of the syllable, rather than by the repetition of stresses within a line of verse (as in accentual meter, characteristic of most English poetry). (See **meter**.) Since words in any language vary as to duration (that is, the time required to pronounce the syllables), quantity influences to some extent the rhythms and meter of any poetry. (See Chapter 3, discussion of Wordsworth's poem.)

QUATRAIN—A stanza of four lines, its uses varying with the meter and rhyme scheme employed. It is commonly used in the ballad and in church hymns (where it is called "hymnal stanza").

RECURRENCE—The principle underlying much of poetical prosody, as in the recurrence of stresses to form meter, the repetition of similar sounds to form rhyme, assonance, alliteration, and so forth, or the patterns of recurrent tones, phonetic sounds, pitch, and syllabic quantity. (See Chapter 3.)

REFRAIN—The repetition of a line or several lines at regular intervals in a poem or song (usually at the end of a stanza). It should be distinguished from **repetend** or **anaphora**, which repeat words or phrases anywhere in a line, and

parallelism (a form of repetend), where the beginning of a succession of lines is repeated, as in Tichborne's "Elegy":

> My prime of youth is but a frost of cares,
> My feast of joy is but a dish of pain,
> My crop of corn is but a field of tares....

REPETEND—A repeated element in a poem, varying from isolated words to groups of words or portions of whole lines. It differs from **refrain** in not appearing as a complete line or lines at the end of a stanza. The repetitions of syntactical **parallelism** are a form of repetend.

RESONANCE—(1) The *sonority* resulting from the depth or richness of **phonetic color** and the poet's **orchestration** of these qualities, as with such words as "alone," "doom," "forever," "flying, flying, flying," "wheeling," "murmur," "the seas incarnadine," and so forth.

(2) The quality deriving from the "tension between ... two images: one of them ... objective; the other, subjective" (Anne Stevenson, *Elizabeth Bishop*, p. 86). This resonance would be set up by the competing associations that the contrasting images create in a reader's mind. The relation between the images, thus, might be compared to that between the connotation and denotation of two or more successive words.

RHETORIC—The phraseology or verbal devices intended to enhance the eloquence or stylistic variety of writing and speech. Many of our commonest kinds of **image** and **figure of speech** serve the purposes of the rhetorician, although their choice may be based more on the commonplace than on originality. Because of the overuse of some of these, or their elaborateness, rhetoric (like **poetic diction**) tends to have pejorative associations for many people.

RHETORICAL STRESS (or *logical stress*)—Stress in a line of verse that tends to conform to the speaking inflections (see pp. 43–45), which may be in conflict with the metrical stress. Thus **free verse** is based on the cadence of speech rather than on metrics or syllabic regularity.

RHYME—The recurrence of similar sounds at various intervals of a poem, usually at the end of a line (terminal rhyme). The most common forms of terminal rhyme are couplets (*a a b b*), interlocking rhyme (*a b a b* or *a b c a b c*), and bracket rhyme (*a b b a*) (see pp. 73–75).

Identical rhyme, or the matching of the same words, occurs usually only at the beginning of lines and is more commonly known as **parallelism**, or in some cases **repetend**. **Beginning rhyme** (cf. **head rhyme**) occurs when only the initial syllable of one line rhymes with the initial syllable of a succeeding or later line. **Rich rhyme**, another category of identical rhyme, occurs when the rhymes are identical in sound but not in meaning (as in the homonyms "lone—loan," "fare—fair," and "led—lead").

Internal rhyme is formed by duplication of terminal rhymes at intervals within a line. (**Assonance** is a repetition of corresponding vowel sounds within the words of a line.) **Leonine rhyme** is an internal rhyme made between the terminal words of each **hemistich**, the half lines formed by a **caesura**.

Rhymes may be on a final syllable alone (**masculine rhyme**), or they may be on two final syllables, the first stressed, the second unstressed (**feminine** or **double rhyme**), or in rare instances, they may be on three syllables (**triple rhyme**). A masculine rhyme is sometimes called a *strong rhyme* or a *strong ending*; a feminine rhyme, a *weak rhyme* or a **weak ending** (also *feminine ending*).

Near rhyme (also called *slant rhyme, approximate rhyme, half rhyme, oblique rhyme,* and *imperfect rhyme*), is the suggested matching, rather than actual duplication, of corresponding syllables between words. **Eye rhymes** and *historical rhymes* match in orthography but not in sound ("wind—find," "prove—love").

Other special kinds of rhyme are *apocapated rhyme, broken rhyme,* and *analyzed rhyme.*

RHYME RICH (or *rich rhyme*)—A form of identical rhyme (in which actual homonyms supply the rhyme) that has its identity in the sound and not in the spelling ("lone—loan," "fare—fair," "bad—bade," led—lead").

RHYME ROYAL—A stanza of seven lines (**septet**) of iambic pentameter, rhyming *a b a b b c c*. An outstanding example of rhyme royal is Chaucer's *Troilus and Criseyde*, which gives the form its alternate name, **Chaucerian stanza**. The injection of the word "royal" probably occurred because James I tried his hand at verses in Chaucerian stanza.

RHYME SCHEME—The pattern of rhymes terminating the lines of a stanza of poetry.

RHYTHM (in poetry)—The natural recurrences, roughly corresponding to the phraseolgy fitting a breath span, in reading or formal speech; the cadence basic to language as spoken. Rhythm appears in conjunction with meter, but meter is regularized while rhythm may exist independently of it. Free verse, as distinguished from metrical verse, conforms to this natural **cadence** rather than to a set number of stresses and feet.

RISING RHYTHM—The rhythmic effect when the stress comes on the last syllable of a metrical foot. Iambic and anapestic feet are the commonest with rising rhythm. (*Cf.* **falling rhythm.**)

RONDEAU—A French form of thirteen lines that makes use of only two rhymes throughout, with an end-refrain taken from part of the opening line. (See similar forms such as **rondel, roundel,** and **rondelet,** mostly varieties of the **roundelay.**)

RONDEL and ROUNDEL—A form of **roundelay** that, like the others, originated in late 14th-century France, and is similar to the **rondeau.** It has thirteen (sometimes fourteen) lines with only two rhymes. The first two lines make the refrain, reappearing as the rhyme in the seventh and eighth lines. The poem closes with one (sometimes both) of these rhymes. An example is Arthur Symon's "A Roundel of Rest."

RONDELET—Unlike the **rondeau, rondel,** and **roundel,** this late 14th-century French form has usually one five-line stanza and two rhymes. The first part of the opening line appears as a refrain after the second and fifth lines. The rhyme scheme might be indicated as *a b R a b b R.*

ROUND—A song, or words to a song, meant to be sung by several voices, in which one voice begins, and as it completes the first line, a second voice begins the first line, and so on with other voices until the last voice reaches and sings the final line of the stanza. Thus, if there are four lines to the stanza and four singers, each will be singing a different line at the same time, the music permitting a sort of counterpoint throughout. A familiar example of a round is the one beginning:

> Row, row, row your boat
> Gently down the stream . . .

ROUNDELAY—A short poem of sophisticated prosody, of early Renaissance origin, and including such special types as **rondeau, rondel, roundel, rondelet**, and (with more recent modifications) **villanelle**.

RUN-ON-LINE (or *enjambment*: from the French "to straddle")— A line of verse that has no grammatical pause (and consequently no punctuation) at the end of the line and thus continues without interruption into the next line. Its opposite is the **end-stopped line**, which has a grammatical pause (hence punctuation) at the end. Enjambment was popular with Hopkins, as illustrated in this excerpt from "The Windhover":

> Because the Holy Ghost over the bent
> World broods with warm breast and
> with ah! bright wings.

SATIRE—Any literary work aimed at exposing by caricature certain aspects of persons or society and its institutions. Satirical poems traditionally compound ridicule and criticism by witty manipulation of the more obvious aspects of prosody, as in easily recognizable meters and rhymed couplets. Since the time of Aristophanes, Catullus, and Juvenal, some of the best known verse satirists lived in or close to the 18th century, such as Dryden, Pope, Swift, and Byron.

SCANSION—The analytical reading of verse, indicating within the line the kinds of metrical feet. Scansion employs certain diacritical symbols: the **ictus** (⁄) to indicate a stressed syllable, the **breve** (◡) to indicate an unstressed syllable. Classical prosody also used the terms *thesis* and *arsis* for downbeat and upbeat, but these are not quite accurately applied to the scansion of accentual meter. In **quantitative meter** the **macron** (–) marks the long syllable, the **mora** (also **breve** (◡) marks the short syllable.

A metrical foot in either accentual or quantitative meter is indicated by a **virgule** in vertical position (|). A **caesura** is indicated by a double virgule (||). A **hovering accent** (or *distributed stress*) is generally indicated by a flattened inverted ∨ above the syllable in question (⌢).

SENSIBILITY—A word usually referring to the degree of awareness of his art by a poet; also to that degree to which the reader captures qualities of the poet's art. Historically there are said to be shifts in this mutual responsiveness, bringing about an alienation between public and poet, as in the latter half of the 19th century in France. (See **dissociation of sensibility.**)

SEPTENARY—See **heptameter.**

SEPTET—A stanza of seven lines, as in **rhyme royal.**

SESTET (sometimes *sextet*)—A stanza of six lines, as in the concluding six-line portion of a **Petrarchan sonnet.**

SHAKESPEAREAN SONNET (or *English sonnet*)—A fourteen-line poem in iambic pentameter, with the rhymes *a b a b c d c d* (the **octave**) and *e f e f g g* (the **sestet**); also considered as three **quatrains** and a **couplet.** Wyatt and Surrey introduced the Petrarchan sonnet in the early 16th century, and its adaptation to the English form may be explained from the fact that it required fewer rhymes on one sound than the Italian original (rhymes being harder to come by in English than in Italian). (See **Petrarchan sonnet.**)

SHAPED FORM (or *carmen figuratum*)—See **visual poetry.**

SIMILE—A brief grammatical comparison as a literary image ("How like a serpent doth envy sting"). Simile is distinguished from the implied comparison of **metaphor** by the grammatical structure, requiring the preposition "like" or "as." The Homeric simile (or epic simile), a regular descriptive device in *The Iliad* and *The Odyssey*, sometimes runs to fifteen or twenty lines, with an extended protasis or thesis beginning somewhat as follows,

> As the invading lion stands watch over his kill . . .

and amplified into a description of such a scene, then concluding with the result clause, or antithesis, to which it has been building up:

> . . . so Hektor towered above the body of Patroklos.

SKELTONICS (sometimes called *tumbling verse*)—Short verses of an irregular meter with two or three stresses, rhyming for several lines on one sound, and conveying an abbreviated and tumbling sort of rhythm, as in these lines from "Colin Clout" by John Skelton, after whom the type of verse was named:

> What can it avail
> To drive forth a snail,

> Or to make a sail
> Of an herring's tail?
> To rhyme or to rail,
> To write or to indite,
> Either for delight
> Or else for despite?

SLACK—Unaccented syllables in metrical verse. (See **scansion**.)

SLANT RHYME—See **near rhyme**.

SONNET—See **Petrarchan** and **Shakespearean sonnet**.

SONORITY—See **resonance**.

SPEAKER—A term for the individual voice or personality (other than the poet's **auctorial voice**) speaking in a poem. The speaker is sometimes identified with the **persona**, a concept of psychologist Jung, representing the archetype of the assumed manner or mask with which one confronts the world; sometimes thought of as an alter ego through whom one acts out an assumed role in life, hence in literature.

SPENSERIAN STANZA—A stanza of nine lines with the interlocking rhymes *a b a b b c b c*, and couplet *c c*, a form invented by Edmund Spenser for his allegorical poem *The Faerie Queene*.

SPONDEE—A metrical foot of two stressed syllables (in quantitative metrics, two long syllables). The two lines from Edna St. Vincent Millay's sonnets contain, respectively, a spondee for the first foot and for the last foot:

> Stróde líke | thĕ sún | ĭntó | thĕ míd | dlĕ ský,

and

> Ĭ stánd | rĕmém | bĕrîng thĕ ís | lănds ând thĕ séa's |
> lóst sóund.

SPRUNG RHYTHM—A term coined by Hopkins for the syncopated effect when stressed syllables are juxtaposed in a line of predominantly regular feet, an effect further accentuated by enjambment from line to line, as in these from "The Windhover":

> Nŏ wón | dĕr óf ĭt: | shéer plód | mâkes plóugh |
> dówn sillĭŏn

263

Shine, | and blue | -bleak em | bers, ah | my dear,
Fall, | gall themselves, | and gash | gold-ver | million.

The words "sheer," "plod," "makes," "plough," "down," and "sillion" have a spondaic effect; that is, the syllables allow of very little **slack**, mostly carrying stresses or at least **hoving accent**, so that this whole section of the line tends to get heavier inflection by the reader. Note also that in all three lines the syncopated effect is emphasized by alliteration and assonantal sound, as with the words "plough—down," "sheer—sillion"; or "blue-bleak," "embers, ah my dear/ Fall"; or "Fall, gall" (an internal rhyme), and "gash gold-ver-million."

Hopkins explained sprung rhythm in a preface to his *Poems* (1876–89), but did not succeed in making the practice quite clear in theory. Variants to the present explanation may be found in other accounts.

STANZA (or *form*; also *stave*, in now archaic terminology)—The arrangement within a poem of lines into a pattern or grouping according to a rhyme scheme and specific kind of meter. Some common **verse forms** or stanzas are the **tercet**, the **quatrain**, **Spenserian stanza**, **ottava rima**, and varying rhyme schemes such as bracket, interlocking, and couplet.

STRESS—The voice stress, accent, or emphasis on certain syllables in the metrical line of verse. In Milton's line from "Lycidas,"

Alas, | what boots | it with | unces | sant care,

the stresses are on the second, fourth, sixth, eighth, and tenth syllables, thus creating iambic feet (in this case the line of five iambic feet is known as iambic pentameter). When stresses fall on the last syllable of a given foot, the line is said to have a **rising rhythm**; when on the first syllable of a foot, a **falling rhythm**.

STRONG ENDING—See **masculine ending**.

STROPHE—(1) Specifically of the **ode**, the first long stanza or group of lines. In the choral movement in a Greek play, it was spoken during or just after the "turn" that the chorus made after entry into the orchestra. (See **ode** for full description.) (2) More generally, any major grouping of lines in a *poem* to form paragraphs, as in a narrative poem such as *Christabel*, the reflective poem "Tintern Abbey," or lengthy monologues such as Browning's "Fra Lippo Lippi."

STRUCTURE—As related to poetry, the relationship of individual parts of a poem to the whole; also, the succession of images or other rhetorical devices that add up to a total effect (as in the balance between opposing ideas that convey the dominant theme of the poem and at the same time produce structural **tension**).

SUBLIMINAL—The unconscious (or subconscious) elements found in some poems, often contributing to the nature of the images. In post-Freudian terminology, unconscious or subliminal images originate in the *id*, or buried part of the mind, and in the process of conceiving and setting down a poem, the poet stimulates that part of the brain which releases these images, which would normally remain quiescent. (See Chapter 7.)

SUBSTITUTION—See also **metrical mutation**. The variation of the normal foot within a line of verse by a different kind of foot, as in the first foot of the second and third lines of Wordsworth's sonnet:

> The world|is too|much with|us; late|and soon,
> Getting|and spen|ding, we|lay waste|our powers:
> Little|we see|in Nature that|is ours. . . .

Substitution is thus another term for the accommodation that a poet makes in the interest of rhythm or speech cadence. By introducing the trochees above in the predominantly iambic lines of the sonnet, Wordsworth keeps a more natural spoken emphasis than by following the iambic meter rigidly. Although the word "substitution" implies conscious deliberation, it is likely that most poets vary their dominant meter in the way illustrated quite unconsciously. Another form of varying a foot in the prevailing meter is known as **compensation**, adding extra unstressed syllables as a means of making up for an absence of stress in a given foot within the line.

SYLLABIC VERSE—The metrical system in which the stresses correspond to the number of syllables alotted to the line (or vice versa). Thus an iambic pentameter line would always have five stresses and ten syllables. Coleridge challenged the predominance of syllabic count inherited from 18th-century metric by discounting **slack** syllables, allowing for **compensation** in some feet, and making the **stress** the basic determinant of the proper number of feet (rather than the mere number of syllables). Thus truly accentual meter and syllabic meter—while they may correspond—may bring about quite different kinds of metric.

SYMBOL—The form that a word, image, or idea may take during recurrences in the same literary work. Symbols function in poetry metaphorically (in the sense that they unite certain likenesses generated in the poet's imagination, while yet retaining the differences within that likeness). They can thus be of varying objectivity or subjectivity. In the first category, symbols are more likely to be signs; in the second, they are more likely to function as literary images. The first might be represented by signs used on roads (a curve, an arrow pointing), by semaphore flags, by certain emblems (the stars and stripes, the red cross, the skull and crossbones). Signs are a shorthand with a fixed conventional significance. The second, or literary, symbol, having no conventional usage, carries a relative and sometimes shifting range of meanings. It thus gives literature more complexity. Literary symbols tend to fall into two general kinds: (1) the traditional and universal variety, and (2) the private or "open-end" variety, many of the latter remaining permanently ambivalent in certain works of art and literature.

In dream symbology, Freud attempted to correlate the recurring mental images of dreamers—typing the actions, persons, situations, and objects as a basis for analyzing the dreamer's psyche. Jung, on the other hand, believed that the persistent images in art and literature through history had a sufficient common denominator to justify an interpretive code (which he offered in the form of archetypes). These persistent images would thus become recurrent at various stages of civilization, providing a kind of universal *lingua france* of symbols running across times and cultures.

When symbols are used in sets, with more or less stable valence and for the duration of a story or poem, they partake of the sign (see above), and function together as **allegory**. Here the symbol is usually a **personification** of abstractions, states of mind, religious principles, and so forth, functioning as an elaborate form of metaphor.

SYMBOLISM—In the general literary sense, the conscious effort by writers to make their work more interesting by complicating the literal meanings through ambivalences; that is,

266

suggesting other than an apparent or literal meaning expressed in an image, word, or idea. Symbolism has occurred at various times in the history of literature. The degree to which one thing may be a symbol for something else often depends upon the intensity of the creative energy expended on the literary work. The presence of symbols, therefore, is not necessarily the result of conscious effort by a writer; rather, it may be a manifestation of the latent symbolism with which people of that time, of that place, invested their feelings about the things and circumstances of life. See Jung's archetypes mentioned under **symbol**.

In the 19th century a succession of French poets revolting from the established conventions of current poetics came to be called Symbolists, and included writers as early as Nerval and Baudelaire and as recent as Mallarmé and Éluard. According to Arthur Symons's *The Symbolist Movement in Literature* (1899), these poets sought to complicate direct meanings in their poems as a way of excluding the despised bourgeois reader (whose tastes were considered banal) and maintaining a more rarified form of communication among themselves.

As a literary influence the Symbolist movement had a profound impact on English poetry near the turn of the century, and upon American poets in the next decades. Its stress upon a highly imaged verse and its practice of ellipsis were features adopted by the **Imagists**, a group attempting to revitalize poetry in both England and America. There were—beyond any particular use of symbols—many by-products of the symbolist movement, not the least of which was the spark given to the poetic renaissance in America of the second and third decades of the 20th century.

SYNESTHESIA–The interchange of sensation, by which color, smell, sound, and so forth, find correspondences in another sense reaction ("dreams of hunting tigers in red weather," "the fly's blue buzz," "an odd dark smell"). The evocation of sophisticated sensibilities by the French Symbolists, as well as their English cousins in the 1890s, stimulated poets to exploit such a mixing of the senses. A poem that has become a famous example of synesthesia is Baudelaire's "Correspondences," written earlier in the century as a demonstration of a poetic phenomenon.

SYNCOPATION—In music, a temporary displacing of the regular beat or cadence; in poetry, a similar displacement to create additional emphasis over and beyond the meter. The effect may be that of concatenated stresses, as in the so-called **sprung rhythm** to which Hopkins subjected many of his poems. Other poets have experimented with some degree of syncopation—Masefield, De la Mare, Edna Millay, Dylan Thomas, and others—but few with the ebullience of Hopkins.

SYNCOPE—The omission of letters (nearly always vowels) within a word (as "ev'ry" for "every," "isn't" for "is not"). See also **elision**, in which words may be run together by means of omission of either an initial or a final letter or syllable.

SYNCRETISM—The running together of words to suggest speed or glibness of diction. This effect of rapidity may often be brought on by a conjunction of several **slack** (or unaccented) syllables in sequence, as in Cummings's poem "Portrait VIII":

Buffalo Bill's
defunct . . .
> who used to
> ride a watersmooth-silver
>> stallion
and break onetwothreefourfive pigeonsjustlikethat. . . .

SYNECDOCHE—A kind of image that designates a whole or an abstract entity or thing by some part or specified aspect of it (for example, "mantle," in "assume the mantle of power," or "bottom," in "our merchant marine lags in the race for new bottoms," that is, ships). Synecdoche expresses the tendency of imagery in general to reduce the broad or abstract to the particular or specific that will stand for it or illustrate it, as a genus for the species ("a courtroom filled with gaping primates"), or an activity by some characteristic element or appendage of it ("a punt that put the pigskin through the posts," or "his men have no heart to face cold steel"). (*Cf.* **metonymy**, several characteristics of which are similar to, if not indistinct from, synecdoche.)

TENOR and VEHICLE—According to I. A. Richards, the two elements of **metaphor** are vehicle and tenor. The *vehicle* is the figure that carries the weight of the comparison, while the subject to which it refers is called the *tenor*. An illustration is given from these lines of Yeats:

> An aged man is but a paltry thing,
> A tattered coat upon a stick, . . .

The aged man is the tenor, "a tattered coat upon a stick" is the vehicle. (*Cf.* Coleridge's well-known critical distinction between *subjective* and *objective* in distinguishing the interactions of imagistic thought.)

TENSION—The result of opposing elements in literary structure. Tension is created by stresses between polarities of emotional attitude, as that for instance between beauty and truth, or permanence and change, or in various paradoxes such as power and gentleness, birth and death, love and hate. The contradictory aspects of accepted views may thus represent the tension between what is and what ought to be, a source in poetry of **irony**, as in the closing lines of Donne's poem:

> All strange wonders that befall thee,
> And swear
> No where
> Lives a woman true and fair.

Tension exists in the ambivalence inherent in many kinds of literary image: **metaphor** (with its balance between likeness and difference), **pun**, **hyperbole**, **oxymoron**, and many kinds of **allusion**. (See Chapter 5.)

TERCET—A unit, or stanza, of three lines. The triplet is a tercet in which all three lines end on a single rhyme. A Petrarchan sonnet often has its sestet divided into two tercets with repeating rhyme pattern (*c d e, c d e*). Dante's *La Commedia* is composed throughout of tercets in the form he invented, called **terza rima**, with interlocking rhymes (*a b a, b c b, c d c,* and so forth).

TERZA RIMA—A series of tercets with the interlocking rhyme scheme *a b a, b c b, c d c, d e d,* and so forth. The form was invented by Dante and used in his *La Commedia* throughout. Because rhymes on one sound are more difficult in English than in Italian, the use of *terza rima* is rare in English poetry, Shelley's "Ode to the West Wind" being one of the few.

TETRAMETER (also called *quatrameter*)—A metrical line of four feet.

269

TEXTURE—A term sometimes used in referring to diction and style, suggesting the parallel of warp and woof in something woven, and in terms of poetry, those elements related to tone, inflection, and various phonetic qualities.

THESIS—Generally applied to quantitative meter. In accentual meter, it may be the name of the unstressed syllable. However, considering the term's Greek meaning of "downbeat," it proves a confusing designation for general purposes of scansion. (See **ictus**.)

THRENODY—A lyrical poem lamenting someone's death (derived from the Greek words *threnos*, a dirge, and *oide*, a song).

TMESIS—The rearrangement of words and their compounds in an abnormal sequence ("what-place-soever" for "whatsoever place" or "party's-of-the-first-part" for "party-of-the-first part's"). It has been used as a diversion in poetry by Cummings and nonsense poets like Ogden Nash. In Cummings's "What if a much of a which of a wind," "Pity this busy monster manunkind," or "Next to of course god america i love you," the twist in conventional phraseology creates attention, emphasis, or mere amused shock.

TRIBRACH—A metrical foot of three unstressed (or short) syllables, as in "finicky," "frippery." Often used for metrical **compensation**.

TRIMETER—A line of verse consisting of three metrical feet.

TRIOLET—A French form of the late 14th century. In its adaptation to English it consists of eight trimetrical lines, rhyming *a b a a a b a b*. An example is Robert Bridge's "When First We Met."

TRIPLE METER—A metrical line of three syllables to the foot. Anapests (⌣⌣/) and dactyls (/⌣⌣) are triple metric feet, and distinguishable from **duple meter**, which consists of two syllable feet, as in iambs and trochees.

TRIPLE RHYME—The rhyming of three final syllables. (*Cf.* **feminine rhyme**.)

TROCHEE—A foot of **duple meter**, with one stressed and one unstressed syllable (/⌣).

TROPE—A term from the Greek verb "to turn," meaning a figure of speech, an image, a rhetorical "turn of speech."

TRUE RHYME (as opposed to **near rhyme**)—Rhyme in which a final syllable in one line matches in sound a final syllable in another line (**masculine rhyme**), or final two syllables (**feminine rhyme**), or final three syllables (**triple rhyme**).

TRUNCATION—The omission of lightly stressed syllables at the beginning of a metrical line, as in Browning's "Saul,"

> 'Till lo, | thŏu aŕt grówn | tŏ ă món | arch; ă péo | plĕ
> iš thińe,

where the predominant meter is anapestic; or in Masefield's "Sea Fever,"

> Ĭ must | gŏ dówn | tŏ thĕ séa | ăgaín, | tŏ thĕ lóne | lў
> séa | ănd thĕ ský

where the first two feet are truncated. When the omission of a syllable comes at the end of a foot, it is called **catalexis**.

TUMBLING VERSE—See **Skeltonics**.

UNDERSTATEMENT (also **litotes** and **meiosis**)—The representation of an assumed state or situation less strongly than expected or in an exaggeratedly weak way ("Just a trifle damp today" to say the weather is teeming outside). In poetry, understatement serves in much the same way as an image; it is the opposite of **hyperbole**, carrying an inversely proportionate amount of irony—as in Mercutio's reply to Romeo when he is asked rather lightly about the wound just received, "No, 'tis not so deep as a well, nor so wide as a church-door; but 'tis enough, 'twill serve."

VALENCE (as used in this text)—The relative capacity of an image to unite, react, or interact with separate ideas or concepts. Related to this potential is our term "ambivalence," by which we mean the double valence when one part of an image is unidentified, as in a **symbol**.

VERSIFICATION—Composition in metrical form or in "verses." (*Cf.* **prosody**.)

VERS LIBRE—See **free verse**.

VERS DE SOCIÉTÉ—Poetry written in a socially sophisticated tone and, presumably, destined for a socially sophisticated audience. Most *vers de societé* has satirical overtones, as in many of the poems of Jules Laforgue or T. S. Eliot (who fell in with LaForgue's manner and tone). Even "The Love Song of J. Alfred Prufrock" achieves considerable irony by the sophisticated indirection of the speaker's built-in social manner, essential to most *vers de societé*.

VILLANELLE—Six tercets of tetrameter lines, in which the first and third lines of the first stanza (or tercet) are repeated alternately in each successive stanza as the final line. The last stanza has four lines (hence, of course, is not a tercet but a quatrain). Dylan Thomas's "Do Not Go Gentle into that Good Night" is a villanelle.

VIRGULE—A single perpendicular or slant line used to indicate an inserted word above a line, or as a separation between two words in the manner of a hyphen. In poetical scansion the virgule is a perpendicular bar or line indicating the separation of syllables or words into metrical feet (|).

VISUAL POETRY (or *eye poetry* or *shaped verse*)—The arrangement of words and lines—frequently regardless of meter or rhyme—into semi-pictorial shapes (diamonds, circles, hourglass, bottles, mushroom clouds, and so forth) as an appeal to the eye. While the form has a venerable tradition as the *carmen figuratem* (*Cf.* George Herbert's "Easter Wings" and Dylan Thomas's shaped poems) of medieval practice, a current revival of bizarre typography into imitation of everything from stars to the female form now goes under the rather inappropriate name of "concrete poetry."

VOCABLE—A word composed of suggestive syllables and spellings without any standard or dictionary meaning. For example, *yahoo*, invented by Swift as a name for his brutelike humans, was originally a vocable. Now, of course, it is in everybody's vocabulary.

VOICE—The aspect of an individual poet's style by which critics hope to differentiate him from fellow poets. (See also **persona**.) *Voice* seems to be roughly interchangeable with what has also been called a poet's "idiom," a mixture perhaps of personal idiosyncracy of speech, stylistic usages, or what is more popularly known of the poet's manner and personality.

WEAK ENDING—A normally unstressed syllable at the end of a line of verse, which by the prevailing metric would be stressed. This is sometimes called a **feminine ending**. (See also **masculine** or **strong ending**.)

INDEX

Poets who are represented in the text by complete poems or considerable sections of poems are indicated by capital letters. Titles of complete poems or considerable sections of poems appearing in the text are also indicated by capital letters. Titles of short poems referred to in the text are in quotation marks. Titles of longer works or books are in italics. Subject entries or term references are in Roman type.